The
Undefended Self

Living The Pathwork
of Spiritual Wholeness

SUSAN THESENGA

The Pathwork Series:

General Editor: Donovan Thesenga

The Pathwork of Self-Transformation.
Eva Pierrakos.
Bantam, 1990. ISBN 0-553-34896-5.

Fear No Evil: The Pathwork Method of Transforming The Lower Self.
Eva Pierrakos and Donovan Thesenga.
Pathwork Press, 1993. ISBN 0-9614777-2-5.

Creating Union: The Pathwork of Relationship.
Eva Pierrakos and Judith Saly.
Pathwork Press, 1993. ISBN 0-9614777-3-3.

The Undefended Self: Living The Pathwork of Spiritual Wholeness.
Susan Thesenga.
Pathwork Press, 1994. ISBN 0-9614777-4-1.

Publisher: **Pathwork Press**
Route 1, Box 86, Madison, Virginia 22727
Phone/Fax 703 948-5508
President: Gene Humphrey
Design, Publicity, and Book Orders: Karen Millnick

The Undefended Self is printed on Lyons Falls *Pathfinder* totally chlorine-free paper as our commitment to and investment in health and the environment. Chlorine compounds commonly used in bleaching wood pulp create organochlorines, including dioxin, which cause genetic defects, immune system suppression and cancer. Our commitment required that we invest in paper inventory far beyond our press run, but we believe in putting our investment where our consciousness lives.
The Pathwork and Pathwork Press

Foreign translations of Pathwork materials are available in Dutch, French, German, Italian, Portuguese and Spanish.

The
Undefended Self

Living The Pathwork
of Spiritual Wholeness

SUSAN THESENGA

Second Edition
Based on the Pathwork material
created by Eva Pierrakos

Pathwork Press
1994

Dedication

This book is dedicated to **Eva Broch Pierrakos**, bringer of the Pathwork wisdom to our world.

Acknowledgments and Appreciations

To the Pathwork Foundation which gave me permission to quote freely from the Pathwork Guide Lectures. The Pathwork Foundation holds the exclusive copyright to these lectures.

To Dr. John Pierrakos who gave me encouragement and permission to use the text and title from Eva Pierrakos's 1965 manuscript, then titled *The Undefended Self*.

To my many supporters along the way both within and outside the Pathwork communities, and especially to the following for editorial and technical help: Asha Greer, Gene Humphrey, D. Patrick Miller, Karen Millnick, and Judith Saly.

To my mother and father who nurtured open-mindedness, integrity, and courage, and to my daughter Pamela who has brought such light and joy into my world.

And, most of all, to my husband and spiritual partner Donovan Thesenga, who is central to how my life and this book have unfolded.

Copyright © 1994 by Susan Thesenga

All rights reserved. No part of this book may be reproduced or transmitted in any form or by any means, electronic or mechanical, including photocopying, recording, or by any information storage and retrieval system, without permission in writing from the publisher.

Library of Congress Catalog Card Number: 94-68275

Psychology/Self-Help/Spirituality/Pathwork

ISBN 0-9614777-4-1

Cover Design: Karen Millnick
          Thanks to Susan Thesenga, Gene Humphrey and Kemper Conwell

Cover Painting: *The Alba Madonna*; RAPHAEL; ©1994 Board of Trustees; National Gallery of Art, Washington; Andrew W. Mellon Collection; c. 1510

Drawings on title pages: Asha Greer

PRINTED IN THE UNITED STATES OF AMERICA

Contents

Summary of Chapters, Susan's Story

Just Susan: Allowing the Flow of Life
Accepting Our Flawed Human Nature; Awakening Our
Spiritual Potential; Expanding Our Sense of Self; Honoring
Our Spiritual Longing; The Path of the Undefended Self

Maureen: Integrating the Child and the Lion-Tamer
The Development of Our Dualities; Growth Into Unity; The
Goal of Spiritual Work; Crisis and the Spiritual Evolution of
Our Species; The Pull of Evolution

James Expanding: The Microscope and the First Aid Kit
The Observer Self; Distortions in Self-Observation; Source
of Our Distortions in Self-Observation; Radical Self-
Acceptance; Two Aspects of the Observer Self: Truth and
Love; Truth: Constructive Attitudes; Love: Constructive
Attitudes; Self-Identification; Tools for Developing the
Observer Self: Meditation and Daily Review; Daily Review

*Bobbi, Barbara, and the Grandmother: Discovering the
Inner Child and the Inner Wise Woman*
Maps of Consciousness; Child Self; The Undifferentiated
Child Mind; Adult Ego Self; Positive and Negative Aspects
of the Ego; Ego in Relation to Others; The Ego in Relation
to God; Need for a Healthy Ego; Soul/ Transpersonal Level;
Positive and Negative Aspects of the Transpersonal Level;
The Soul/Transpersonal Level Distinguished from Other
Levels; Unitive Level; Surrender; Stages Co-exist; The
Paradox of Spiritual Evolution

Charts included in this Chapter:

"Every human being senses an inner longing that goes deeper than the longings for emotional and creative fulfillment. This longing comes from sensing that another, more fulfilling state of consciousness and a larger capacity to experience life must exist."

—*the Pathwork Guide*

Bill and Joanne: Untangling the Sexual Knots in Relationship
An Image Defined; Origin of Images; Origin of Images at
the Soul Level; Kinds of Images; More Examples of Images
at Work; Compulsion to Re-Create Childhood Hurts; How
to Find an Image; Shame Indicates an Image; The Main
Image or Soul Splits; How to Dissolve Images and Resulting
Vicious Circles; The Benign Circle

Connie's Mask: Dropping the Idealized Self-Image
The Mask and the Journey of Transformation; What is the
Mask?; Origin of the Idealized Self Image; Connection
Between an Image and the Mask; The Defense; Secondary
Defense Reactions; The Mask and the Re-Creation of
Childhood Hurts; Three Types of Mask; 1) The Mask of
Love; 2) The Mask of Power; 3) The Mask of Serenity; 4) A
Combination Mask; Transformation of the Mask Self; The
Mask as a Distortion of the Higher Self

Charts included in this Chapter:

Albert's Ghosts: Meeting the Lower Self
What Is the Lower Self?; What Is Evil?; Denial of the Lower
Self; Three Aspects of the Lower Self: Pride, Self-Will, and
Fear; What the Lower Self Is Not; Lower-Self Anger;
Uncovering the Lower Self; The Creative Power of the
Lower Self; Origins of the Lower Self; The Innate Lower
Self of the Child; Karma and the Lower Self; The Origin
of Evil; The Christian Myth; Non-Christian Perspectives;
The Pathwork Perspective

Susan's Heart: Opening to the Higher Self
What Is the Higher Self?; The Experience of the Higher Self;
The Higher Self and the Lower Self; Denial and Shame of
the Higher Self; The Higher Self and the Mask; What the

Higher Self Is Not; The Emanations of the Three Selves; What Is God?; The Higher Self as Cosmic Consciousness; The Higher Self and the God Image; Surrender and Resistance to the Higher Self

Michael's Devil: Exploring the Roots of Forbidden Fruit
Negative Intent, Negative Will; Making Negative Intentions Conscious; Why We Choose Negativity; Relinquishing Negative Intentions; Affirming Positive Intentions; Understanding the Deeper Levels of Our Negativity; Negative Pleasure; What Is Pleasure?; Attachment of the Life Force to Negative Situations; Origin of Negative Pleasure; Distortions in Sexuality; Working with Our Negative Pleasure; The Transformation of Negative Pleasure

Michael's Devil: Transforming Lust into Love
Activating Higher-Self Energies; Letting Go of the Lower Self; Activating Lower-Self Energies; Feeling Our Feelings; Seeing Evil as a Defense Against Pain; Feeling the Pain of Real Guilt; Patience in Healing the Lower Self; Meditation to Re-Educate the Lower Self; Seeing Divine Qualities Behind Faults; Taking Full Self-Responsibility; Letting Go to God

Susan's Retreat: Journeying Toward the Feminine
Self-Creation and Self-Responsibility; Identification with the Higher Self; Meditation for Positive Creation; Summary of Self-Work Required for Positive Life Creation; The Creative Dance of Spiritual Evolution; Creating Heaven on Earth

Preface

The deep longing that exists in every human heart for a more fulfilling state of consciousness and a larger capacity to experience life must, sooner or later, impel us to look within ourselves. When we learn that our happiness will never be realized by outer possessions, achievements, or even relationships, we at last turn our attention inside and begin to ask, "Who am I? What is real happiness and how can I remove my obstructions to it?" And beyond personal happiness we begin to ask, "What am I doing here on earth? What is God and how can I experience it/him/her?" Such questions will impel us on a psychological search to know ourselves and on a spiritual search to discover the answers to ultimate questions about the nature of reality. Sooner or later we will need to find and pursue a path that has aided other travelers in finding inner fulfillment and meaning in their lives.

This book outlines the Pathwork, a contemporary spiritual discipline which promotes our personal growth toward knowing and integrating our vast inner reality. The Pathwork emphasizes the need to accept all our dualities, including our evil as well as our good sides, our limited ego as well as our divinity. Through such self-acceptance, we learn to live in unity, love, and truth—the place of the undefended self. This book summarizes the Pathwork for the individual reader working seriously on his or her own spiritual development.

The Pathwork is based conceptually on material channelled by Eva Broch Pierrakos from 1955 until her death in 1979.[1] Eva was an extraordinary spiritual teacher with whom I studied for seven years. The entity or energy whom Eva channelled is known simply as the Guide. The process developed from the Guide's teachings—which continues to evolve through the contributions of many therapists, healers, and spiritual teachers—is known as the Pathwork. This work is taught and practiced at two rural retreat centers in the U.S. and at other centers in the U.S., Europe, and South America which offer Pathwork counseling and teaching programs. Small groups of people in many parts of the world meet to study and apply these spiritual principles.[2]

---

[1] A complete listing of the Pathwork Guide Lecture titles begins on page 284. These lectures can be ordered individually from the centers listed on page 290.

[2] See page 290 for a listing of groups and centers where the Pathwork is practiced and taught.

The Pathwork, which I have taught and practiced for over twenty years, offers maps and processes for many stages of the universal spiritual path. The unique gift of the Pathwork is a profound understanding of the nature of evil and the personal lower self, and an effective process for transforming the dark side of our nature. This book offers help for many steps on the spiritual path, but its most original contribution will come in those chapters summarizing the work with the lower self. The Pathwork process for transforming the lower self offers a clarion call of hope for deliverance from evil in ourselves and in our world.

This book mixes my summary of the Pathwork material with quotes from the Pathwork Guide. I write from my particular human perspective; the quoted Guide material is from the viewpoint of a non-incarnated spiritual entity. I also include many stories from my spiritual journey and many illustrations of personal transformation which I have witnessed while helping other people on their spiritual paths through my counseling and workshops. The names in the stories have been changed to protect confidentiality. Stories introduce each chapter and are woven throughout the text. Exercises to deepen one's understanding of the material conclude each chapter.

Summary of Chapters

The chapters of this book follow the stages of spiritual work as I see them. Chapter One encourages us to accept our flawed dualistic human nature and to honor our spiritual longing. Chapter Two reinforces our need to follow the path of our personal and collective evolution, and helps us align with our longing to unify ourselves. Chapter Three shows us how to develop and to identify with the observer self, the most important tool for transformation work. Meditation and daily review are presented as tools for strengthening our capacity for objective and compassionate self-observation.

Chapter Four outlines four developmental stages of consciousness—child, adult ego, soul, and unitive consciousness— and how we can recognize their very different realities within us. Chapter Five shows us how we are constantly re-creating in the present our past childhood issues and conclusions about life, and how we can release these false illusions and "images." Chapter Six begins exploring the major map of consciousness to be followed in the rest of the journey outlined in this book, that of the three selves: mask, lower self, and higher self. Chapter Six also gives us a thorough presentation of the mask and the work to be done to understand and release our attachment to it. Chapter Seven introduces the lower self and guides us into facing this vital, though distorted, creative energy in our souls. Chapter Eight helps us to come home to the higher self, our original divine nature. Chapters Nine and Ten show us how to release our attachments to negative will and negative excitement and thus how to transform the lower self. Chapter Eleven affirms our work of shifting our self-identification from the ego to the higher self. From this secure anchor, we can embrace the totality of ourselves and use higher self energy to work with spirit in creating positive new life.

That you might better understand how I view the perennial wisdom offered by the Pathwork teachings, I share my story, revealing the historical and personal context which shaped the particular lens through which I view reality.

Susan's Story

I was born the month after Hitler invaded Poland, and was nearly six years old when World War II finally ended. As I threw my homemade confetti into the air, the celebration of Victory left me trembling with an excitement I could not understand. I knew that something important had happened; some terrible darkness had been lifted from the world.

Though I could not have known it at the time, Hitler and his Holocaust would become for me both a metaphor and a koan that I have devoted my life to understanding. Had I been more intellectual, the impact of Hitler might have led me to a life as an historian. Had I been more combative, it might have led to a life devoted to social justice. Instead my passion has been more personal and emotional, to understand the Hitler who lives in me, and in every human heart, especially in those ones of us too well-fed to use economic desperation as an excuse for the innumerable grand and petty cruelties we perpetrate and condone, singly and collectively, every day.

Issues of good and bad preoccupied me from as far back as I can remember. I was an earnest child and, from age nine to eleven, kept a diary of the good and the bad that I did or witnessed every day, with prayers for the bad and thanks for the good. When I could not find my bike, I assumed that I was being punished for not helping my mother with household chores. When I ran from a fire in the woods, I searched my soul over whether this was an act of cowardice or of courage.

At home I was always seeking to break out of the emotional cotton batting in which my safe, suburban life was swaddled. Even as I young child I was the sort who would crawl under the carefully set table to investigate the nose pickings we children had deposited on the table's underbelly and then proclaim my find to the polite company. The truths to be found under the table of life's surfaces were always the ones that interested me most.

Despite my parents' honest, intelligent agnosticism, I became avidly interested in religion. When I was ten, my nine-year-old Catholic cousin died in a bicycle accident; death, that close, was a powerful teaching for me. When my father bought me an ice cream cone and tried to assure me that "Johnny was in heaven now," we looked at each other and both knew this was only a convenient lie that covered our mutual ignorance. So I experimented with different churches trying to find out more— what is death, and what is good and what is bad?

After rejecting the Catholic church, I went for a while to an Episcopal church where my heart had been won by a single powerful ritual that still moves me in memory. On Good Friday an enormous black wooden cross was raised at the front of the church, the reality of death now obliterating the pretty pictures and the lacy white coverings of the altar. I once sat in the church for hours, absorbing the message of that black cross. As I merged with the blackness, I saw the ground underneath the cross open up and reveal numerous grand rooms richly decorated with mysterious furnishings from all over the world, including many Oriental treasures, all very different from the mundane suburban apartment complex where I lived. Whatever lay beyond death seemed unutterably vast and no longer so frightening.

Then on Easter Sunday everyone in the congregation brought flowers to pin, tape, or stick onto that cross until it fairly bloomed with bright spring flowers. This symbol of Christ's resurrection confirmed my own vision that death, which we fear as the end

point to the line of our lives, might be only a dot on the circumference of a wheel. Everyone knew that birth was followed by
death, but I began to glimpse that birth might also follow death.
The mystery that spirit transcended body, that physical incarnation was only the beginning of a much deeper reality—all of this
moved my serious young soul to a pious joy and reverence.

When the more pressing concerns of adolescence hit,
I stopped going to church. But I started going camping. Being in
nature not only spared me some teenage madness, it became my
preferred way of worshipping God. Also during my teen years I
first met Jews and became obsessed with reading personal
accounts of the Holocaust. I was trying to understand how such
evil could have taken root in people who "knew better." What
was the overwhelming attraction of evil?

I was through college and graduate school before I started to
question seriously whether all this learning had anything to do
with my real concern—becoming a better person. I wondered if
education was just another mask, irrelevant to the deeper lessons
I somehow knew were awaiting me.

While teaching English to college freshmen at Howard
University, I was offered my first opportunity to "do good" in the
world. The civil rights movement was in full swing, and I jumped
on the moral bandwagon. Becoming immersed in African-
American culture stretched me culturally, and I shared in many
peak historical moments of the mid 1960's. I had an experience
of enormous consciousness expansion while participating in the
1963 "March on Washington" in which Dr. Martin Luther King
gave his unforgettable "I Have a Dream" speech. In the summer
of 1964, I went south (along with many other well-intentioned,
hopelessly naïve northern middle class white people), where
I taught at a small black college outside of Jackson, Mississippi.
I had my first brush with real terror after being arrested there
while riding in a racially mixed car.

My ongoing work with the civil rights movement intensified
my hatred for oppressors, whom I saw as white men, particularly
white men in authority who worked for the "Establishment."
Like my beloved father. Eventually I realized that my hatred was
neurotic; my moral fervor had as much to do with unresolved
feelings for my father as with the political issues to which my
feelings had become attached. This realization led me into
therapy and eventually into alternative therapies.

My first encounter group in 1967 was an experience of coming home. I was suddenly given permission to speak what I'd always known: that underneath all our civilized politeness and masks of niceness, people are full of all kinds of wild and woolly feelings, rages and tears, and mountains of pain. And these inner realities cause us to do all sorts of things we later regret, and keep us from the happiness we say we want. The inner world of feelings had always been more palpable for me than outer rules and roles; I just hadn't known how to name what I knew was real.

From then on I gobbled up therapeutic and group experiences—Tavistock, Gestalt, humanistic psychology, sensory awareness, bio-energetics. I felt that a deep well of emotional deprivation was at last being filled. But still I sensed there was more. On a trip to California in 1969, reading R.D. Laing, listening to one of the first Ram Dass tapes, I knew my mind was opening to a reality far vaster than I had ever imagined. I began to sense that a powerful spiritual influx was penetrating the collective consciousness. By the time I arrived at Esalen Institute at Big Sur, I knew a deeper, unnamable part of me was in charge. I had a vision of being tied to one end of a rope, the other end of which was wrapped around a giant winch pulling me, inexorably, home to something I could not name.

In an intensely dramatic encounter group at Esalen, I met Donovan Thesenga, my future husband. Donovan's years of study and practice of Zen Buddhism and his serious exploration of transcendent experiences via LSD had brought him to spiritual understandings that far surpassed what I had known. On the other hand, my emotional openness led him into depths of feeling that were new for him. Together we stretched—and continue to stretch—each other.

Donovan and I were married in 1970 and then moved to rural Virginia, to start leading encounter and bio-energetics groups. We bought land and started a growth center which eventually became Sevenoaks Pathwork Center, where we still live and work.

I was training in bio-energetics with Drs. Alexander Lowen and John Pierrakos when I met Eva Broch Pierrakos in the summer of 1972. Instantly I knew she was to be my spiritual teacher.

How does one know these things? Everything about her attracted me. She was born Jewish in Austria, and had fled to

Zurich during World War II. Beautiful and earthy, she was also engaged in the deepest kind of spiritual search. She was, of all things, a "channel" for a spirit entity, and she had begun this work while I was still stumbling around in high school.

While attending Guide lectures given by Eva, I was filled with spiritual electricity, the most incredible excitement combined with the deepest calm. Never had I felt more alive, more filled with the presence of God.[3] Eva herself was vital, vibrant, excited about life, and yet also more serene than anyone I had known. She truly seemed to have, and to live, the answers to questions that I was only just now forming.

At the time I met Eva I felt adrift on a raft that was slowly splitting down the middle. One half of the raft was my deep immersion in my personal therapy; the other half was my equally deep involvement in the practice of Zen Buddhism. The first ignored my spiritual potential; the latter was oblivious to my personality. I knew that each discipline held only part of the truth for me, and I had been unable to find resolution.

In meeting Eva, and in my subsequent reading of the Pathwork Guide lectures, I found the union my soul sought of the philosophic contradictions between Western psychology and Eastern mysticism. Here I could explore my preoccupations with evil and with death, reconcile my sexuality with my spirituality, and join my outer activity with my inner quiet. Here I might move toward unity by accepting my dualities, and move toward freedom by intimately knowing my defenses. My inner raft began to mend.

But being with Eva was not always easy. She was demanding and authoritative, and she was pleasure-loving and sexy. Both these aspects of her nature threatened and challenged me. Frequently I would come to sessions with Eva after several hours of deep meditation at the New York Zen Center, only to be greeted by her cheery question, "How is sex with Donovan?" It was certainly the subject I was least prepared to discuss at that moment! She clearly believed that my spiritual path had a lot to do with my deepening surrender to my husband; I came to believe that too.

During a period of serious trouble in my marriage, she confronted me with my desire to control Donovan and forced me to

---

[3] I use the word "God" to refer to the "Ground of Being," the "Higher Power," the "Life Force," the "Great Spirit," or however others might want to name the unnamable Mystery at the heart and center of all existence.

look within at my dependency and withholding as the source of my unhappiness. I had to turn my stance around 180 degrees, away from blame and toward self-responsibility. It was not the only time that Eva and the Pathwork would tell me something I didn't want to hear, but it was precisely the truth I needed.

I loved Eva deeply. No adult relationship, other than with my husband Donovan, has affected or changed me so profoundly. She was my model, helper, and teacher for seven years until her death from cancer in 1979. Yet my relationship with her, during her lifetime, remained that of an adoring child. Eva was my spiritual mother, the wise and giving woman I had needed so badly to help me fill emotional voids and answer questions that had gripped me since earliest childhood. The community which had gathered around her and her husband John Pierrakos became for me the intimate, emotionally honest family I never had.

But, since I never grew up with Eva, or with the community, her death was thoroughly devastating to me, and it initiated another, yet deeper, spiritual journey. After a brief period of denial, our Pathwork communities suffered profound grief and disorientation. Membership dropped and financial crises loomed. The early 1980's were a scary and depressing time for me.

My rosy image of Eva started to fade. I had to rail and rage and grieve the loss of my idealized spiritual mother. I hated that I now had to be responsible for myself and my own spiritual growth. For a while I wanted to die rather than grow up spiritually, and I was indeed quite sick with despair for several years.

During this time I found myself spiritually adrift again, having let go of the Pathwork in a bewildering but necessary surrender. Sometimes I was terrified of drowning in meaninglessness, but I was equally determined not to compromise my integrity by holding on to an unseaworthy craft. I found that the practice of letting go and drifting became my new spiritual discipline. Now I was floating in the open sea without a raft of any kind, letting go of my illusions like so many useless planks of wood. Every so often I would find one of the timbers of my former beliefs floating back and I would rest there for a while. And despite my confusion about the Pathwork, the process of honest self-facing was so ingrained in me that I could not help but continue to work on myself in the Pathwork way that had always worked so well.

In the time since Eva's death, I have gradually discovered a deep faith that comes from within me and that is remarkably similar to the teachings of the Pathwork Guide. I have found myself reconstructing the Pathwork for myself, from the inside out. The more I looked around at other spiritual beliefs and practices, the more I became convinced of the essential truth and depth of the Pathwork.

I now see Eva as a real person with profound spiritual gifts which she developed through her devotion and perseverance as a channel and a spiritual helper, and which culminated in her founding of the Pathwork, which has helped and will continue to help so many people. As my idol crumbled, an extraordinary human being remained.

The Undefended Self

My process in writing this book has been a microcosm of my spiritual journey the past twelve years. At first, as Eva's adoring student, I started to edit a manuscript she wrote in 1965 entitled *The Undefended Self*. But then my Pathwork world fell apart, and I didn't know if I would have a home or a job, much less the ability to write a book. Eventually I knew I was called to write my own summary of the Pathwork lectures, also entitled *The Undefended Self*, for use primarily at Pathwork Centers and for other spiritual trainings led by those familiar with the Pathwork. In that book I included some of my own stories, disguised by other names. This book, which is an edited version of my former one, is intended for a much wider audience of therapists, healers, and anyone else interested in a vibrant path of psychological and spiritual self-discovery. Here, true to the name I have kept for the book, I share more openly my own undefended self in three of the stories that introduce the chapters.

This book is my gift of gratitude to Eva. And it is also my goodbye to her, though not to her legacy. With this gift and this goodbye, I let go once again to the drift, to the not-knowing. I assume I will continue to be driven by my apparent need to face the reality (and illusion) of evil and the reality (and illusion) of death. I still think about Hitler and the lessons about evil and its masks which we so desperately need to learn in order to survive and flourish together on this planet. Whatever awaits me on my path, I know I will be guided by the inner teacher, pulled along by the winch of my spiritual destiny.

I offer this book to your heart as well as to your mind. I invite you to look deep within, to accept all of what you find there, and to never stop looking. I share with you a commitment to follow the deepest truth and most loving path we can find.

If this book strikes a chord in you, then perhaps this is a path for you to explore more fully. If not, keep searching, because we are each inexorably drawn toward the light of our inner spiritual source, as surely and dependably as a flower is drawn toward the sun. The inner path to God is a reality. All of our life experiences are no more and no less than an exact teaching to help us reach the source within.

Be blessed on your journey,

Susan Thesenga
Sevenoaks Pathwork Center
Madison, Virginia

CHAPTER 1

Accepting Our Dualities

"An inner voice tells you that there is
much more to your life and yourself than you are
capable of experiencing at the present time."

—Pathwork Guide Lecture 204, *"What is the Path?"*

Just Susan: Allowing the Flow of Life

I walk through the wintry woods of a January morning in Virginia. Brown leaves outlined with frost crunch under my black Reeboks. Around me oaks and elms, a few white pines, and clear blue sky above. Now a patch of bright green creeping cedar vine covers the ground. Moving fast, toward our stretch of the state road just past these woods. Awareness of my pace makes me choose to stop, to listen. It's hard to get quiet enough inside to listen to these winter woods with no singing birds, no whistling wind, no scratching animals, no outward sounds at all except the dull background shoosh of the highway. But I begin to hear or perhaps sense something, a steady, low heartbeat which feels like the pulsation of life within these trees, and I sense that my human presence is disturbing something that would be better left alone. So I return to a hurried pace. Who hears this message? Who is this Susan who rushes through crisp woods on a frosty morning?

I've always liked that my name is ordinary. It helps me keep the affliction of grandiosity, which affects me from time to time, from lasting any longer than an average case of the flu. I do have a more hidden name, one which only I call myself, Looks-Within-Woman. It came to me while reading **Seven Arrows** *years ago, but this name feels acceptably modest. It makes no claim to know my essence as Shanti or Ananda or Shakti. Sometimes, when I find myself stuck in one of the thorn-filled pits of anxiety and self-doubt just on the other side of the mountain of grandiosity, I wish for a sacred name or a magical mantra to assure me of my divine essence. But then I remember the job is to bring my divinity through "just Susan."*

Years ago, when I was self-consciously enjoying an identity as a Zen Buddhist practitioner, I expressed in an encounter group my desire to manifest more perfectly the inner calm I could achieve in extended zazen sitting. I was extremely impatient with my ordinary scattered and frantic states of mind. Someone suggested that I talk to a pillow representing my anxious, imperfect self and tell it in no uncertain terms how it should shape up. Shifting to sit on the pillow, I felt the pain of my self-judgment and cried like the rejected child I also knew within me. The critical parent and the rejected child, the top dog and the underdog. An impasse. A friend intervened and tenderly offered that maybe being just Susan, as she was in each moment, was the essence of Zen. Nothing more (or less) was required than full acceptance of my experience moment to moment. A revelation. Just so. Just Susan.

On the state road, I begin my chosen task—to pick up the trash left by passing motorists since the last time I walked this part of the road that we at Sevenoaks have "adopted." Walking briskly I bend many times to stuff the discards of our throw-away civilization into my heavy-duty orange plastic bag—the paper and aluminum wrappers from McDonald's, Taco Bell, Tastee Freeze; the beer cans and bottles; the cigarette pack wrappers. In between the bending and the stuffing, my awareness is with walking and breathing, made visible by frosty puffs of each exhalation. Just walking, just breathing.

And then I remember my ten-year old daughter Pamela's story about two kids on the schoolyard just before Christmas break puffing on candy cigarettes and exhaling frosty smoke. And they fooled a teacher who thought they were real cigarettes. Kids and candy cigarettes. I can still taste the powdery white sweetness from my own childhood when I too alternated sucking the candy with puffing out cold morning air. Nothing's changed since then, even though forty-two years separate me and my daughter. Except that I wouldn't have had the daring or the playfulness to try to fool the teacher. A scared, uptight, goody-good kid I was.

And then, just below the surface of awareness, I pick up a slight tension or strain. What is it? Ah, a little moral superiority trying to assert itself as I walk along doing good, picking up my neighbors' trash. Why this straining to do good? Doing good to make me special? What for? To justify my existence in some way because just being me isn't quite enough? I recall my super-critical and super-conscientious father and how I tried so hard to get his approval, never believing I had it, or enough of it to make me feel worthwhile. I worked so hard to fulfill all the outward criteria for his approbation. Which of course never gave me that feeling of security and worth, that whatever-it-is feeling that we all seem to want from parents and magically, and mistakenly, believe is theirs to confer. I know now that there are no more Mommies and Daddies. Can that trip of proving my goodness finally be over? Can I let myself off the hook? Can I walk this road because I walk this road, not to do good, or to improve the world, but just because walking this road and clearing trash is what is happening?

A car passes and I wave to my neighbor and new friend. A black woman, or is it now African-American? I, whose family may very well be more recently American than hers, don't call myself Scottish-American. Yet among black Americans the search for cultural self-definition is so much more urgent and carries so much racial pain. Shifting words reflect the ongoing search for an identity with dignity. How much am I defined by my white skin? Inwardly I feel multi-cultural, rainbow-hued, dual-gendered. And yet I am aware of perceptual limits stemming from my outer identity in this life as a middle-aged white woman. Can I let go of the idea of a fixed self?

My awareness simplifies, outwardly watching black Reeboks climbing the hill of grey-black road, inwardly watching breath, panting some now, keeping pace. Then I notice sun-glistened frost covering long tufts of yellowed grasses by the side of the road. Light coming through icy sheaths creating a thousand tiny prisms. Sun illuminating water, whether through raindrops, dew or frost, always moves me. I stop, my legs weak and watery, my body vibrating with the same electric shimmering as frost reflecting sunlight. My visual field softens, energy pulsates up my legs, begins to dissolve my skin-defined sense of self, extending me outward to embrace the beauty of this frosty moment. Awe fills the space that until a moment before had been bounded by sneakers and headband. Frozen water reflecting sun's light becomes a graced gift of Creation. And with this gift the ordinary becomes extraordinary.

Back again now to sharpened focus, seeing the trash at the base of these frosty grasses, a Styrofoam coffee cup from a Seven-Eleven store promising "We keep you revvin'." The sound of the highway closer, the revving of life nearer. A flash of contempt for the revving and for the litterers. Yet it isn't hard to shift my awareness a little and remember the times when slowing down feels scary, and all that's safe is inside a car getting away or going toward something, whatever it is or is imagined to be, just so long as it isn't here now, and everything outside the car, especially the ground, is "other" and doesn't matter, since it is just a place to receive our refuse. If I can enter the places in me where cruelty dwells, as I have done, then surely I can find the consciousness of the litterer. He too is me.

There's a sharp pain in my heart as I remember a recent encounter with Pamela. As she does sometimes when we aren't getting along or she needs to declare her separateness, yesterday afternoon Pam "ran away from home" carrying a suitcase down to another residence on the Sevenoaks property. As is usually the case, she called me a half hour later to ask me to come pick her up, and I said, "No, someone big enough to run away from home is also big enough to walk back." But she'd come back without the suitcase and later I'd relented to drive her down to go pick it up, all the time thinking that I was probably making a mistake in aiding her willful manipulation.

As soon as we got in the car, Pamela said, "I love you, Mom." I responded cynically, "You mean you're glad I'm doing you this favor?" She replied, without apparent hurt, "No, I just thought you needed to know I love you." "Oh," letting in what she had said, I answered truthfully, "I'm not feeling very lovable at this moment." "I know, that's why I told you I love you." "Well, thanks." I slowed down, but only a second, going on to ask her why she had been in such a lousy mood after returning this morning from her friend Sonia's overnight birthday party. She told me that seeing how her friend was able to ask her mom to leave the girls alone, and that her mom did so, "madified" her towards me. "How come you don't let me and my friends alone during overnights? How come you tell us when to go to bed and don't let us decide when?" Still in my defensive mood, I snapped back, "That's because you still act less mature than Sonia when friends are over." The words bored and aggrieved even me as soon as they were out of my mouth. Pam just answered sadly, "That's what you always say." Conversation ceased.

Only now could I hear the tight meanness in my voice, and regret the missed opportunity to talk about how we might honor our mutual need to negotiate our boundaries. Having glanced this morning at another Alice Miller book on child abuse, I'm acutely aware how easy it is to fall into an unconscious parental superiority, rather than open to the truth that my child is struggling to express, to honor her awareness that something needs to change between us and to consider that together we might be able to figure out how to make things better. It never crossed my mind that she was anything but the inferior partner in our discussion. Maybe I'll have another chance at it this evening; maybe not. That moment has passed. A sharp pang of sadness and an itchy self-disapproval tangle up together in my heart, even as I keep my aerobic walking pace. A big sigh. So be it.

I'm back at our Sevenoaks mailbox now, where I leave my orange bag full of trash for the Highway Department to pick up later. I'm free now to walk back to my house, to feel the woods floor now damp and spongy from thawed frost, rich with my favorite smell of decaying leaves. As I lay down my orange burden, I wonder how many inner burdens can I release with each breath, each step home? Just so much and no more. I am, after all, just Susan.

Accepting Our Dualities

As I walk a country road, I am asking "Who am I?" I sense in me a nature mystic attuning to a presence in the woods. I also find an anxious child still needing to please her father. I admit to a judgmental ego-mind critical of the litterers and our revved-up throw-away culture, but I discover also the litterer's consciousness within me. As I wave to my African-American friend, I am aware of both my white skin and my multi-colored soul. I am a thoughtful mother upset at a thoughtless exchange with my daughter. And then, in a graced moment, I am nothing at all, just a space through which awe can flow in harmony with mid-January frosty grasses on a country road.

Which is the real Susan? Is it this awe-filled moment, in which there is no separate Susan, only the seamless fabric of life into which my awareness is woven? Or am I the judgmental ego mind filled with contempt and criticism for other travelers on this road? Surely I am both. Frosty breath and memories of candy cigarettes bring a rush of loving connection with my daughter. And yet moments later I remember a Susan lost in a parental control trip. Am I a good mother or a bad mother? Surely I am both. Am I limited by my outward identity as a white American woman, or am I a soul whose experience goes beyond this particular outward package? Both, surely.

Any time I answer the question "Who am I?" the response must be partial and limited. Even if I am sitting in an open space, feeling united with all life, that too will pass, and soon I will experience myself as a disconnected fragment, evidence of my inevitably flawed human nature. The ever-changing flow of inner experience available to me freezes the minute I label some of these experiences (usually only those I approve of) as "me" and the others "not me."

All spiritual and psychological paths are attempts to answer the question, "Who am I?" Different paths focus on different levels of consciousness, different parts of the totality of our experience of being human. Psychological work will help us integrate the inner child and strengthen the positive ego. Some spiritual work will help us develop our intuition and enter into shamanic and transpersonal realms. Other meditative practices will aid our ability to get our separate egos out of the way and experience our innate harmony with life directly.

All inner work is valid which deepens our experience and hence expands our understanding of the question "Who am I?" But work which attempts to freeze us into a single answer to the question about who we are does not serve the evolutionary task of expanding our idea of what it means to be human. When we are told that "we are all terrible sinners," we shrink into a dark and limited identity based on self-rejection. But when we are given an answer that "we are really all angels in disguise," we may also pull away from parts of ourselves and deny our darkness. Surely we are both—sinners and angels—and much, much more.

It is extremely difficult to contain in our awareness the many contradictions of being human. We easily fall into the temptation to oversimplify our experience. When we see our flaws, we lose sight of our magnificence. When we recognize our beauty, we forget our pain and vulnerability. Yet both extremes, and everything in between, is part of the human experience, our experience, our true nature as human and spiritual beings.

As a species we have developed an incredible and unprecedented ability to ask questions about ourselves. And yet as a species we constantly seek to define and thus restrict our complexity. Our minds are still limited by the dualistic illusion that we are **either** this **or** that. We define ourselves and others in terms of the dualities our minds have been structured to recognize. We label ourselves and other people as either happy or unhappy, either sane or insane, either trustworthy or untrustworthy. We seek to place labels and have definitive answers about ourselves that will keep our identity secure and fixed.

We are all like children watching a Shakespearean play. When we get scared by the raging of King Lear on the stormy moor, we urgently demand to know, "Is he a good guy or a bad guy?"—as if to answer the question definitively could allay the anxiety central to our complex nature as both good and bad. We need gradually to educate our immature, dualistic minds to embrace the whole of our human experience, to transcend oppositional "either/or" thinking, and allow the wisdom of "both/and." This is the next evolutionary leap for our species.

On the social level we need to challenge the either/or mentality that has produced wars and the mentality of war, in which our relationships with other people are reduced to the simplicity of seeing everyone as either an ally or an enemy. This mentality of me *versus* the other is also central to the planetary crisis of ecological exploitation, in which we see humans as separate from the earth, rather than as part of the matrix in which we and the future generations of our species must live in harmony if we are to thrive. We need to understand that our well-being as individuals and as a species depends on a healthy respect for and connection with all other humans and with all the other non-human species with whom we share this planet.

This expanded understanding of interconnectedness begins with admitting the truth of our own complex nature. When we reclaim those negative attributes within ourselves that we project onto the "other," we will have fewer enemies. When we allow ourselves to expand our individual boundaries to include an identity with other humans and with nature, we will be able to live in greater harmony with the whole of life. "Love thy neighbor as thyself" is not so much a moral injunction as an invitation to see life as it really is. We are asked to expand our awareness of self to include our neighbors, to know that to love our neighbor is to love ourselves, and vice versa. Love is the experience that expands our boundaries of apparent self-interest to include more and more of what was previously deemed outside ourselves as "other." Conversely, when we learn to love all of our inner selves, to not reject whatever is within us, it will be easy to love our neighbors and our neighboring earth.

The expansion of our self-understanding must begin with becoming exceptionally truthful with ourselves, especially about our personal faults and negativities.

Accepting Our Flawed Human Nature

To be human is to be flawed and imperfect. We all make mistakes, occasionally hurt the people closest to us, and sometimes behave very badly. And yet this simple truth seems very hard for us to accept.

When I realize I have hurt my daughter by a careless exchange, I cringe inwardly, as if trying to fend off the pain that is an inevitable part of the awareness of my action. We are even more reluctant to accept the messages about our flaws that come from other people. Our defenses go up immediately, as if our bodily person were under attack. Indeed the very same fight/flight physiological defenses, appropriate to situations where there is immediate threat of direct bodily harm, have become attached to protecting our idealized self image, needing to appear right and good rather than wrong or bad. We shrink from looking at our mistakes and flaws because they are a painful, though unavoidable, part of who we are. Only when I relax my perfectionism can I feel the simple sadness of having done something hurtful to my daughter. I breathe deeply, relax my automatic defenses, and feel the simple pain. Only then can I experience forgiveness. I come to a deeper level of self-acceptance.

When we deny our faults and selfishness, we stay trapped in trying to appear better than we are and to place the blame for our difficulties elsewhere. "It's not my fault," is the first cry of the child in us whenever we are confronted by our mistakes. When something unpleasant happens, we respond inwardly like the young child who heard his mother's voice calling out to him after an earthquake had shaken the house. His first response was "I didn't do it, Mommy." The child in us fears that to acknowledge our bad or imperfect qualities means we are only bad, or that we are colossally bad, and will incur the judgment or rejection of those parental "others" who, we imagine, are responsible for our wellbeing.

Out of fear of our flawed self, we create a mask self, an idealized self, the self we think we ought to be, rather than admitting the imperfect human self that we are. We're all quick to say "I'm fine" when asked, no matter how depressed we may be by our boss's recent criticism, or delighted we are by our recent business success. We are quick to assure ourselves and others that "I'm o.k., I'm competent, I can handle it" no matter how needy or unhappy we actually are. As a child I was the over-achieving good girl, eager to appear always smart and competent, to earn my father's love and guarantee his approval. This mask still appears in the adult I am whenever I see myself as "doing good," and as therefore better than others, such as the litterers whose trash I am picking up.

Whether we create the mask of the good girl or boy, or the powerful man or woman, the striving student or the self-assured teacher, the needy child or the competent adult, the naïve seeker or the worldly cynic, our masks are an attempt to rise above our faults and our pain, to deny our ordinariness and our pettiness. We create a mask whenever we attempt to portray ourselves as more loving or powerful, more competent or needy, more compassionate or cynical, than the feelings or motives we are actually experiencing at that moment.

The avoidance of our true experience in the moment wastes enormous energy that can be reclaimed by the simple act of choosing to open to the truth of ourselves as we are, moment to moment. Such self-acceptance includes understanding our need for the mask, created as it is out of a need for the child in us to establish an acceptable persona when our self-esteem feels fragile and threatened.

As we deepen our commitment to being honest with ourselves and others, we develop a more reliable basis for self-esteem. Thinking well of ourselves then no longer depends on meeting the unrealistic demands of a perfectionistic mask, but is anchored in the courage to face our present imperfect human reality. The vastness of our human potential can become ours only when we first dare to be exactly and only who we are moment to moment, however petty or fearful, grand or holy, this might temporarily be.

"If you do not pretend to be more than you are, you will dare to be all that you are." These words, spoken to me by the Pathwork Guide years ago, continue to guide me.

Awakening Our Spiritual Potential

Being human also means that we can experience within us an inherent wholeness and perfection; we can know ourselves to be one with the Life Force, with spirit, with God.

While walking on the road, I noticed that my act of picking up trash had become an effort to be "good" that kept me locked in my identification with my good girl mask. The moment I could release that self-conscious idea of myself, I became empty, no more important a presence in that scene than the munching cows on the other side of the fence or the glistening grasses at my feet. I was then open to experience a melting of self into the beauty and perfection of the moment that temporarily obliterated my separateness, expanding my sense of self as being in harmony with the whole of life.

We can feel ourselves to be one with all that is, an individualized expression of the Universal Spirit moving through all things. Most religions, and the mystical traditions of all religions, recognize our inherent divinity as our truest nature. "Godself," "Buddha nature," or "Christ self" are all names for the higher self, or higher power, within each human being. There is in us a wholeness behind our usual fragmented, separated experience of ourselves.

We are so much more than we think we are. In each moment, whether or not we are aware of our inner vastness, we extend beyond our known selves and deeper than our present personality. The issue of enhancing our self-esteem then broadens into an inquiry about who is this "self." In such an inquiry we will discover inner identities of greater dignity and more nobility of spirit than we dreamed possible. We can experience states of consciousness where we know that every moment of our experience is a perfect expression of a totality much larger than we can even imagine.

> In the nucleus of your innermost self you will find the eternal presence of God. . . . [There is an inner] universe in which all is well and nothing is to be feared. In it you will find a sense of wholeness and of eternal life, the power of healing and emotional fulfillment on the deepest possible level. *(PGL 200, "The Cosmic Feeling")*[1]

But just as we defend against knowing our imperfect human self for fear of being nothing more than our limitations, so also do we defend against knowing our innately divine self for fear of losing our comfortable, circumscribed idea of who we are. We have come to believe that our limited human personality, bounded by the surface of our skin, is our identity, and we resist knowing that we are more. We live on the surface of life, identifying our "self" with our experience of separation. We are afraid to plunge to the depths of ourselves where we are so much more than our usual experience of ourselves.

We fear acknowledging our faults and unconscious negativity because this awareness shakes up our pride and our identification with the pretenses of the mask. But we equally fear awakening the unconscious positive, expanded self because we do not want to challenge our known universe or be disappointed by wanting more than we can have. In this way, fear and pride narrow our personal perimeters of experience and keep our awareness fragmented and partial.

> The reality you experience as a human being and on this human plane is an infinitesimally fragmentary aspect of total reality. . . . When consciousness is not connected with the deeper meaning of things, life must be a struggle. This applies to every human being, to some degree at least. For even the most aware and developed individuals have periods when they, too, get lost in the maze of their own disconnectedness and lack of understanding. *(PGL 181)*

---

[1] Hereafter, throughout the text of this book, only the number of the Pathwork Guide Lecture will be given after a direct quote from the Pathwork material. The title of that lecture may be found by consulting the complete list of Pathwork Guide Lectures, arranged in numerical sequence beginning on page 284.

Thus, we live most of our lives in a state of defense, building walls around our awareness as we attempt to keep "out there" whatever threatens us, and which we do not claim as part of ourselves. On the one hand, we push away awareness of our simple flawed humanity, with its petty evils, frequent mistakes, common pain, and intense vulnerability. We enclose ourselves in a mask which we hope will keep our flaws and pain outside our awareness. And on the other hand, we deny our deepest spiritual core, where we are whole, magnificent expressions of the All.

Expanding Our Sense of Self

Spiritual work is the discipline of slowly, steadily expanding the boundaries of self to integrate into awareness more and more of who we are. It takes dedication and courage to expand our idea of ourselves. We must be willing to remove our defenses against our buried pain in order to grow.

Harriet was exploring her resistance to expanding her idea of herself. She could feel an inner wall, a rigid and defiant "no" to knowing herself as other than a grimly competent adult or, conversely, a depressed lost child. Both of these identities felt familiar; anything else was unknown and scary.

In a guided visualization she could see her thinking mind as a sentinel that stood on top of the gray stone wall surrounding the known territory of self, warning her against straying into dangerous territories of feeling or spirit. Whenever she felt the smallest inkling for more in her life, the sentinel would issue his command, "Watch out! That's dangerous territory out there. Get back inside the familiar fortress. You'll never survive out there."

And yet Harriet could remember a time long ago when, as a young child, she lived in a very different world. This was a bright magic world, where teddy bears talked, where she had tea with her happy imaginary friends, and where the woods glowed with spirit life. The world was safe then, and Mommy and Daddy were there to protect her; she hadn't needed a wall or a sentinel then.

Harriet could also remember when this bright, happy world turned into total, inexplicable blackness. The precipitating event was the death of Harriet's father when she was only six years old. After her father's death, her mother had become quite unstable and emotionally dependent. Little Harriet's security was threatened and the light was extinguished in her psychic world. She had made the unconscious choice to grow up as quickly as possible to survive this terrible loss. She suppressed her grief and strained to act like the competent grown-up her mother needed.

Harriet began to see that her feelings and sense of self had become frozen at the moment of her father's death. Unconsciously she had made the decision to flatten her emotional world, color it gray, live inside the safe fortress of her depression. She had unconsciously concluded that her sunny, lively elation was unsafe; it left her too vulnerable to terrible, black disappointment. Better to shut down all extremes of feeling. She had erected the wall and invited the sentinel to be the protector of her vulnerable feelings, the guardian of her defense. This long-forgotten decision now came to the foreground.

In a Pathwork session with me, Harriet talked to the sentinel as though he were another person, and thanked him for having protected her from feelings and awarenesses that might have overwhelmed her as a child. Then she asked him to let her venture beyond the narrow boundary of the self she had known. Harriet told him she was truly grown now and had the ego strength to risk the fall into the feared abyss of her feelings; she now had some faith that she could land safely at the bottom of the well which had once meant sure annihilation.

Harriet allowed the energy of her grief and anger; she wept and she raged. She now had the courage to embrace her feeling self. As she opened up to her deeper feelings, Harriet felt herself flooded with brightness and hope. She was slowly reclaiming the childhood innocence and openness that lay behind the terrible pain of her father's loss. The wall would close in again, but never quite so tightly as before. Each time she opened to her pain or to her longing, her life was a little less gray and forbidding than it had once been.

Our experience of life is an exact reflection of who we are within. Wherever our lives are constricted and unfulfilling, we need to go deeper into our inner territory, to uncover where we have frozen our potential for a richer experience of life. Every time we expand our inner territory, our outer lives will expand. Our best spiritual teacher is always the life that is right in front of us; our most important spiritual lessons always come in the form of our life experience.

To expand our lives, we must be willing to move into the unknown within us.

> It always seems at first frightening to go beyond the
> present ego-confines. New land is unaccustomed,

foreign, unknown. The ego is under the illusion that
to stay in the narrow confines of the known territory
is easy, relaxing, effortless. This feeling is an illusion
because the stagnant state is really effortful. Stagnation
requires an enormous amount of often unconscious
effort in order to sustain the resistance against the
natural inclination of the soul to grow. (*PGL 199*)

Honoring Our Spiritual Longing

The call of the soul to grow spiritually comes to us in the
form of our personal longings. Every human being longs for
something which we believe would make our lives more fulfilling. This may come to us as longing for a deep mutuality with
a mate or for meaningful work or for a more loving family. Or
our desires may be for spiritual fulfillment, for a deeper relationship with God, or Christ, or the Earth. Behind these specific
desires is "a feeling or a sensing that another more fulfilling
state of consciousness and a larger capacity to experience life
must exist." (*PGL 204*)

All longing is ultimately the same longing—to experience a
more loving relatedness to self, to others, to our environment,
and to God. We may be ashamed of our longing because it opens
us to feeling vulnerable, the way we felt as children when our
longings were frustrated or even crushed. We may fear our longing because it opens us to the possibility of disappointment. Yet
only by awakening and honoring our longing will we have the
motivation to do the inner work to expand our lives.

Most of our longings can be expressed as a desire to love (self,
another person, work, nature, or God) and to be loved (by self,
another person, our environment, or God). The first step is to
learn to love, and be loved by, ourselves. In this way we establish
a foundation for fulfilling all our longings. We learn to identify
with a part of ourselves that can love, and then direct that loving into those parts of ourselves that feel unlovable. Learning to
love and accept all of ourselves is the primary, ongoing tool for
self-healing.

Our longings to love and be loved lead us toward expanding ourselves and our lives. But we must also be willing to pay
the price of strict inner honesty and self-confrontation, to look
at how we constrict ourselves. We learn to see where we have
been hateful instead of loving (toward ourselves as well as

toward others), where we limit ourselves due to fear or pride, where we believe we are helpless victims and others are respon-sible for our unhappiness.

> Your longing is realistic when you start from the
> premise that the clue to fulfillment must lie in you;
> when you wish to find the attitudes in you that pre-
> vent you from experiencing life in a fulfilled and
> meaningful way; when you interpret the longing as a
> message from the core of your inner being, sending
> you on a path that helps you to find your real self.
> (*PGL 204*)

The Path of the Undefended Self

The path to the real self includes learning to shed our mask, accepting our "lower" imperfect human nature and embracing our "higher" perfect spiritual nature. Spiritual growth is move-ment toward the undefended self, the self that neither masks our human flaws nor denies our spiritual essence. Expanding our self-awareness and self-acceptance in these ways will bring us the deepest possible harmony and contentment in life, and will pro-vide the most solid basis for true self-esteem.

This book outlines an approach to personal and spiritual growth that emphasizes the need to explore all the opposites and extremes of our nature—the devil and the angel, the vulnerable child and the competent adult, the pettiness of ego and the grandness of spirit. We learn to accept the multiplicity of our human identities and experiences. We learn to relinquish our defenses against knowing all of who we are—the undesirable as well as the desirable sides of our nature. To reclaim our human-ity, we must let go of our defensive masks and acknowledge our inherent limitation and imperfection. To develop our spiritual-ity, we need to drop our pretense of already knowing who we are and be open to the vast unknown depths of self.

Exercises for Chapter 1:

1. What do you most long for in your life? Write down your specific longings. Then see how they represent an underlying longing for more expanded and loving states of consciousness. Put into words your deepest longing.

2. a. Make a list of what you think are your specific flaws or faults. Ask one other person to share what they think are your faults and write these down.

   b. Make a list of your good qualities. Ask another person to share what they think are your good qualities and write these down. Sit with the lists of both your "good" and flawed aspects and see how fully you can allow yourself to claim both sides of yourself.

3. a. Write about an area of your life that is troubling you. Relate this area to your list of faults. Do you find a relationship?

   b. Write about an area of your life that is working well. Relate this area to your list of good qualities. Do you find a relationship?

4. Ask for the help of your inner Godself in directing you on your path. Sit quietly and ask for help, making specific your request for spiritual guidance. Listen inside for a voice. If you hear something, write it down. Ask for a dream to guide you on your spiritual path and write down whatever comes.

5. In what area(s) of your life would you most like to focus your personal growth work now? What aspects of your higher self need strengthening? What aspects of your mask and lower self need to be understood more fully?

CHAPTER 2

Choosing to Unify Our Selves

*"When you undertake inner exploration as your
main task in life, restlessness disappears
and a deep sense of meaning and direction
come into your soul."*

—Pathwork Guide Lecture 208, *"The Innate Capacity to Create"*

Maureen: Integrating The Child and the Lion-Tamer

"I love my husband very much," Maureen blurts out, between sobs. *"But ever since our children were born, I have had little or no sexual desire for Jim. It feels like a terrible loss. When we were dating, I couldn't keep my hands off him, but now I feel affectionate and fond, but hardly ever actively desire him. And it isn't just sexual desire,"* she confesses, *"I just don't have much feeling with him anymore, even though I know I love him, lots."* Maureen's large brown eyes fill with tears again, as she looks pleadingly toward me and Alan, my co-leader. She concludes, *"I don't understand what's happening."* Maureen, a successful therapist and pretty woman in her mid-thirties, then shares a little about her Irish Catholic family, in which she was the oldest of five children, with a domineering alcoholic father subject to wild mood swings and a bitter submissive mother who seemed perpetually tired.

We ask Maureen to choose a "father" from among the men in the group, and she chooses Bob, whose father had also been alcoholic. With a little coaching from Maureen, Bob knows the role well. Bob swaggers across the room, imitating a manic mood, and bellows at his "daughter" Maureen. *"Been a great day today. Made lots of sales. Isn't that great Maurie?"* With a question that is more like a command, he slaps her on the back. *"C'mon now, let's see some smiles outta you today. Whatta you givin' me that droopy look for?"* Maureen starts to reply, but her "Dad" quickly interrupts, *"C'mon, Huh, say 'huh' back to me."* This had been her father's trick to make his rather somber and serious daughter laugh. He would tell her to say *"huh,"* then he would return with *"huh, huh"* and she would have to respond again with *"huh, huh, huh,"* until she would produce the obligatory laugh. His nickname for her had become *"Huh."* This time Maureen tries to protest. *"Listen to me, Dad, I want to tell you about my day."* Bob, as father, jumps up and starts to tickle Maureen. *"Come on, Huh, don't gimme that sad sack routine. It's a great day today; let's have some fun."* Maureen, reliving the feelings of her inner child, feels the defeat keenly and retreats to the other side of the room, crying softly. Alan and I encourage her to express her sadness fully, but only a few tears trickle out.

Then Bob and Maureen act out a situation in which her father's mood was reversed. Bob comes into the room with a scowl on his face, barking out a command, *"Get me my slippers, Maurie."* When she delays and attempts to talk with him, he yells, *"Now!"* She slinks away but comes back a minute later with the slippers and a school project to show *him. Bob waves her away. "Not today. Can't look at anything today. Terrible day. No sales." And then, raising his voice, "Can't you see I'm in no mood to put up with you kids. If things keep on this way, we'll pull you all out of that expensive Catholic school your mother insists you go to. Terrible time for sales. Go tell your mother to bring me a drink before dinner." Again Maureen moves away, sad and pained. But this time there are no tears.*

Suddenly Maureen straightens up and reveals, "I remember a moment, in the hallway, outside my parents' bedroom. He was in one of his foul moods and had yelled at me because I hadn't brought him the right slippers or something. Then, carrying his before-dinner drink, he went into the bedroom and slammed the door, making me feel I had done something really awful to him. I started to sink inside, the way I always did when I knew I had failed to please him, and then something snapped. Or hardened. Or let go. I can't tell which, but anyway, I remember thinking, 'I'm not going to let him get to me again, not ever again.' And I didn't. I don't think I ever cried again until I was in college and met Jim, my husband. I just shut down and wouldn't feel anything when Dad went into one of his moods."

Alan takes her hand in his and urges Maureen to look at him. When she does, the tears start again softly and she almost whispers to him, "I think I've shut down with Jim just like I did with my father. Now that Jim is the father to our children, I love him even more than I ever did. He matters to me so much, I think I'm more afraid now that he could really hurt me, hurt me as deeply as my Dad did."

Alan and I urge her now to make a choice different from the one she made as a child to withhold her feelings from her father. Alan stands next to Bob and encourages Maureen to give to the two men the full range of her feelings toward her Dad. First she hisses, "Do you have any idea how much you hurt me? You ignored me, you self-centered bastard. You didn't pay any attention to who I really was. I was just a prop in your drama. You never really saw any of us, we were just background, just 'the kids' to you." Her voice gets louder. "What about me, Dad? What about me? I count for something, don't I? Don't I, Dad?" Now, pointing her finger at herself, she stamps her feet and yells, "See me! See **me** *dammit! You aren't the only person on earth. I matter too." But by now her voice has become a high squeak. Fear and grief have eroded her certainty. She collapses onto a couch, and into the arms of one of the other women in the group, sobbing, "I'm not so sure I do matter. If he couldn't love me, maybe I'm not lovable." Now the grief comes forth more fully, the sobs unchecked.*

When Maureen gets to her feet again, I comment, "I think you can consciously make a new choice now, the choice to have all of your feelings, for yourself. Your father cannot hurt you like that any more. And Jim is so much better able to receive and love you." Then I ask softly, "Can you make this new commitment now?" Maureen searches inside and says truthfully, "Almost, but not quite. Something seems to be missing."

I make a guess at what is missing. "Maybe you need to experience the reverse of your victimized child. Maybe you need to find the ways you still want to punish your father, even to victimize him. Is there a part that still wants revenge?" Maureen's eyes light up in recognition. "That sounds true!"

She asks Bob to help her again, only this time as her present sixty-five-year old father, aging and aware of his frailty. Bob asks Maureen to be kind to him now, to forgive him the faults of his youth. "No way!" she bellows. "Now it's my turn to boss you around! Now I'm in charge and you'll do things my way." With emphatic tone, she adds, "Do you hear?" Bob meekly whines, "But I need you now; please be nice, Huh." With a sharp burst of "Ha!", Maureen repeats, "No way! You'll jump when I say jump now. Now go, go fetch me my slippers." He does so. "I feel like I've finally tamed the lion," she shares. "He's an old man now and I have the power to hurt him."

Alan and I look around for something to be a lion-tamer's whip for Maureen. A young man pulls a length of rope from out of his pants loops, and gives it to Maureen. We encourage her to let out her lion-tamer more fully. She slaps the floor with the rope, and shouts out demands to her compliant "father" Bob. "Laugh now, Dad, go 'huh, huh.' Do it, now." Bob complies. "OK, do it again, only with more feeling," Maureen commands, slapping the rope several times again on the floor near Bob. She laughs a cruel laugh, finding herself enjoying the role of lion-tamer. She makes several more demands to which Bob accedes, and then she sums up, exultantly, "You'll do what I tell you to do and only what I tell you to do, when and where I tell you to do it!"

Maureen's movement from the role of sad child victim into the role of cruel adult perpetrator is now complete. We ask her to feel the negative pleasure in her new role, and she easily accesses the delight she feels in the power to order her father around, to be totally in control of him. She acknowledges too the satisfaction she feels in having cut off her human feelings for him. "No compassion, only power and control," she announces in triumph. She strides around some more, striking the rope on the floor and allowing the full pleasure of her "sweet" revenge. Several women in the room acknowledge their delight at Maureen's taking revenge against her father.

But after a few minutes the mood palpably shifts, within Maureen and in the room. "I feel empty," she shares. "This isn't really much fun. I don't feel any more loved or lovable this way, and I certainly don't feel the kind of connection I longed for with my Dad. Now I just feel sad. Sad for myself, my own loss of my father and sad for how I want to hurt him back. Sad about how men and women keep doing this to each other. This terrible hurting game, back and forth. It all feels enormously sad to me right now, a terrible waste of energy."

The tears start again, as she walks slowly toward Alan and Bob. Standing vulnerably in front of them, she says simply, "I'm sorry. I'm so sorry." Alan, speaking the words we all know must be buried in Maureen's Dad's heart, returns, "Me too. I'm sorry too." Maureen falls sobbing into Alan's arms and they sit on the couch together, with Alan holding her, for a long time. A number of people around the room, also crying, have sought the arms of another next to them for holding and for comfort. We are all feeling the sadness of our shared human losses and the pain of our vengeful feelings. After Maureen's crying eventually subsides, she looks up into Alan's face, and adds, to Alan, to Jim, and to her Dad, "It's over now. We don't need to do this any more. It's so sad, but it's over now. I can love me. I can forgive you. It will take time, but I can do it. Now I know."

Choosing to Unify Our Selves

Even after Maureen opened up the previously buried feelings of her wounded inner child, this healing experience was not complete. A step had been skipped. She needed to meet the opposite of the hurt child, the vengeful adult, before she could release the childhood pain and forgive her father.

Our healing depends on just such a process of incorporating opposites. The competent adult steps aside and reveals the damaged child. The wounded victim yields to uncover the cruel perpetrator. Our spiritual path will lead us to embrace every pair of inner opposites, bringing out of the shadow whatever has been hidden away as unacceptable, mean, petty, or weak. Only in that way can the dark, undeveloped side be integrated into consciousness and the excitement and pleasure that are locked in the negative shadow be released back into the pool of our available energy.

But precisely because the human mind sees life in dualities, we often experience even our longing for personal and spiritual growth as a desire to enhance positive experience and eliminate the negative. We want to have health, pleasure, and happiness, and to exclude sickness, pain, and unhappiness.

Nor is it an error to want the positive things that human life has to offer. It could not be otherwise since that is how human consciousness is organized. However, the spiritual problem comes when we seek to repress what is negative or vulnerable in us, to deny or live "above" our mortality, fallibility, negativity, or pain.

> It is wishful thinking that concentrating on divinity
> automatically deals with the dark side of human nature.
> This cannot be so. You cannot overcome what you have
> not consciously and fully experienced. (*PGL 193*)

We perpetuate non-awareness when we struggle to embrace only the positive side of human life and to deny or avoid the other half. If we focus only on our good qualities and ignore the problems that our lives reveal must exist in us, or if we hope for fulfillment without actually facing whatever in us blocks this fulfillment, we will stay in perpetual illusion, and our spiritual growth will remain incomplete.

> When you seek only one side of a pair of opposites,
> you must oppose the other side. In that opposition,
> your soul is agitated and fearful, and in that state
> you can never reach a unified state. As long as you
> oppose one side and cling to the other, self-realization
> or liberation—that is, the unitive principle—is
> unattainable. (*PGL 144*)

If we want love and power, pleasure and creative expansion, we must also be willing to feel fear and helplessness, pain and contraction, because trying to exclude these "bad" states will so constrict our capacity for experience that the "good" will also be unavailable. When we close off awareness of any one side of ourselves, we also close off its opposite side. When we open, we open to it all.

The Development of Our Dualities

Our usual human experience is of a limited and partial reality, in which the vastness of consciousness has been narrowed within the limits of person, time, and place. Some-times consciousness temporarily frees itself from the constraints of the limited, dualistic mind and carries us into the broader knowing of our essential state of Being, behind and beyond duality, from which we can know our oneness with other humans and with all life. But then we come back to our squeezed and partial ordinary state of knowing, our "me" separate from whatever is perceived as "not me."

Each human birth is an entrance into a separate identity. Just how separated and alienated we become from parts of ourselves, from other humans, and from our environment is a result of what dualistic issues we have come into life to resolve. These issues become manifest in the course of our growth from infant to adulthood.

At birth the infant does not have an ego; "self" and "not-self" are not differentiated. But the infant does experience duality on the physical level. Some things (hunger, wetness, cold, rough touch) are unpleasant and bring dissatisfaction and pain. The baby cries. Some others (feeding, dryness, warmth, gentle touch) are pleasant and induce satisfaction and pleasure. The baby coos. Instinctively the infant seeks to maximize those experiences that support his physical survival and that produce pleasure, and to minimize experiences of pain and deprivation. Our earliest experiences of human duality on the physical level are imprinted on us and often determine how we relate to eating and hunger, warmth and cold, cleanliness and uncleanliness for the rest of our lives.

Little by little the developing child enters further dualities—on the emotional level—as he discovers that certain ways he behaves and feels produce negative or unpleasant consequences in his world, as defined primarily by the reactions of his parents. Physical survival now becomes emotional survival and more dualities about "what is emotionally safe" *versus* "what is emotionally unsafe" proliferate as he attempts to enhance those reactions from parents which feel good and to avoid or reduce those which feel bad. We begin to define our particular emotional dualities, our psychological issues, our neuroses and our problems, as we struggle to achieve emotional survival and well-being. From our early childhood experiences with our parents, family, and our immediate world, we define for ourselves "what is good" *versus* "what is not good" behavior and feelings on the basis of the kinds of reactions they arouse in us.

The developing person defines himself in the mental sphere as well as in the physical and emotional realms. He learns to accept some ideas as "o.k." and to reject others as "not o.k." Not only are certain ideas judged wrong, it becomes unacceptable to even have these thoughts, and so they are relegated to the unconscious mind.

The physical/emotional/mental self—which we would like to limit to acceptable bodily sensations, agreeable feelings, and approved thoughts, and which we believe ends at the edge of our skin—is perceived as separate from the environment. All outside this boundary is perceived as "other," different from self. Just how distant or cut off we feel from all that is deemed "other" is largely a result of how relatively dangerous or benign we perceived our childhood environment to be. Once we identify ourselves as a separate ego, our needs for physical, emotional, and mental well-being are incorporated into the need for ego enhancement and self-esteem. With the development of an ego, yet more dualistic beliefs come into existence about what is desirable (ego-enhancing) *versus* what is undesirable (ego-diminishing).

In the course of our growth into a separate adult human being, we erect more and more barriers to our knowing of ourselves. We have labeled many experiences of our physical, emotional, and mental reality, and many aspects of our relationship with others, as undesirable, even intolerable. By the time we are adults, these rejected aspects of ourselves have become buried in the unconscious. We have limited our self-definition to a more or less small territory of experience that we have found acceptable. We have come to believe that we are only our idealized image of ourselves.

Growth Into Unity

The spiritual path requires that we explore the personal dualities which become manifest in childhood and are carried over into adulthood. We need to unravel and reverse the process by which we have become alienated from ourselves and our environment. We make the journey from the limited identity of our idealized self image back to the expansiveness of our real self.

On this journey we awaken the longing to experience an expanded identity, to touch our central core, to know the place of unity within. From our normal ego perception we see life in terms of opposites, one of which we deem desirable and the other undesirable. However:

> In the unified plane of consciousness, there are no opposites. There is only good, only right, only life. Yet it is not the kind of good, or the kind of right, or the kind of life that comprises but one half of the opposites on the dualistic plane. The unified "good" transcends the opposites, and is of a completely different nature. The good that exists on the unified plane of consciousness combines both aspects so that the opposites no longer conflict with one another. (PGL 143)

We can only arrive at this deeper unity when we learn to accept what we have rejected in ourselves, to go toward what we have tried to avoid. We come to unity through accepting our dualities.

Dorothy asked for a dream to guide her on her spiritual path. She had achieved considerable worldly stature as a successful businesswoman and was a committed spiritual seeker. She felt ready to go deeper; her dream laid out her path with exquisite clarity:

"I come up from a place in the basement of a building, a cramped narrow space where I had been living. I have a friend with me who is very worldly and sophisticated We ascend steps into a building which is much larger than I had imagined possible.

"At the very center of this building is a small garden with a tiny fence around it. The only thing growing here is an enormous squash plant, with a large, sturdy central core and twelve or more vines coming out from this thick stem. At the end of each vine is a fruit, like a squash, but each squash is split in half. I sense that the plant represents unity and duality, the central unified core of life and the dualistic manifestation of life's fruits. In the presence of this plant I have a great feeling of serenity. I then discover that the plant is being tended by an old couple, wise and serene, whom I recognize as the eternal guardians of this plant. I want to stay and be taught by this beautiful couple, but my friend is impatient and wants to move on. She does not even notice this plant which has so captured my attention; she is eager to explore the building.

"I go with my friend and we move around the house, eventually going upstairs and out onto a side porch into the outer darkness. Here I meet a man who seems to be the mate of the woman who has been accompanying me from the basement. They do not act like a couple; they are so lost in their own narcissistic concerns. Some years ago I had a compulsive affair with this man, who is now worried and anxiously pacing around the porch. I try to soothe him, comfort him, but he is unable to re-center himself. I cannot get through to him; he is lost in his negative space and unable to connect with me or his mate. I leave them pacing anxiously on the darkened porch; she is prattling on about the architecture of the house.

"I come back inside the lighted building. As I look down from the top of the stairs at the building inside, I am awed at its beauty. The large squash plant gracefully fills the central core, and all around the large room surrounding the plant are tables covered with luminous emerald green, moss-colored tablecloths where people are waiting to be fed from the fruits of the plant growing in the core of this space. I am filled with contentment as I view the plant and this room, feeling what a healthy, sweet place this is. How good for everyone to be nourished by this space as well as by the plant at the center.

"Drinking in the richness of the space, I feel myself becoming more beautiful, graceful, and healthy. As I come downstairs to spend more time with the plant, I see a man. We look at each other, and I recognize this man as my true partner. He feels like both the real partner for whom I long and also the masculine part of myself.

"I return to the plant, joined now by the man who is to be my partner, and begin my new task of caring for this plant. I will be instructed by the wise old couple who are the eternal care-takers of the plant, and who I sense are my unified masculine/feminine higher self. I will work with my partner to feed the people who have come to this building for nourishment. These guests have a role in my own completion; they are part of the mutuality that exists between myself and those whom I serve.

"I know, however, that my task does not stop here, but includes my continuing to reach out to the couple trapped out on the dark porch, who seem to represent the distorted masculine and feminine aspects of both my mask and lower self. My mask is one of sophisticated, worldly competence. My lower self manifests in my compulsive grasping energy and my fearful distrust of others. I lack faith in my spiritual self and have a compulsive need for my little ego to be in control. In this place of relying solely on my ego, I have immense anxiety. I know I will need to carry to this couple the food of spiritual nourishment from the squash plant. I will need to go back and forth from my new home in this beautiful build-

ing out to the darkness where these two are still trapped in their igno-
rance and anxiety, until they are ready, which I trust they sometime will
be, to come inside with me."

Dorothy's dream showed her clearly that she needed to leave her limited outer worldly life and enter the richness of her inner house. There she would discover the spiritual center within her symbolized by the squash plant—unified at the source, and dualistic in its expression. Dorothy finds the outpicturing of her negative, lower self male-female split in the compulsive couple, and she commits to working with them as long as needed in order to bring them home. She also discovers her central task of contemplating and tending the inner plant with the guidance of her unified male-female higher self. To do this she will need to meet her mate, that is, to unify her own masculine and feminine aspects. Further, she is meant to serve others who have come to this house of spiritual nourishment.

The dream beautifully illustrates how the spiritual path includes both meeting our flaws and our dualities and opening to our central core of unity.

> When you undertake inner exploration as your main
> task in life, restlessness disappears and a deep sense of
> meaning and direction come into your soul. With that,
> slowly but surely, life's frustrations begin to disappear
> and rich fulfillment begins to take their place. You can
> find your place in life only when you focus your atten-
> tion on the reason for coming into this plane of exis-
> tence in the first place. (*PGL 208*)

The Goal of Spiritual Work

We come into manifestation, into a separate human existence, in order to purify and unify those aspects of ourselves
which are disconnected from the whole. Our disconnection
becomes evident during the course of our childhood experiences
during which we cut off from aspects of ourselves, rejecting them
as intolerable. Those parts of ourselves which we reject exist in
the unconscious, as separated aspects, not knowing their true
origin in God. These are parts which have become alienated from
their true identity as expressions of the All. These are the lost

sheep of our psyches and we must become the good shepherd who welcomes them home.

The goal of spiritual growth is union. Union is accomplished by "the re-unification of every piece and fragment of consciousness that has ever split itself off" from the original union with God. (*PGL 193*)

> True spiritual growth is always a unifying process. It always implies bridging a chasm, mastering a conflict, resolving a contradiction or apparent contradiction. All of life is a progression to attain further unity and eliminate more and more areas of disunity. (*PGL 178*)

Thus, following a spiritual path is not just seeking experiences of union. It is also about getting to know all those negative fragments of self that have been split off from unitive consciousness. This requires our commitment to self-purification, to becoming aware of our flaws and limitations. Then we can transform our blind spots by carefully unraveling the process by which those aspects got buried in the unconscious and thus took on a separate identity.

> When you adopt the limited ego state, you do so for very specific purposes. You come into and manifest yourself in this limited state for the purpose of purification and unification. (*PGL 208*)

Human manifestation allows us to focus on our faults and imperfections in a way that is not possible in other forms or at other levels of our being. In the unitive state of consciousness, beyond human form, we know that our flaws are merely specks of dust on the luminous gown of Being. Only in human life do our faults loom large enough for us to examine and transform them fully. We need to focus on our difficulties and limitations, to see them "as large as life," as it were, so they can get our full attention and be welcomed back into our total being.

We choose to incarnate to know our humanness intimately. The job of transformation is to keep choosing to incarnate more and more of ourselves, to expand what it means to be human, to release our flaws at their origin. While in human form we can activate both our higher and our lower natures.

It is possible to activate the capacities of the larger spiritual or higher self, to focus in its direction and be receptive to its ever-present voice. Similarly, it is possible to focus on and be receptive to negative aspects of your personality that lie deeply buried and that also need to be tackled on your evolutionary road. This path teaches you to contact all these hidden layers and deal with them appropriately. Some parts are more developed and other parts are less developed. The more developed aspects are in the position and have the equipment to explore, to bring out and to unify with the other, less developed parts which are not yet actualized at this time. (*PGL 208*)

The developed aspects of ourselves welcome into consciousness the undeveloped parts ready to come into awareness. All human beings, however evolved, have human flaws. No one is immune from the blindness and limitations of the human condition. However enlightened we may be in certain aspects, other aspects remain undeveloped as long as we are in the human state. The undeveloped aspects are brought into incarnation for purification and our spiritual task is to focus specifically on these faults in order to transform and integrate them. Our dreams often reveal where our paths must focus next.

A young man, newly embarking on his inner path, reported the following dream:

"I am in a large outdoor nature sanctuary—enormous but enclosed—with a very high roof. I discover that I can fly. I am part human/ part creature with reptilian wings, lumbering and powerful, yet also vulnerable and self-doubting. I do not know what I am to do, except that I am sure I need to fly to the top of the enclosure, as high as I am able. There, I think, is where I must build my nest.

"But in order to get there I must fly past a sleeping creature that looks like a dinosaur—a rust-colored lump of flesh. I want to creep past without waking him, because I know he is unevolved, stupid, territorial, and evil. Yet somehow I know I will have to engage him—there is no way around him. And he will not stay asleep if I pass him."

The dream calls on the dreamer to build his nest high in his inner sanctuary. And yet to get there he must incorporate the power of his primitive self, and claim fully the unconscious beast that blocks his way to the heights.

As in "The Beauty and the Beast" fairytale, we can redeem the beast within only by love and acceptance. The "good news" of the path outlined in this book is that there is nothing so dark within the human psyche that it cannot be transformed if brought to the light of awareness. Negativity that is met within the self can be embraced, forgiven, and released. The essential vitality within the negative energy can be reclaimed and integrated with consciousness to add to our sum total of available energy.

Every fault acknowledged, every defense dismantled, and every pain felt and released, gives us powerful new reserves of thought and feeling for creating our lives in positive new directions. And, on the other hand, every negative attitude unconsciously perpetrated, every defense held on to, and every pain denied, ties up our life energies and limits our consciousness.

> Most human beings totally forget or ignore the fact
> that what is worst in them is essentially creative power,
> universal flow and energy that are highly desirable. . . .
> When you shut off the undesirable part, this same part
> cannot change and remains stagnant and paralyzed.
> (*PGL 184*)

Our work on our flawed selves releases enormous positive energy because nothing within us is ultimately separate from our original unity.

An older woman, who experienced her life as a tangled mess of neurotic involvements, had this dream: "I am caught in a sticky spider's web which has ensnared my whole body. I am feeling pretty hopeless until I turn around and see right beside me another spider's web, perfectly formed, glistening with crystal drops of dew. This web is breathtakingly beautiful; I cannot take my eyes off it. I notice too that it is connected to the web that has me caught and, from there, to all the beams of the house I am in. I feel greatly reassured."

She woke up knowing that even though she sometimes feels totally wrapped up in all her sticky neurotic webs, the stuff in which she is stuck is not fundamentally different from the stuff out of which the most glori-

ous webs are woven. In reclaiming and releasing more of her own neurotic aspects she will release more of her divine essence.

Crisis and the Spiritual Evolution of Our Species

We are at a critical point in the evolution of the human species. Our collective lower-self negativity expresses itself in our potential for suicidal pollution of the planet and in our capacity for armed self-destruction. The expression of our higher-self longing to live in love and peace with one another, even with those closest to us, is still severely retarded. Never has the need for spiritual growth, in the individual and in the species, been more compelling. We cannot survive on this planet without it. Evolution is clearly and urgently calling us to this task.

We are also experiencing the breakdown of many certainties—in religion, economics, social organization, and even in science. New paradigms are emerging. Not only are the changes rapid; they are accelerating. In times of such rapid change, crisis is inevitable.

All crisis—on the personal as well as on the species and global levels—is a message about the need for spiritual evolution.

> Crisis is an attempt of nature—of the natural, cosmic lawfulness of the universe—to effect change. Crisis in any form attempts to break down the old balance structures which are based on false conclusions and on negativity. It shakes loose ingrained, frozen lifestyles so that new growth becomes possible. It tears down and breaks up, which is momentarily painful, but transformation is unthinkable without it. (*PGL 183*)

Crisis helps break down the old to create room for the new. Actually it can be a step in growth when we allow the lessons of crisis and disruption in our lives to reveal to us deeper levels of buried distortion that require our attention and transformation. When we meet negativity (or sin or neurosis or limitation or ignorance) in our own souls, then we can see it for the defense that it is, and lose our fear of it.

> The inner negativities and stagnation which create crisis are often unconscious. The first part of any path of honesty with the self is to make these unconscious aspects conscious. They are misconceptions; destructive

> emotions and attitudes, and behavior patterns that
> arise from them; and pretenses and defenses erected
> to hide them. (*PGL 183*)

Spiritual growth requires that we face the negative within. Each time we delay self-facing, the manifestation of crisis and difficulty in our outer lives will escalate.

Harry was a middle-aged Vietnam vet whose life was suddenly erupting with problems, including long-suppressed hostilities toward authority, which were coming out in inappropriate ways in his work. He felt judgmental and frightened of his violent feelings and was strongly tempted to deny them.

He reported the following dream: "I am beside a river and this guru figure appears. Suddenly the river is very tumultuous, choppy and dangerous-looking. The guru beckons me to jump into the river, but I say 'No!' The guru jumps in and swims gracefully downstream about 20 yards and surfaces, again inviting me to jump in. Again I say 'No.' Suddenly the river dries up and there are sticks all over the bottom of the river bed which then change to snakes. The guru beckons me to jump in and walk through the snakes. I say 'No!' Again, the guru walks right in through the snakes with no problem and again invites me to join him and I again say 'No.' At that point the snakes begin to turn and start coming after me, and I wake up."

Harry's interpretation: I have been trying to avoid taking responsibility for my feelings of violence all my life. But the dream clearly says that the more I try to avoid the tumultuous feelings, the more the crisis escalates. When I was in Vietnam I acted out my violence with justification. But now I have to face it as a part of myself that is no longer serving me. My higher self is trying to show me that it is safe to jump into the river of my own inner violence, and I keep resisting. I think I need to make the choice to jump, to do the inner work, before things get worse!

After Harry began serious Pathwork with me to uncover his violent feelings, he had the following dream:

"I am swimming along in a lake that is also some kind of marine research facility, where there are a lot of fish. I see a large fish that I think is a barracuda and I feel afraid; but as I swim nearer to the fish I lose my fear and feel reassured that he will not harm me. Then I see a huge fish

with sharp teeth right in front of me, bigger than a shark, but not as big as a whale. I am startled and am quite afraid. But again I notice that the closer I get the less scary it appears. I relax and notice there are lots of kinds of fish swimming all around me, but none of them will bite me. I give a sigh of relief and dive deeper. Then I am swimming underwater and I notice I can hold my breath a lot longer than I thought I could. I get to the other side of the lake and enter into a kind of laboratory room where a woman assists me to start breathing normally again."

In the laboratory of his personal process work with me, Harry is embracing his inner violence, diving deep into his unconscious and learning to swim with what he finds there.

The Pull of Evolution

Spiritual growth—growth toward unification of all our disharmonious aspects—is not just urgently called for at our current stage of evolution. Spiritual growth is the meaning and purpose of human life on earth. The task of growing spiritually links humanity with all life on the planet whose meaning is fulfilled through participating in the patterns of evolution, manifesting the Cosmic Mind in forms of greater and greater complexity and self-awareness.

The human condition is a state of accelerated evolution, of constant "becoming." The state of non-human nature, by contrast, is one of more simply "being," where the forces of evolution move slowly, having not yet reached the stage of self-consciousness or free will. On the other end of the evolutionary spectrum, beyond our normal human consciousness, are beings of pure spirit who have evolved beyond the duality of the human condition and exist in complete unity and self-awareness, in a state of "conscious being." Human consciousness is neither simple nature nor pure spirit. We are, instead, in the middle stages of evolution, beings of both spirit and matter, of partial but not complete self-awareness, caught in restless incompleteness and inner division. We are in a state of disequilibrium seeking balance, of disunity and duality evolving toward unity.

Unlike non-self-conscious nature, we human beings have the capacity—though only temporarily—to resist our own evolution. Unlike a tree, we can say "no" to growing. We can refuse to feel the life force in our bodies by creating muscular armor which keeps out pleasure and pain, numbing us to the realities of physical life. We can refuse to grow emotionally, and thus get caught in inappropriate and childishly outdated responses to life. We can decide not to expand our minds, and thus keep thinking in limiting concepts which become hardened into prejudices and preconceptions. We can close ourselves off from all that life has to offer, and instead feel victimized and inhibited as we cling to old and outworn attitudes. We can try to cheat life by wanting to get more than we are willing to give.

Sooner or later, however, all such refusals to grow or to give up old attitudes will backfire. Because life cannot be cheated. Wherever we refuse to grow—mentally, emotionally, spiritually—our life experience will be correspondingly shallow and unsatisfying. Whenever we resist the call of evolution for more expansion and greater personal development, we end up creating more pain and difficulty for ourselves. We have to keep learning, again and again, that our happiness lies in choosing the path of personal evolution, in spite of our fears.

The call of the life force toward evolution is a reality. It can be resisted, but it cannot be denied. Personal growth is not just desirable; it is inevitable. It is part of the inexorable cosmic pull of evolution.

> There is a great pull in the manifest universe in which
> you live. This pull must exist in every human individual.
> This pull is directed toward union—toward unifying,
> bringing together, individual fragments of conscious-
> ness. . . . This pull manifests as a tremendous force,
> moving everyone toward inner union and union with
> others, making separateness painful and empty. . . .
> Life, pleasure, oneness with self and others are the
> goals of the cosmic plan of evolution. (*PGL 149*)

The force of evolution is constantly impelling us toward growth, toward opening up more and more areas of ourselves in order to create greater consciousness and more unity. When we choose consciously to share in the universal task of evolution by pursuing our own spiritual growth, our lives become filled with meaning and purpose, as we joyfully participate in the cosmic drama.

Exercises for Chapter 2:

1. Explore some of your personal dualities. What parts of yourself or your life do you reject or judge as: a. intolerable, b. unacceptable, or c. undesirable? Imagine welcoming these rejected parts of yourself or your life back home, as the father did for his prodigal son, or as the good shepherd does for his lost sheep.

2. What parts of yourself or your life do you judge as: a. tolerable, b. acceptable, c. desirable? How might you strengthen your acceptance of yourself and of life?

3. Describe any experiences you have had of your "core" self, the unified center of life that flows through you.

4. Look back at the course of your own spiritual evolution. What events or people have served to awaken you to follow your inner path? Write a brief letter of thanks to whoever or whatever has served in your awakening. Especially notice when crises and difficulties in life provided the incentive for your spiritual learning and allow yourself retroactive gratitude for these events.

5. Look back at some past crisis in your life and see if you can now summarize the lesson that it held for you. What inner duality did it serve to illuminate? How did resolution of the crisis bring more unity into your life?

5. Make a conscious commitment to your own personal evolution, including a commitment to bringing all the undeveloped aspects of your personality into consciousness. Put the commitment into your own words, and create a ritual of commitment for yourself, inviting (if feasible) one or more other people to witness your commitment.

Developing the Observer Self

"There is a real self that equals neither your
negative aspects, nor your adamant self-judgment,
nor the pretense that covers up the negativity.
To find this real self is our concern."

—Pathwork Guide Lecture 189,
"Self-Identification Determined through Stages of Consciousness"

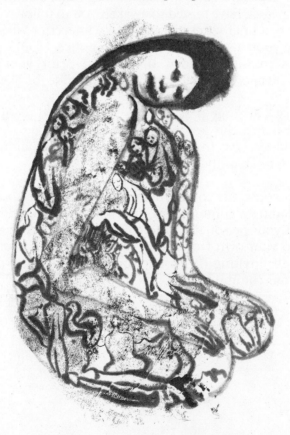

James Expanding: The Microscope and the First Aid Kit

At age fifty, James knew who he was. Or thought he did. He had struggled out of a narrow, lower-class upbringing to finish college and graduate school, and had worked to establish a culturally sophisticated and financially successful life. He had outgrown an early, immature marriage to a dependent and controlling woman, leaving her to raise their two sons.

As a child James had taken seriously his family's rigid Catholicism, even becoming a devoted altar boy. He could never understand the other boys' jokes about missing mass or using the Lord's name in vain. For James the possibility of eternal damnation for committing such sins was a very serious threat. In adolescence, James was gripped in a viselike contradiction between his powerful emergent sexuality and the prohibitions of the Church. At the same time his mind was challenging the superstitions of his religion. He eventually rejected Catholicism and become an adamant atheist.

However, he never stopped searching for answers to the ultimate questions about the meaning of life and death. In his late twenties James had discovered Eastern mystical religions with their mind-stopping answers to the questions he still had. James then began a committed practice of Zen Buddhism and, after many years of meditation, had a powerful enlightenment experience in which his ego-bound sense of separateness dissolved into the state of unitive consciousness, God-realization. Since that time, he was rarely anxious and had lost all fear of death. In his thirties James had found the Pathwork and had done considerable work on trying to bring his personality more into alignment with his spiritual awakening.

But lately James had been feeling bored with his life. While enjoying his competence, independence, and intellectual maturity, he felt he had achieved all his worldly goals. His spiritual knowledge felt secure, and he rarely felt personal distress. Reasonably content with his life and relation-ships, James had been semi-consciously praying for something to shake him up and get him fully engaged with his path of spiritual growth again.

Then his twenty-five-year-old son Matthew arrived for a visit. James had seen Matthew only rarely since he had left his wife many years ago. Father and son had never been close. Although he was fond of Matthew, James had never felt deeply loving toward this gentle boy, who had been a physically fragile child and had never been aggressive or successful enough to please his father. James's ambivalence toward his son also contained a strong dose of guilt about his own inadequacy as a father.

Shortly after his arrival, Matthew told his father that he was gay and had AIDS, a disease that would likely kill him within the year.

Reacting with shock and emotional numbness, James tried to observe in himself the feelings he expected to have in the wake of Matthew's tragic news. But all he could sense was a cold, hard place around his heart which shut out all feeling.

James encouraged his son to talk, and over the next week Matthew cautiously began to open up, first describing his anxiety toward his father and the resentment he had felt when James left the family. He described how his sense of feeling trapped and restricted while growing up with his mother had resumed now that he had recently returned to live with her. Matthew admitted his terror of death, saying that his own rejection of Catholicism had not been replaced by any other spiritual perspective. He confessed that his gay sexual life had mostly been frantic and unhappy, furtive and unfulfilling, until the previous year when he had met and briefly settled in with a man whom he loved deeply. But when Matthew was diagnosed with AIDS, the relationship had crumbled under the strain and he had returned to live with his mother.

James listened through all of this with very little reaction, the chill around his heart solidifying into a wintry numbness. While he wished his son well and felt no judgment about Matthew's homosexuality, James could find nothing reassuring to say to his son about death; he could not articulate any words of comfort. His voice seemed lost deep inside an icy well. When Matthew left a week later to return to his mother's care, the only feeling James could find were twinges of old guilt about his poor fathering.

Then the nightmares began. James awoke several nights in a row trembling and sweating. In one dream: "I am surrounded by nuns or maybe witches, terrifying oversized women, dressed all in black, cackling and pointing accusing fingers at me. I am sure I am about to be killed for some heinous crime. As they start to come toward me, I magically find in my hand a microscope. When I look through the microscope, the whole dream scene changes and I am now viewing myself and the oversized women from a long way away, through the microscope, observing them the way a scientist might, calmly studying some natural phenomenon."

In another dream: "I am stranded alone on a cold, dark field where I will have to spend the night. I somehow know there are vampires here, who might come and suck my blood. I wish for a friend with a first aid kit."

After several weeks of nightmares, James returned to regular Path-work sessions, hoping to find the tools that his dreams suggested might help him. His helper urged him to keep a daily journal, recording all his dreams and feelings. As James worked on his dreams he understood that the microscope in his first dream represented the tool of the objective scientist in him, which had helped him from being overwhelmed by the threatening dream women. In the second nightmare James had hoped for a compassionate friend to bring "the first aid kit," which would help him to heal himself. It was clear to both James and his helper that deep, ancient feelings were now needing to surface. They both knew James needed the clarity of the scientist with a microscope and the compassion of a friend with a first aid kit to see and record what was happening to him, without judgment and without fear. With the help of his observer self, James could welcome the growing unconscious turmoil as signaling a new phase of his spiritual work. He soon had a dream about the state of his "inner house":

"I am in a falling-down house. Coming down the steps, I see curtains fall to the ground, and then part of the steps collapses. A young guy laughs. The owner of the house says, 'It's rough. You don't know how I struggled to put this place together. For years I've been buying and selling small pieces of real estate, knowing that out of each transaction I'd only make a little profit. I kept putting aside the profits to buy this place, and now it's falling apart. I'll never get as much for it as it is really worth.'

"I go out with the owner of this falling-down house and several of his friends. We go through city streets with lots of twists and turns, and I comment on what a hard journey this is. We arrive at a bar, and I order a Bud, but the bartender laughs and says, 'That's the one thing you won't get here.' I say, 'Give me whatever you've got.' The bartender leers, leans over toward me, and replies, 'I've got lots of other things I could give you.' Feeling ill at ease, I leave the bar alone to wander through deserted streets, feeling completely lost."

In the ensuing months James uncovered his fear that the careful ego structure he had crafted by considerable hard work over many years was, like the house of his dream, in danger of falling down and becoming worthless. Letting go of some of his ego defenses meant allowing himself to feel temporarily lost. Behind his fear of the homosexual bartender, he discovered his longing for a "Bud," a brotherly friend. A lifelong competitiveness with men began to relax into a desire for real masculine closeness.

James also found the little boy in him who grew up feeling overpowered by his moralistic mother and by the nuns who surrounded him during his twelve years at Catholic schools. Growing up, James had been terrified of threats of hell and damnation for his sexual impulses. Even now, unconsciously, James feared that his sexuality condemned him to being "bad blood." The vampire threat in his dream arose from this ancient terror, and was related to his unconscious fear that his son's AIDS was a punishment for sexuality.

James felt his rage at the abusive power these Catholic women had wielded over him, and then he reviewed his years of unconscious revenge, his own vampire which had inflicted retributive emotional cruelty on the women he had been close to. Now he felt a real, adult guilt for having closed his heart to women for fear of being hurt or controlled by them.

He reviewed his relationships with men and realized he had pushed away many who had reached out to him in friendship. James felt within him the little boy frightened of his father—a big, athletic man who constantly ridiculed James's sensitivity. Still painful were the memories of going dove hunting with his father and being told to go fetch the fallen birds. He wept remembering the sight of a particularly pathetic dying dove, its wounded breast heaving its last breaths, and he, the obedient bird-dog son, an accomplice to its killing. He had finally refused to go hunting with his father and adopted a mask of contempt and superiority toward his father and his sports. But now James felt the pain of his estrangement from his father, and in his anguish he found an opening to feeling the pain of his own rejection of his sensitive son Matthew.

James's life was certainly not boring now. His inner life was very full as he opened up the vast hidden rooms of his emotional being. He had another dream about his inner house: "I am in a room of the crumbling house of the earlier dream, but I know there is a larger room behind this one, a room that is in good shape. A different kind of business is going on in that room; there are lots of men, of all ages and descriptions, talking about making a movie together, and they want me to be in it. I wonder if I will."

The dream helped him see that, behind the crumbling old rigid structure of his mask, there was a room in good shape which contained a large "cast of characters" in his psychic house, and he was being invited to join the inner drama being enacted here.

In his dreams and in his personal work James was opening up to many previously hidden aspects—his fear of and longing for closeness with a man, his childhood sexual terrors, and his real adult guilt. He was entering unknown territory that felt more feminine and vulnerable than the familiar masculine stoic strength he had known.

He dreamed, "I am outside the door to my sister's house. I have only been to her house a few times and, even then, I have never been inside.

But this time, in the dream, she invites me in and I enter it with a kind of sacredness, as if entering a church."

Here is new room of James's inner house, the room of his previously denied feminine nature, now at last letting itself be known to him. Soon after this spiritual entrance, he dreamed:

"I am on my way to an ancient sacred site in South America. On the airplane a woman comes to me, saying she is the first Peruvian Native stewardess. I feel awkward with her, not knowing what to say. Yet I have a sense that this journey has been made to meet her." A central purpose of James's recent unconscious turmoil was now revealed: he was journeying to meet his buried native feminine nature.

In his Pathwork sessions he continued to explore new feelings and meet many sub-personalities that had chafed under the rule of his rigid limiting ego mask. Through this kaleidoscopic experience of change, James always kept intact a part of himself which could ride any wave, allow any feeling, and admit any unconscious information. This part was his observer self, a spiritual anchor in the choppy seas of growth. His emotional life, which seemed frozen just a few months ago, had fully thawed.

Integrating more of his previously hidden nature soon afforded James a new capacity for sharing feelings with his son. Toward the end of Matthew's life, James was able to cry with him, admit his regrets about his fathering, and thank his son for being in his life. Staying close to Matthew's hospital bed during his last few days, James was able, for the first time, to stroke and comfort Matthew, talking softly to his son whom he had known so little. The tragic, early death of this gentle homosexual young man helped his father reclaim his own gentleness and moved James toward wholeness.

Developing the Observer Self

Every human being is, in reality, many beings. Like James, we each exist simultaneously at many levels of consciousness. While this is confusing, it also helps us to make sense of the many apparent contradictions that coexist within us. The adult James wanted to feel compassion for his son. But James's own inner child was still paralyzed by residual fear of being ridiculed for his emotional sensitivity. James's spiritual self knew that death was an illusion, but his frozen grief and fear for his son made him unable to express what another part of him knew so well. His masculine ego self had struggled and coped and built a strong sense of himself; his feminine feeling self was breaking down the rigidity of that structure to allow the waters of his unconscious to flow more freely. Our many inner selves contradict our limited idea of who we are, and the different levels often contradict one another.

This inner complexity can be likened to having a "cast of characters" within us, each with its own beliefs, attitudes, and feelings. Each character lives in a separate room of our psychic house, inhabiting a different reality. Or we might say that each of these levels of consciousness exists at a different frequency, available as different channels on a radio dial. When we are tuned into one station we may be unaware that an entirely different frequency is available with a brief switch of the inner dial.

In becoming acquainted with our inner cast of characters, or inner psychic frequencies, we especially need to accept the apparently undesirable ones, including the scared, sensitive child and the hostile, vengeful adult. These characters live in hiding, as our shadow-self, which can be repressed but never eliminated.

While we may understand that diverse and contradictory levels of consciousness coexist in us, we often do not perceive that each one of them is innately creative. Our lives are a manifestation of the sum total of all the different characters or levels of consciousness that we are, whether or not we are aware of them. Bringing the inner worlds of our personal cast of characters into awareness allows us to understand how we create our lives.

The Observer Self

How do we begin the inner journey of self-transformation? If we are to meet our wounded child and release our negative ego, discard our mask and transform our lower self, who does the work? Which self works on these other selves?

The parts of ourselves that are already developed take on the task of welcoming into consciousness and transforming the other parts. The mature parts of ourselves become the "helpers" to the undeveloped parts. All our helping selves guide us on our evolutionary journey toward maturity and wholeness. We do need the help of outer teachers, healers, therapists, and guides, but we must remember that the goal is also to awaken the inner teacher/healer who is ever-present and ready to guide us.

Even if we do not feel mature, and even if we cannot contact the inner teacher, anyone can, with practice, develop an observer self. The observer self is made up of the tools which James discovered in the course of his work on himself—objectivity and detachment (the microscope of the scientist) along with love and compassion (the first-aid kit of the friend) toward our many other selves. The observer stands "outside," as it were, of our selves and our lives, and notes what is experienced. This stance is a place we can plant ourselves psychically and from which we can view all the rest of our lives. It is a place we can identify with while we are learning to notice and name other parts of the self. **The ability to observe ourselves objectively and compassionately is the single most important skill to develop in walking the spiritual path.**

The objective observer is a positive ego function. It is an aspect of the higher self that we can experience in ordinary ego reality. It is a benign witness to our inner processes and outer events. It simply notes, without judgment, whatever comes to the surface of our awareness. It welcomes especially those messages from the unconscious which bring us potentially new information about ourselves. It does not discriminate between the "good" and the "bad" that emerge from within; it welcomes all to awareness.

Laura was moving from a city life as a dancer and dance teacher, in which she maintained a polished professional image, to a simpler life in the country with her new husband. She had the following dream:

"I come out of a Pathwork session to the parking lot where three vehicles are parked, all of which I know are mine. One is a slick white Cadillac, one is a black Harley-Davidson motorcycle, and one is a little red pick-up truck. All the stuff I own is in these three vehicles. Several masked robbers are trying to steal my belongings from the vehicles and I start yelling at them. 'You can't take that; it's mine.' I know some of the stuff isn't worth anything; in fact, it's stuff I would probably throw away when I get home. But I don't want them to have it; I know it's mine and I'm determined to claim it. Eventually I yell at them enough to get them to stop stealing, and they leave. I feel triumphant at having claimed it all as mine."

Laura felt that the three vehicles represented aspects of herself. The white Cadillac was her mask as a professional dancer: sleek and fancy. The motorcycle was her idea of her negative lower self: exciting but dangerous. And the little red pick-up was her higher self leading her now to a life in the country. She was following her heart rather than her idealized self-image. She felt the masked robbers were the defensive (mask) part of her that wanted to deny other aspects of her identity. And she felt wonderful at having insisted that all three vehicles and their contents were hers. The dream solidified her claim to all of herself—the mask, lower self, and higher self. The dream also incorporates where she had been and where she was going. In the Plains Indian medicine wheel symbolism, white is the color for the north, for letting go and for death (of her old life) and red is the color for the east, for birth and new beginnings.

The Laura in the dream, who claims all three cars, is the self which can identify other aspects without becoming identified **with** any one of them. This observer self may also be called the "fair witness," who sees and records all without distortion. The observer sits at the edge of the vast terrain of our inner selves, paying attention to whatever comes up.

We might visualize the immensity of self by seeing ourselves as a container in which aspects of universal consciousness "float around," as it were, expressing themselves now through me, and then through you, and then through someone else. Such a visualization can help us detach a little from the particular contents of our own personal container of consciousness.

> Every trait familiar to human understanding, every attitude known in creation, every aspect of personality, is one of the many manifestations of consciousness. Every one of them that is not yet integrated into the whole needs to be unified, synthesized, made part of the harmonious whole. . . . Can you imagine for a moment that many traits familiar to you, which you have always associated with the person, as existing only **through** a person, are not the person *per se*, but are actually in themselves free-floating particles of the overall consciousness, whether these be good or evil traits? Take love or malice, perseverance or sloth. They are all free-floating particles of the overall consciousness which need to be incorporated into the manifesting personality. Only then does purification, harmonization, and enrichment of the manifesting consciousness take place which create the evolutionary process of unifying the separated particles of consciousness. (*PGL 189*)

This understanding of ourselves as "containers" of many diverse particles of consciousness, some of which are superficial or negative or destructive, will especially help us in learning to view ourselves with greater compassion and greater detachment.

We can learn to shift our identity away from all the floating fragments of consciousness and toward the one who observes them all, This is comparable to identifying with being in the audience as we watch the whole cast of characters come onto our inner stage. Or, in another metaphor, we become the owner of the house who opens the doors of the separate rooms where the inner characters dwell.

Negative and unproductive attitudes toward the self always come from a wrong belief that we are only some limited or negative part of ourselves rather than the whole of who we are. The bridge to knowing our inner wholeness is the observer self, that part of ourselves which accepts **whatever is** within us. As we learn to identify with the observer self, we develop self-acceptance. Total self-acceptance is the most curative habit we can develop on the spiritual path.

Distortions in Self-Observation

When we first start observing ourselves, we tend to make dualistic judgments about what we see—judging our selves and our attributes as either good or bad, weak or strong, silly or profound. Yet the moment we judge ourselves, we are not observing any more, we are judging. The process of observation then needs to shift back "behind" the judge, so we can calmly observe the self-judgment. If we find ourselves becoming hopeless about what we observe, then we "step back" and observe the hopelessness.

Our attitude is often one of alarm or disapproval or even despair when we discover ourselves acting or feeling in ways that do not conform to our idealized self image. But we cannot change behavior stemming from our undeveloped selves until the behavior and the underlying attitudes are brought into consciousness. Self-condemnation throws us back into denial of our negativity where it can never be transformed.

Source of Our Distortions in Self-Observation

More often than not, our negative judgments of what we see in ourselves are the internalized voices of parents or early authority figures, or of rigid cultural and religious codes of conduct. These judgments are not the true self-observer, but come from the idealized self image that has embodied unrealistic standards of perfectionism against which we constantly measure ourselves. The first step in true self-observation is, therefore, to observe this perfectionism in ourselves. Whenever we lapse into harsh self-judgment, we need to step back and compassionately observe this process as well.

Martha was moving into a new apartment. She picked up some boxes at work for packing, and decided to take along the small Styrofoam "peanuts" in the boxes in case she wanted to pack something fragile. When she got home, however, she realized that she didn't need all the Styrofoam; it just cluttered up the available packing space, and now she would have to discard it.

At this point, however, she got terribly depressed and could hardly go on packing at all. When she tuned into herself, she became aware of an inner voice accusing her: "You're so stupid! How could you possibly have thought that Styrofoam would be useful? What a stupid thought." The strength of this self-condemnation struck Martha as absurd and comical, even as she suffered its real painfulness.

As she stopped to listen to this debilitating self-criticism, she realized it sounded like the voice of her mother, who had constantly criticized her as a child. Martha had internalized her mother's voice and was using it now to destroy her own self-esteem. Even though she could not immediately alter this inner self-destructiveness, she did manage to step back from her critical judge, into the real self-observer, who simply noted what was going on within her: the old drama of the critical mother and hurt child playing itself out again.

She then started a dialogue between that mother and child; the latter voice felt victimized while the first voice felt "on top." Suddenly the victim part of Martha asserted herself and said that she would not sit still for this self-abuse any longer; she stood up to the critic, who then backed down. Martha immediately felt better and could resume her packing. Her objective observer self had facilitated this healing through acting as a benign and detached helper to Martha as she worked with her different inner characters.

The voices of perfectionism, self-doubt, and self-denigration are most often negative parental voices that we have internalized. Gestalt theory calls this the voice of the "top dog" which is always critical of the "underdog"; other therapies call this the voice of the "parent" who is critical of the "child" self. The demand for perfectionism by the internalized judge makes even the simplest, most innocent mistakes into catastrophes for our self-esteem.

Martha pursued her critical voice further in a Pathwork session and learned the secret to its perpetuation: the belief that "if it hurts, it must be true." She accorded more credibility to her self-critical voices than she did to any self-praising ones.

*As she looked at this still more deeply, she realized how much as a child she had craved her mother's approval, believing that she would be o.k. only if she could live up to her mother's perfectionistic standards. Until that time, however, she must suffer being unloved by her mother. It was difficult to accept that in reality she would never be loved by her mother in the way she had wanted, and that the lack of acceptance of her was actually **her mother's** problem. Her need for acceptance was real, even if unfulfilled. The truth was that her mother had been an imperfect parent; she an imperfect child.*

Martha had to let go of the illusion that she was the bad one and her mother was the good or perfect one, whose love Martha could earn by someday being as perfect as her mother demanded. She had to accept that she had not been loved well, had not been accepted for who she was, and that it was not her fault. It simply happened that way.

She sobbed harshly with the grief of giving up the illusion that she might someday be loved by her mother, if only she were perfect. And then, more gently, she cried with the pain of the lonely little girl within her whom she had been beating up on so often in her thoughts. Martha visualized her higher self as the good mother, "re-parenting" her little girl, holding her and reassuring her, loving her unconditionally, allowing her to make mistakes.

We need to be able to identify the negative self-critical voices, but learn not to identify **with** them; they are merely part of our inner landscape, no more "true" than any other part of ourselves.

Many of us have misconceptions about self-awareness, such as "if it hurts, it must be true," or, equally falsely, "if it hurts, it can't be true." In truth, awareness, especially awareness of the lower self, can be painful. However, such pain, simply felt, is both temporary and cleansing. And awareness, especially of the higher self and of unified states of being, can be deeply pleasurable. Behind the temporary feelings of pain or pleasure, which pass through us, awareness simply is, an empty container for all life experience.

Radical Self-Acceptance

Twenty years ago I was given a dramatic example of the stance of benign self-observation. When I was newly a member of the Pathwork community, going to Guide lectures given by Eva Pierrakos in New York City, a woman I'll call Penny, whose leg had been amputated because of cancer, also attended the lectures. Some months later, as Penny was facing a terminal diagnosis from her cancer, Eva asked Penny how she felt about her impending death. "Is it o.k. to die, Penny, or not o.k.?" Penny responded simply, "It isn't o.k. or not o.k., Eva, it just is." That "just is-ness" of death has been a model for me of radical self-acceptance for whatever is observed within the self at any time.

I believe the Pathwork teachings can do for our understanding of negativity and evil what other, recently popular spiritual teachings have done for our acceptance of death. Evil, like death, just is. At the dualistic level at which we live most of the time, both benign and evil energies live within us. But we deny our negativity even more vociferously than we deny our death. We cannot ultimately believe we will not die. But we can perpetuate the illusion that we do not contain evil. Yet to live in this illusion is as detrimental to our spiritual health as to deny our mortality. We can safely learn to allow awareness of the negative and evil aspects of ourselves with dignified self-acceptance.

Nothing within us is ultimately unacceptable. It just is, whatever it is. The most important work we do on ourselves is to align our attitude with honest and compassionate self-observation.

> How different your attitude to yourself must be when you realize that it is the task of human entities to carry negative aspects with them for the purpose of integrating and synthesizing them! This affords truthfulness without hopelessness. What a dignity it lends to you when you consider that you undertake an important task for the sake of evolution. When you come into this life, you specifically bring negative aspects with you for the purpose of transformation. . . . Every human being fulfills an immense task within the universal scale of evolution. (*PGL 189*)

Impatience and demands on the self to change are always counter-productive. Self-judgment creates an attitude of rebellion against a harsh super-ego. If, however, we see clearly (without self-deception) and compassionately (without self-indulgence), then we can choose to change negative aspects. We are much more likely to want to change if we can simply and benignly assess who and what we are expressing at any moment, knowing that this is not all of who we are.

> If you attempt growth rather than perfection, you will live in the now. You will dispense with superimposed values, and find your own. You will dispense with subtle pretenses and superimpositions. This leads to selfhood and away from self-alienation. All this will bring you to a state of identifying with your real self, being anchored in your real self, rather than on peripheral layers. (*PGL 97*)

Two Aspects of the Observer Self: Truth and Love

The practice of honest self-observation will teach us about **truth** and **love**: we learn **total honesty with the self** combined with **total acceptance of the self**.

Learning to be honest with ourselves, not to flinch from anything we see in our hidden thoughts and feelings as well as in our behavior, is the same as learning to live in truth with ourselves. In strengthening our ability to be in truth with ourselves, we also strengthen our capacity to be truthful with others and to stand by the truth of issues in the world.

Learning to accept ourselves, to forgive and have compassion for every hidden thought and feeling, and every action, no matter how apparently unacceptable, is the same as learning to live in love. In strengthening our capacity to accept and forgive ourselves, to not reject, judge, or compare ourselves to others, we also strengthen our ability to love others. We can learn to love others unconditionally, without blindness, indulgence, or dependency, only when we can first learn to love ourselves.

Learning the universal values of **love** and **truth** must begin by practicing the attitudes of absolute truthfulness and unconditional acceptance toward ourselves. As we learn to identify with the observer self, rather than with any particular piece of distorted thinking or feeling, we can learn to welcome everything that comes to us in life as part of our spiritual growth.

Truth: Constructive Attitudes

Being truthful with the self means welcoming unconscious material into consciousness even if this material comes in the form of frightening dreams, negative thoughts, or unpleasant feelings. Every act of bringing unconscious or only dimly conscious material into the full light of awareness furthers the evolution of consciousness, the movement from ignorance to awareness, from limitation to wholeness, from disunity to unity.

Unconscious negative emotions and unconscious limited thinking are powerful creative forces in the universe. On the personal level, our own unexamined prejudices toward the opposite sex undermine our conscious efforts to establish an intimate relationship with a mate. On the social level, our unexamined or rationalized prejudices toward people of different color, culture, or religion continue to create negative relationships among people. As long as this negativity is rationalized or denied, then its results are created unconsciously. And then we are surprised by the results, e.g., a failed marriage or a world at war. These negative results can only be prevented if the negativity is allowed to become conscious.

At first this may seem scary. The uncovering of previously unacknowledged negative thoughts and feelings, and the awareness that this negativity does indeed produce our undesirable life experience, often creates an initial recoiling from the process and a desire to repress the material. However, repression makes impossible the connection of cause and effect which is essential to the growth of self-responsibility and spiritual consciousness. **Awareness is always a more desirable state than ignorance**, even if the content of awareness is not always pleasant. Reality is preferable to illusion, however temporarily painful our reality may seem.

We gradually learn to distinguish between truthful self-observation, including moral discernment about ourselves, and harsh or punitive self-criticism. The latter always feels bad, provoking unnecessary, false, and mind-clouding guilt, whereas truth, even painful truth, feels clarifying.

Love: Constructive Attitudes

In developing genuine self-acceptance, we need first to confront certain common attitudes masquerading as love. Self-indulgence, denial, or rationalization are not real love; they only keep us from unpleasant truths. We falsely believe that by not looking at the lower self we are being kind to ourselves (or others), emphasizing the positive, or building self-esteem. While we do need to be careful about the right timing in confronting our (and others') negativity, to deny or rationalize it does not come from love. It comes from fear of the lower self.

Denial of our negativity only feeds this fear of ourselves and hence undermines self-esteem. We deny or rationalize our lower self out of fear that this is all we are. In each of us **is** a rock-bottom fear that we are, in essence, bad or hopeless or unlovable. And we fear that seeing our despair or our badness will bring about our annihilation. **This deepest illusion of the human personality must be faced**. As we face our negativity and realize that it is not all of who we really are, the apparent need to deny or indulge through avoidance will also gradually dissolve.

The way out of our fear of ourselves is the gradual recognition that we are not any of our inner "characters," including the mask and the lower self. We gradually shift our identification away from the observed aspects of self and toward the observer who identifies these aspects. We become the mapper, not the mapped. We become awareness, not that of which we are aware.

To become a loving self-observer is comparable to becoming a good parent to ourselves. Slowly we learn to give unconditional love to ourselves, especially to the parts of ourselves that are childish, weak, or immature. The good parent reflects back the child's strengths and helps her to develop areas that are weak. The good parent accepts the child in her entirety, including her negative feelings, even as the parent also puts limits on the child's acting-out of her negativity and helps her learn appropriate self-expression. The parent teaches that the negativity is not her essential nature, without also denying or colluding with these aspects. Our negative aspects can be seen as immature children within us that need our attention and love in order to "grow up" into mature self-expression.

I believe that when we can love all of our selves we will fulfill the promise offered in the 23rd Psalm: "Lo, though I walk through the valley of the shadow of death, I shall fear no evil, for thou art with me." The "thou" of the psalmist is a being of unconditional love who can be present with us even as we face fear, death, and evil. This "thou," while it may signify God or Christ or any angelic being perceived as outside the self, can also be experienced within the self. We can perceive this presence as our own higher self, the companion of our soul, the inner God-self. When we offer this spiritual companionship to ourselves, we can face anything.

When we give gentle acceptance and love to our own imma-ture aspects, we give them what they most need to grow. "We have been waiting all our lives to hear the words 'I love you' spoken by our own voice."[1] When we practice love rather than denial we give ourselves room to expand. We create a spacious bowl of acceptance for whatever we experience in ourselves. Then our negative or painful or undesirable aspects do not need to go into hiding. Away from the light of our love, they fester unseen. When we direct the light of love and truth toward them, they can grow.

In developing positive attitudes of truthfulness and self-acceptance, we build a bridge to the greater self within us. The objective observer starts out as an ego function, as we discipline a part of ourselves to stand outside and watch our-selves. However, as our capacity to be both truthful and loving with ourselves matures, we become more and more identified with that truthful, loving self which is our personal expression of these divine forces in the universe. We come to know ourselves as our higher self, who observes and transforms all else that we are.

> To the extent the conscious self uses its already exist-ing knowledge of truth, its already existing power to execute its good will, its already existing capacity to
> . . . **choose the attitude to the problem**, to that exact degree the consciousness expands and becomes increasingly more infiltrated by the spiritual con-sciousness. **The spiritual consciousness cannot mani-fest when the already existing consciousness is not fully put to use in the process of self-observation.**
> (PGL 189)

Self-Identification

Learning to identify ourselves with the objective observer self, and to dis-identify with the many disparate aspects of ourselves, creates inner freedom.

---

[1] Quoted from Stephen Levine's book, *Healing Into Life and Death,* Doubleday, 1987.

Through the act of acknowledgment of some heretofore disowned aspect of the self, a subtle but distinct
shift in identification occurs. Before such acknowledgment, you were blind to the destructive aspects, which
indicated that you believed them to be you. Hence you
could not afford to acknowledge them. . . . But the
moment you acknowledge the heretofore unacceptable,
you cease to **be** the unacceptable, and instead you are
identified with that in you that is capable of the
acknowledgment. . . . It is a totally different situation
when you are identified with the ugly traits or when
you identify them. **The moment you identify them,
you cease being identified with them**. This is why it
is so liberating to acknowledge the worst in the personality, after having battled the ever-present resistance to
do so. . . . . The moment you identify the destructive
aspects, name them, state them, articulate them,
observe them; it is that which identifies, names, states,
articulates, and observes that is the self with which you
can truly and safely and realistically identify. This self
holds many options, possibilities and choices. Therefore you no longer need to persecute yourself so
mercilessly with your self-hate. There seems to be no
way out but hating yourself as long as you have missed
out on this all-important process of identifying with
that in you that is capable of observing, stating,
naming, choosing, determining, facing, dealing with,
recognizing, without devastating self-judgment.
(*PGL 189*)

*Kathy was full of self-doubt about her marriage. At times she felt like
leaving her husband, as she felt so impatient with him. He seemed so
undeveloped spiritually and emotionally. At other times, she felt that the
fault was hers, that she was ungiving and blocked in her love. She would
push herself to change, only to discover her resistance to opening up her
feelings with him was greater than ever.*

*When I asked Kathy to search for a self which could accept all these
contradictions and ambivalences, she visualized a valley filled with
swirling mists going in different directions and obscuring her vision into
the real floor of the valley. She then imagined herself sitting on the top of
one of the hills, looking benignly down into the valley of her inner turmoil,
watching the mists and calmly waiting for them to clear.*

*Kathy's visualization changed then from hills containing a valley to
four walls containing her prison. One wall she felt was the barrier of her*

awakening consciousness. She could not go back behind that to a time of being unaware of herself; she was barred from the "innocence" of uncon-sciousness. The wall opposite was her resistance, her fear of the future of her relationship. She found she could "sit" upon on the roof of her prison carefully studying the walls of her past unconsciousness and her resistance to the future. As she contemplated the walls of her inner prison, she found peace from her frantic ambivalence, and even a measure of self-acceptance.

Knowing we are not our flaws helps us be both gentle and compassionate and also non-defensive. If we do become defensive or embarrassed about our flaws, then the observer goes back yet another step and simply observes compassionately these attitudes of defensiveness or embarrassment. We continue to "step behind ourselves," as it were, until we can find a place where we can rest in serene self-acceptance. No matter how bleak we may be feeling about ourselves, we can learn to move our awareness back to identify with the bowl of spacious, loving awareness that can accept it.

In learning to identify with the observer self, we educate all the other temporary negative selves to realize that they are not our true identity.

> You learn that which observes is you and not that
> which is being observed. Thus, no matter how undesir-
> able any particular aspect is, it becomes wholly possible
> to deal with it, accept it, explore it, work with it, no
> longer be frightened by it. The capacity to observe and
> adjudge, to note and evaluate and, last but not least, to
> choose the best possible attitude as to what to do with
> the observed—that is the true power of your real self,
> as it already exists right now. Freedom, liberation, the
> knowledge of self, the finding of self are the first steps
> toward realizing the greater consciousness, the universal,
> divine consciousness in you. (*PGL 189*)

Tools for Developing the Observer Self: Meditation and Daily Review

It takes discipline to develop the objective, compassionate observer self. To focus the mind inward and witness whatever is within the self requires practice. The most useful spiritual disciplines are meditation and daily review.

Even a few minutes of daily meditation, in which we relax the outer, busy mind and tune into our deeper selves, has tremendous physical, emotional, and spiritual benefits. Meditation can take us to every level of our inner being. We can listen to the voices of the inner child and lower self as well as make contact with the higher self. We can use it to re-educate the immature aspects and release tensions. And we can, in moments of divine grace, contact the place of unified awareness.

The first task in meditation is to release the busyness of our chattering outer ego mind, full of the preoccupations of the past and the future, and discover a calm presence who can witness ourselves in the moment. So, we take some time each day alone and in a quiet place, sitting relaxed and alert, in a symmetrical posture, with back erect, feet grounded on the floor. We take time to tune inside, free of outer distractions, to get centered. I find the following practices most helpful.

1) <u>Meditation with Breath</u>: Focus all attention on the breath, the in-breath and the out-breath, as it happens, moment by moment. The breath is where voluntary and involuntary processes converge, where the boundary between "inner" and "outer" dissolves, and hence a powerful meeting ground of mind and body, the separate self and the All. While focusing on the breath, observe and let go of all other thoughts, thus bringing about a gradual one-pointedness of attention in the moment, the present awareness of each breath as it happens. Do not attempt to change anything; just focus on becoming aware of the breathing as it is. You may either count each out-breath, up to 10, and then begin again, or you can simply focus on one spot in the body—nostril, chest or abdomen—from which to observe each in-breath and each out-breath. To observe the breath as it is in the moment gradually shifts awareness away from the contents of consciousness and toward the observer self.[2]

2) <u>Mindfulness Meditation</u>: Another centering practice is to see yourself at the threshold of the thinking mind. Identifying yourself as a sentinel at the edge of the mind, observe each thought, feeling, or sensation at the instant that it arises. Note it

---

[2] For an excellent introduction to breathing and mindfulness meditation, see *Mindfulness in Plain English*, by Venerable Henepola Gunaratana.

and let it go, not becoming attached to whatever arises. Continually refocus on the sentinel awareness, that which does the observing. This gradually slows down the body-mind so you can eventually pay attention to each discrete inner experience and let it pass without judgment or attachment. Again, do not attempt to change anything, only to be aware of **what is**.

Both these centering practices will strengthen identification with the objective, compassionate self-observer. Once you have the ability to identify with the witness, you can use your period of meditation for working with your immature selves, and for listening to the guidance of your enlightened selves.

In Chapter Ten we will talk about using meditation to help transform the lower self by engaging in a three-way inner dialogue between the positive ego, the lower self, and the higher life. Chapter Eleven will present a visualization for creating a more positive and fulfilling life. But these are complex tasks to be attempted only after we have calmed the outer mind and become identified with the observer self.

3) <u>Prayer</u>: Prayer can easily be woven into periods of quiet meditation. Prayer comes from the spontaneous desire of the personality to seek alignment with, or protection or guidance from, some higher power or spirit. Prayer can, of course, take many forms—from the innocent expression of a sincere wish to a complex and elaborate ritual of evocation. As our spiritual evolution progresses, prayer evolves from a simple petition to a higher power viewed as outside the self into a means of issuing our requests deep into our own creative soul substance, while evoking the help of universal powers.

Like meditation, prayer is a path for surrender of the little ego to the greater energies of life. But where meditation is more receptive and quiet, prayer is directed toward some goal in a more active engagement of divinity. For me, the ultimate prayer for aligning individual ego and purpose to the larger design of God is "Not my will, but Thine, be done."

Daily Review

In addition to daily meditation and prayer, daily review is the most important spiritual practice for strengthening our self-awareness. We take time every day to review our day's inner as well as outer life. This is best done by keeping a written journal, but time spent in quiet contemplation of the day is also useful. Keeping a journal or a diary is always a good way to build focused self-awareness. We can include dreams, written guidance, and self-reflection in a journal.

The discipline of daily review, however, goes beyond a simple record of the outer (or inner) events of the day. It is a specific practice that furthers our ability to identify with the observer self and to work with our other selves.

Here is how it is done: Let the events of the day pass in front of you, and **specifically note any incidents which gave you a disharmonious feeling or reaction**. Make notes about these and only these occurrences, knowing they provide clues to the inner states that gave rise to these manifestations.

Every negative experience is an invitation to look deeper into ourselves and discover the day's lessons. In making a daily review, we learn to become aware of how we really react, so these thoughts/feelings do not have a chance to accumulate in the unconscious. We learn to "come clean" with ourselves every day, thus performing a kind of emotional hygiene as important to our spiritual well-being as physical hygiene is to our bodies.

In doing daily review we strengthen our desire for truth, as we give ourselves permission to experience and note whatever we actually thought and felt, rather than what we think we ought to have done, felt, or thought. When we encounter resistance, we note it just as we would any other aspect of ourselves. Daily review prevents self-deception, pretense, and repression—all the ingredients of mental disturbance and confusion.

> If you follow this through for some time, and not just once or twice, but faithfully, you will see after a while a clear pattern coming out of it. At first these incidents [in which you experience disharmony] will appear entirely unconnected and isolated. (*PGL 17*)

> [But after a while,] you will discover that certain kinds of incidents are repeated. Then a pattern will evolve from which you will have clues as to your own inner make-up. If something recurs constantly, it is an important clue to your own soul. (*PGL 28*)

Once we have begun to see a pattern in our experience, then we can begin to look more deeply into ourselves for the origin of this pattern. We ask ourselves, "Who is the person within me who reacts in this way?" And then we can work with the different selves that emerge, initiating a dialogue between the part of ourselves in need of healing and the higher self which can direct the healing. After a while, daily review will become our regular time to engage the selves which have emerged during the day.

We can do a lot of work on our own through the practices of daily meditation, prayer, and daily review. I must add, however, that every person consciously following the spiritual path also needs an outside helper at some times to assist in the work of transformation. We are all blinded to aspects of ourselves which can only be accurately perceived by others. And we need the safety and support of other human beings who witness our pain and acknowledge our struggle. We need other humans to reflect the "thou" of our observer self, able to stand by us as we face our pain and distortions.

Our spiritual development will be greatly facilitated by regular spiritual practice, but such discipline cannot be forced. Daily spiritual practice is, I believe, a real need of human beings seeking to become more conscious. However, spiritual discipline must evolve slowly and organically, usually over years of at first sporadic practice. Developing a spiritual practice should not become yet another club used by our perfectionism to beat up on ourselves. ("See how terrible you are, you aren't working hard enough on yourself or meditating enough," or whatever.)

The ego is necessary to establish self-discipline, but it cannot do the job alone. Evoking the energies of the higher self can ease the process. The practice of self-observation will collapse quickly if it is forced and unpleasant. If we feel our real need for self-understanding, the experience of a spiritual discipline will bring feelings of pleasure and success. When we are meditating because it feels good, and working on ourselves because we really know the relief of being in truth rather than in ignorance about ourselves, then our practice will be truly grounded.

Jody had developed her spiritual practice during her early work in the Pathwork, but more recently she had let her daily meditation slide as her outer life had become much more busy and fulfilled. She meditated less frequently and only when she felt particularly uncentered. In a session with me, Jody spoke of an inner tension she felt by being "caught," as she put in, "in the jaws of the day," pushed by the demands of her outer life. When, with my encouragement, Jody returned to daily meditation practice, she noticed her tension lessening. Her life began to turn more smoothly. Putting meditation into the center of her life felt, Jody said, "like snapping the center into an old 45 RPM record which otherwise just flopped around on the turntable."

On the spiritual path of self-knowledge we will encounter many states and levels of consciousness within the self. We may find ourselves thinking unfamiliar thoughts—loftier, or crazier, or meaner thoughts than we ever dreamed we would think. We may find ourselves feeling feelings we would never have dreamed possible—unbearable agony or unexpected ecstasy. The spiritual path requires that we open to all our multiple selves, journeying always toward the center of self, toward the unitive state of consciousness. The practice of self-observation is the bridge from our ordinary scattered selves to the core of our unified self.

Exercises for Chapter 3:

1. Pick an issue of some concern in your life now. Identify two of your inner "cast of characters," preferably ones which have opposing points of view on this issue. First describe briefly these two characters and their points of view. Then create a written dialogue between these two opposing characters inside you in relation to this issue. Explore fully each side's point of view, and see if you can learn more about your own conflicts or ambivalence in this area.

2. Practice written daily review for five days, summarizing at least one time each day when you experienced disharmonious thoughts and feelings. At the end of five days, see if you find the common denominators of these experiences.

3. Practice daily meditation for at least ten minutes each day for five days. Write out when you did it each day, and summarize each day's experience. You may use either of the centering practices discussed in this chapter, but say clearly which one you tried—either following the breath, or standing at the threshold of the mind observing thoughts/feelings/sensations.

4. Practice identifying with your objective observer-self during some daily routine act, like brushing your teeth, for five days. During these times, observe your outer actions, and observe your inner experience. Write about your experiences.

CHAPTER 4

Embracing the Child, Adult Ego, and Transpersonal Selves

"Only when you are fully in possession of your
outer self, your ego, can you then dispense
with it and reach your real self.

—Pathwork Guide Lecture 132, *"The Function of the Ego
in Relationship to the Real Self"*

Bobbi, Barbara, and the Grandmother:
Discovering the Inner Child and the Inner Wise Woman

Barbara had been battling cancer for five years. First she had a breast removed, and then she had extensive removal of her lymph nodes. Now the cancer had spread to her liver, and she had been given less than six months to live. She undertook a seven-day retreat for intensive personal work at Sevenoaks with me and her helper Donovan, in an effort to penetrate more deeply into the emotional roots of her disease, and to prepare herself spiritually for whatever might come. She wanted to live, but knew realistically that she might not have much time left.

To the Pathwork Barbara brought her own well developed spiritual outlook—a blend of her cultural Judaism, her own psychic abilities, and a deep respect for the teachings of nature as understood by the Native Americans. She had separated from her husband, which had been a wrenching emotional loss for her, shortly before her first bout with cancer.

At the outset of the intensive, Barbara wrote in her journal:

"The autumn air smells so good. I am sitting on the wooden bench under the circle of seven sacred oak trees, facing the mountains. Smells of crisping leaves and grass, insects and aging acorns. A sweet smell, but not the flowery scent of spring and summer; instead, the odor of decaying earth and of things becoming earth. Watching the brown oak leaves fall so smoothly and gracefully through the breath of wind to the waiting earth mother. Recognizing the parts of me that have fallen through the years like twigs and branches from a tree. Not wanting yet to fall completely free. But hoping that when I do, I shall fall as effortlessly and gracefully as a leaf whose season is done. My body will become ash to nourish the earth with calcium and minerals. And then my spirit will rise on the wings of eagles, soaring over this land."

Barbara was aware of her inner wise woman who accepted the natural place of death and loss in the cycle of life. At the same time her adult ego did not want to die, and her inner child was frightened that she might never have the chance to grow up. Barbara's inner child, little Bobbi, was still frozen inside her, having never recovered from her early traumas. In the intensive, Barbara used her adult ego to evoke and talk with little Bobbi, so wounded by her childhood losses. And she used the ego to evoke her spiritual self, who came to her in the form of an ancient Grandmother of the Earth. This wise woman was able to reassure and comfort the child Bobbi and the adult Barbara, who were both so scared of dying. All three selves were present in her work.

Early on, Barbara worked on her unfinished emotional business with her father who had shot himself when little Bobbi was only four years old. In the child's voice, she wrote in her journal:

"My lovely Daddy. If only you'd lived. But maybe then my love for you would have turned as sour as Mom's did, into something hurtful and evil.

"I never would have stopped loving you, Daddy! NEVER!! No matter what happened. I wouldn't listen to Mommy. I never will listen to my Mommy. She lies to me. She lies to me for her own convenience and I won't listen to her. I won't ever believe her. She's cold and hard and not sexy and hates men and I'll never listen to her. I'll never be that way to you. I love you. We're both alike. Sweet and warm and alive and sexy and playful. Let's be together, like that, forever, o.k.? Let's run away and play, and never grow up."

In her sessions with Donovan and me, Barbara gradually allowed herself to regress more and more to the little girl inside. Donovan and I sometimes played the role of her Daddy and Mommy, and we supported her need to discharge the rage and grief left over from her childhood. She screamed out anger at her mother and sobbed her grief at the loss of her Daddy.

Barbara's father had been a disturbed, childish, and irresponsible man who could never hold down a job or support his family. He had felt like a failure for a long time before he eventually killed himself. In her journal, Barbara described some of her work with us:

"Donovan held me and was my Daddy for a long time. He told me I am o.k. and that whatever happens to me, I'll be all right and he, my helper, is glad I came into his life and he, my Daddy, was very glad I was born. My Daddy. My lovely, sad, crazy, sweet, warm, lost, out-of-control, confused, loving Daddy.

"Donovan, as my Daddy, said that my love was the only joy in his life, but all the love in the world, if I could have had it and given it all to him, would not have kept him alive because one person can't give enough love to another person when they can't receive it. Donovan/Daddy said, 'I just can't get it together with a job or with a woman. I love you. You are the brightness and sweetness of my life, but my troubles are so deep they overwhelm me and I'm confused and out-of-control and I'm going to have to go, but it's not your fault.' That sounded like me. Substitute man for woman.

"The only adult male person I have ever loved with anything close to or akin to the fierce, wild love I felt for my father, my Daddy, was my husband. Perhaps that is why the dissolution of that relationship was so hard and preposterously painful.

"I have this love again for Donovan. I am afraid for him. I am frightened that our deep experience of each other at this time will somehow put him in danger. My 'fate' will cause harm to come to him. He might . . . I cannot say it. Do not want to put thought to word and perhaps lend weight to deed. But I am very afraid."

Barbara's father had often threatened to leave, many times before he actually committed suicide, and she was experiencing again the fear that Donovan might leave, and the shame that it would be her fault. She felt also the terror that followed her father's death, when her mother was overwhelmed and unable to care for her properly. Barbara re-discovered the grief and anger attached to the memory that her mother had destroyed all her father's belongings immediately after his death, including a letter her father had written to Bobbi just before he shot himself.

"Felt the very great loss of never seeing the letter my father had left for me. What was it?! However simple or profound the words might have been . . . and the betrayal by my mother who took to her bed after his death, destroying all trace of him. She has always been so self-centered, absorbed in the drama of her own hard times. How I hated her!

"Told Donovan for the first time how my mother had burned my father's last letter to me. Donovan spontaneously started crying which touched me deeply. His crying honored the magnitude of my childhood loss. The pinching and weakness in my back—that familiar, scary cancer kind of pain—is gone since this morning's session. I believe it went with Donovan's warm hand on my lower back—the exact spot—as I experienced and released the anger and hurt of my bewildered, aching child."

By beating up pillows and wringing the "necks" of towels, Barbara discharged a lot of her childhood anger at her father for killing himself and at her mother for collapsing after his death and for diminishing her relationship with her father. The work that followed involved helping her adult ego to comprehend her experiences, particularly the intensity of the impact of her father's death on her inner child. His suicide occurred just as Bobbi was at the developmental stage when the little girl awakens her sexual and loving feelings for her Daddy and just as she rejects total dependency on Mommy, and long before she can see either of them as real people. At that time he was still her perfect Daddy, and Mommy was the villain.

Barbara then descended into her child's mind and found the simple generalizations and false conclusions which are so typical of childhood thinking: "**If bad things happen to me, I must be bad.**" In her unconscious child mind, she believed her father's death must have been punishment for her badness; probably she was being punished for loving Daddy and rejecting Mommy. This false conclusion then led to, **"Since I deserve punishment, I will punish myself. If I punish myself first, then maybe God won't."** Barbara's suffering from cancer, and especially from a dreadful round of chemotherapy, had always felt like a form of self-punishment to her, an atonement for she knew not what. Now her adult mind could look deeply at the irrationality of her childhood conclusions and start to challenge them and to have compassion for the disturbed child who had held such painful misconceptions and suffered such excessive self-punishment.

As her adult mind was comprehending little Bobbi's distortions more fully, she dropped even more deeply into the inner child and found the following:

"I'm just like him. I hate Mommy and I want her dead. He should have killed her instead of himself. Then we could go off together, me and my Daddy, and leave that cold, mean woman. But he didn't kill her. So, if I grow up and become a woman, then I'll have to kill her, because she killed him, his spirit, and he didn't want to live anymore. So I better kill myself, before I kill her.

"Women are cold and mean and make men kill themselves, so I better kill myself before I get to be a woman like my mother. My husband left me. It must have been my fault. I was cold and demanding and critical and so he started drinking. Then one night he had a car accident and might have been killed and it would have been my fault. I've become a woman just like my Mommy, and she made my Daddy die, and then I hurt my husband. So I'm doing it too. I am killing. I better kill me quick so I don't kill anybody else."

Barbara went to sleep after writing this, but woke up in the middle of the night, frightened, and wrote:

"Something comes to get me at night.

No one else can hear or see it.

They won't believe me.

It may be me."

The little girl was speaking, letting adult Barbara know her fear of her demon, her destructiveness, the killer within. Then the voice of the four-year-old child spoke again, revealing more of the hidden negative thoughts that had resided in her since the trauma of her father's suicide:

"It's over.

I'm glad it's over.

I wish they were both dead.

I wish everybody was dead.
Who'll take care of me?
I wish I was dead too."

And then again the clear revelation of what the destructive part of Barbara was doing to herself and why:

"We're doing this because if we get out of control we'll kill somebody else. So we're letting this cancer be out of control inside us so we won't be out of control outside us."

Barbara arrived at one of the roots of her cancer, the fear of her own killer which she had turned against herself. And then, that same night, the child spoke again, talking to the Grandmother, the guardian of her soul's journey.

"It hurts, Grandmother. I don't want to hurt me any more."

She asked to hear the voice of the Grandmother who replied:

"Yes, my child. The psychic and even physical pain you have given yourself to atone for your hidden guilt and fear of your badness can stop now. You need no longer punish yourself or withhold love from yourself. You have suffered more than enough. You can let go of hurting yourself. You are beloved of God, just as you are. You are entirely forgiven, and always were. The killer you were so afraid of is not as bad as you feared. It was a natural childish response to your real childhood pain. You can see now its innocent childishness. You need be afraid no more. You are safe and free and utterly loved."

Reflecting later on her discovery of her destructive child, Barbara realized that she felt much more powerful than ever before in her life. She wrote later about this awareness from the place of her intelligent adult ego-self.

"I have felt powerless because of not acknowledging my lower self— my unconscious killer. By not owning my killer, her power has been locked away in a dark place where she has slowly been killing me. Ah! The joy of having her for an ally, of re-claiming her energy. Now I know her secret thoughts, her killing thoughts, and can re-claim the power of my hate without acting out the self-punishment."

Near the end of the intensive, Barbara wrote in the voice of her adult self:

"O.K., little girl, I'm going to take care of you. I'm really going to try to care for you in the best, most loving way I can, recognizing that I am imperfect. I may die of cancer, but I will not kill myself with cancer. I will love myself—all of my selves!

"If we stick together—our higher and lower selves—we will manage and someday arrive at the God and the Goddess of whom we are a part. Our darkness is only the pain of our partial knowing. So draw

on the energies of the earth for cleansing and healing. The eagle will fly even as the sun sets and our grandmother the earth gives off such a sweet, rich smell."

Barbara also began to make peace with her mother.

"I can see now that my mother has been evolving into a truer attempt at selfless caring and there is growing a sweet delicate love, from her for me-as-I-am. And my task now is to trust and accept that from her, to let her give to me in my present need, and to let her be, as her pain was certainly as great as mine. I can feel my compassion for her now. And I can also grieve, with her, the painful past. But that is done with.

"My Mommy will never put me to bed, and my Daddy will never hold me in his arms, but my helpers did both, and they were my parents for this short time and they were also themselves. And now I am leaving them to be my own parent, to take care of me. In this time I was little Bobbi, the higher and lower self child, and at the same time me, adult Barbara. And, as always, the Grandmother was here too.

"So hooray for us, all of the 'us-es' so present in these few precious days. Hooray!!"

Barbara's intensive ended with a ritual at the Sevenoaks medicine wheel. Photos of her child self and adult self were put in the center of the circle, along with an eagle feather to symbolize her spirit. The powers of the directions were invoked for healing and strengthening her body and soul.

Barbara lived a year longer than expected, with very little pain. This year was time well spent in spiritual deepening. During her last few months her mother took exquisite care of Barbara, and the love between mother and daughter flowed sweetly. Toward the end of Barbara's life her spirit would often travel "out of body," and she lived with the Grandmother more of the time. Her ego consciousness did not know that the body was dying, but she spoke often of being with the Grandmother, seeing the mountains, and soaring with the eagles. After her death, her ashes were scattered under the seven oaks and at the medicine wheel.

Embracing the Child, Adult Ego, and Transpersonal Selves

Like Barbara, we each need to meet and care for our inner child. And, also like her, we can evoke our spiritual grandmothers and grandfathers, our guardian angels, teachers or guides, who come to us from beyond the level of our ordinary adult ego personality.

As we journey within we discover many different inner selves. We need maps to sort out the many kinds of consciousness that make up our totality.

Maps of Consciousness

In this book we will lay out two maps of consciousness for the individual human psyche that provide reliable guides for the spiritual work of personal transformation. Every individual's journey traverses distinct inner terrain, and therefore produces a unique experiential map. Only by going on your own journey can you affirm the validity of the maps presented here and adapt them to your needs. Yet having a map of the territory that has been encountered by countless other explorers will give you some guideposts and boundaries to look for when you step into your own inner landscape.

The major map presented in this book is one of the three selves: the mask self, the lower self, and the higher self. The mask, which will be discussed in detail in Chapter 6, is a false outer self, the one we put on for the world to see, the person we think we ought to be. The mask is roughly equivalent to the Jungian concept of the *persona*. Hidden beneath the mask is the lower self, the negative aspect of the Jungian *shadow*, a pool of dark and usually unconscious energy, consisting of all our distortions and misconceptions. The lower self and its transformation will be specifically addressed in Chapters 7, 9, and 10.

The mask self is reactive; it was created in response to others' impact on us. By contrast, the lower self is an active, spontaneous, and innate center of destructiveness stemming from our long-forgotten choice to separate from our heart, and from the wholeness of creation, from God. At our core, or center, is the higher self (which Jung called the *Self*), a pool of spontaneous positive life energy, which is our true self. As will be discussed in Chapters 8 and 11, the higher self has unlimited vitality available for creating positive life experience.

The mask and lower self are accretions, or defenses, which keep us from knowing our true identity as emanations of God. And yet the mask and lower self are also very real on the human level. The division of consciousness into these three selves—mask, lower self, and higher self—is central to the principles, process, and practices of the path of the undefended self. The spiritual journey begins with the penetration of the mask, progressing through exposing and transforming the lower self, and coming to know and anchor in the higher self. On this path we come to know God within and meet, honestly and lovingly, our obstructions to God in the form of the mask and lower selves.

Here is a visualization of the three selves, with the mask pictured as our "outer" identity, beneath which is the lower self which defends our core identity, our higher self. At our center is God.

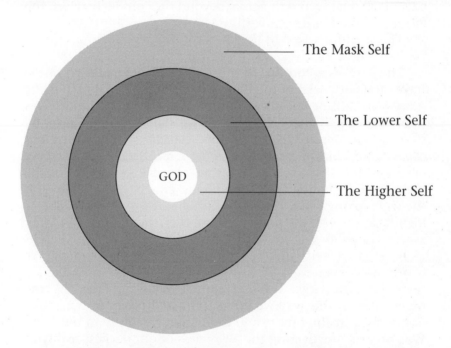

The Mask Self

The Lower Self

GOD

The Higher Self

A second map of the human psyche is described in this chapter and referred to throughout the rest of the book. It is a map of four stages in the spiritual evolution of human beings, which are also four different ways of experiencing and knowing the world. Although these represent four successive stages of spiritual development, they also co-exist simultaneously in our psyche as 1) the inner child or primitive consciousness, 2) the adult or ego awareness, 3) the soul or transpersonal level, which contains the karmic history of our own soul's journey and is also an expression of the collective, archetypal consciousness of all humanity, and 4) the unitive level, which is synonymous with cosmic consciousness. There is different inner work to be done at each of these developmental stages.

The map of the three selves interacts with the map of the developmental stages of child, adult ego, transpersonal soul, and unitive consciousness. The mask, the lower self and the higher self express themselves at both the child and the ego levels. The mask disappears at the transpersonal level, but the lower self continues to express itself in this dimension. However, the dark side of our nature disappears at the unitive level, which is beyond all duality and therefore beyond the conflict between the lower self and higher self within us.[1]

This is summarized in the chart on the next page.

This book is an outline of the work to be done at each of the stages and with each of the three selves. The spiritual path is the process of shifting our identification (who we believe ourselves to be) into the higher self column. We start at the ego level by shifting our identity to the positive ego, by strengthening our capacity for objective, compassionate self-observation. Then we drop our anchor of self into deeper and deeper aspects of the higher self, including the spontaneous, creative inner child and the wise, loving inner parent and teacher. From our safe base of identification with the higher self, we then incorporate the other aspects of who we are—our fragmented and defensive self-identities that exist in the mask and lower self columns. We invite these less developed aspects into awareness and integrate them into the larger bowl of consciousness provided by the higher self. In this way we bring splintered pieces of our selves home, thus creating more and more manifest unity in our lives. We also keep uncovering the awareness of our deepest reality as already living in unity and wholeness, one with God.

Do not attempt to understand all of this at once; let it seep in as we proceed through the stages of the path in the following chapters. All will become clear!

---

[1] While these maps of consciousness come from the teachings of the Guide of the Pathwork, my background thinking has been influenced by Ken Wilber's books, especially *The Spectrum of Consciousness, No Boundary,* and his more recent books quoted in *Grace and Grit,* all of which so usefully make distinctions among the different levels of consciousness. I suspect the Pathwork Guide's three evolutionary levels of consciousness—child/primitive, adult ego, and universal self or soul—also correspond rather closely to what Wilber describes as the pre-rational, rational, and post-rational stages in evolutionary self-identification. He and others have also named these levels as pre-personal, personal, and transpersonal; or preconscious, conscious, and supra-conscious. I have called these three levels "child," "adult ego," and "transpersonal" only because I think these phrases are simple and clear.

MAP OF THE HUMAN PSYCHE

Developmental Stage and Task:	THE THREE SELVES		
	The Mask Self	The Lower Self	The Higher Self
Child Self *Re-educate inner child to become autonomous adult*	Phony child behaving in reaction to expectations of others, trying to avoid vulnerability of being real. Submissive or rebellious child, in reaction to parental authority projected onto others.	Selfish, willful child who wants only his/her own way. Negative, wounded child defended against feeling pain and disappointment. Superstitious and not autonomous.	Spontaneous, loving, creative child, in touch with spirit. Open, undefended child, able to feel and be vulnerable. Open to spiritual reality, without preconceptions.
Adult Ego *Strengthen Positive Ego Mind;* *Align with* *Spiritual Self*	Idealized self-image of ourselves, which we present to the world and want to believe is who we are. Perfectionistic demands on self and others. Character defenses of the Mask: a distortion of a divine quality: submission (Love), aggression (Power), or withdrawal (Serenity)	Personality faults. Egotistical, selfish ego which wants to be master of all it surveys. Alternately, a weak dependent ego which will not take responsibility or lay claim to what it deserves. Pride, self-will, and fear (aspects of lower self on all levels)	Good qualities of the personality. Positive ego will, serving the Spiritual Self. Makes positive choices. Observes and accepts all aspects of the self. Pursues spiritual discipline and follows through on guidance received. Personal strength: Love, Power, or Serenity.
Soul/ Transpersonal Level *Heal Personal and Collective Soul;* *Surrender to God*	No more mask.	Personal soul: Negative soul directions, with intent to perpetuate duality. Personal soul dents, karmic distortions. Collective soul: Negative archetypes & demonic impulses. Attachment to negative power and separation (evil).	Personal soul: Positive soul directions, with intent to unify. Personal soul gifts and desire to serve. Collective soul: Positive archetypes and angelic essences. Surrender to inner guides and to God.
Unitive Level BE IN GOD	No more mask.	No more separating impulses; no more lower self.	Creative Presence; Love and Truth; BEING HERE NOW

Note: At the end of this book—on pages 282-283—I have included an expanded version of this chart called "Steps on the Spiritual Path", which includes a summary of the work to be done at each stage and the stance of the helper toward the worker at each stage.

Child Self

An inner child lives within each of us. Actually, we have many inner children, corresponding to the different developmental levels we have passed through in our lifetime. Of particular importance for our personal healing are those inner children whose emotional development got stuck at one stage or another due to neglect, invasion, or trauma. When emotional development has been incomplete, the adult will act out the unresolved childhood issues until we pay attention to them. The consciousness of these inner children can be re-experienced by the adult we are, in order to bring about their healing.

The infant in us was utterly dependent on her caretakers, and her craving for care, love, and comfort were life-and-death needs. When these were not properly met, the inner child will still be attempting to get others to care for her, or, alternately, refusing to feel the need for care from others, long after we are no longer children physically. The demand for immediate gratification was a real need in the infant; in the adult it is neither appropriate nor achievable. Only by allowing ourselves to feel the full impact of not having had our early needs met and the immensity of our pain at this unfulfillment can we begin to re-parent our infant and allow her to grow and mature into a self-nurturing adult state.

The toddler in us needed to assert independence and begin to control her own bodily functioning. If our need for differentiation was thwarted, the child in us will keep fearing invasion by others, unconsciously asserting her right to be separate which may undermine our attempts at adult closeness. Only by re-experiencing our childhood rage at being held back from our spontaneous need to grow apart from parents can we find the proper balance between separateness and togetherness in adulthood.

A part of our psyche gets frozen at any point in the developmental process from infancy through adolescence when what is experienced is too unsafe or traumatic or threatening to be fully felt and released at the time. The disturbance may be from unmet physical and emotional needs in infancy, or from lack of support for differentiation as a toddler or from invasion of boundaries and personal integrity later on in our development. The child usually does not have the perspective to know that what is happening to her is not right; the child conforms to the environment in which she is raised and represses her distress or

protest. If she does know that what is happening to her is not right, but has no one to talk to about her situation, the loneliness can itself become unbearable, and the precipitating negative situation similarly repressed.

Later, however, when we observe our adult behavior closely, we can see clearly that certain stages of our developmental process were disturbed or incomplete. Then we can go back into the mind and feelings of the child who still lives in us and complete the growth process. Barbara, whose story introduces this chapter, found her inner child and let her speak. Her inner Bobbi spoke, as we would expect, in a child's voice. The adult Barbara, along with her helpers, listened in a way that no one had listened to her when she was a child in grave distress over her father's suicide. This very listening helped the child to heal from her secret murderous feelings, which she had judged so severely and punished so painfully.

In Chapter 5 we will discuss more about the process for working with our inner children, but in this chapter we will discuss the child mind in general, even though we realize there are vast differences between an infant and a ten-year-old. Nonetheless, both are developmentally still in the process of getting their dependency needs met and slowly releasing their dependency. Both are still in varying degrees of fusion with their environment, gradually becoming separate individuated people.

The Undifferentiated Child Mind

The child in us has not only all the characteristics of the particular child we once were, but also the universal qualities of all children. The child self is spontaneous, creative, playful, sensitive, responsive both emotionally and physically, and full of delight, wonder, and love. These are the higher-self qualities of the child. But the child is also self-centered, demanding, dependent, irresponsible, undiscriminating, chaotic, immature, and superstitious. These are the lower-self qualities of the child.

> The child at birth does not yet possess an ego. Without the ego, it is possible to perceive the message from the real self quite clearly. But without the ego, the meaning of the message must be distorted. The child experiences the longing for utter perfection, utter power, and utter

> pleasure. But in the undeveloped ego, these desires are
> not only illusory, but selfish and destructive. (*PGL 132*)

The child spontaneously knows the unlimited potential of the invisible world of spirit, from which she has so recently come. But these messages are distorted by the demands of the child to be gratified instantly, from the outside, without having to create this fulfillment from within herself.

The mentality of the child is close to that of the primitive or collective mind.[2] It is largely unconscious, operating out of automatic or instinctual responses rather than from conscious choice or self-reflection. It lives on the physical and emotional levels primarily, and lives utterly in the moment. The child knows only her own experience and makes generalizations about the nature of the world from the limited perspective of her personal world. (Chapter 5 will explore more fully how the generalizations that we make in childhood color and even define our present experience of reality.)

The child's consciousness is fused with her environment— with family, tribe, and nature. Out of this fusion the child has illusions of omnipotence. Before realizing her limited separateness, she believes she can do anything, and she does not know or fear death. Her sense of mortality begins with the awareness of existing as a separate body and ego. As adults we fear the inner child because of the powerful, spontaneous energies she lives in, and which unconsciously control much of our actions today as adults.

And we fear our inner child because her primitive impulses and actions originate not just from the higher self but also from the lower self. The young child's primitive idea of "good" is what feels good in the moment; "bad" is the thwarting of immediate gratification. The pre-egoic child mind does not make independent moral judgments and may have trouble understanding what she is doing wrong when an action is called "bad." She lives as the customs of her

---

[2] I want to make clear that, by connecting the child and primitive mind states, I am not implying that indigenous or primitive peoples think only with the child mind. This is a **kind** of thinking or awareness—the undeveloped or child-like aspect of all peoples. All human cultures, in fact, have elements of all three aspects—the child mind, the ego mind, and the transpersonal mind. In many indigenous cultures, however, the ego or discriminating mind is the least developed. Both the childishly superstitious and the maturely spiritual aspects are more fully expressed. Since our typical Western culture has, by contrast, over-emphasized the development of the separated ego mind, a needed balance can be found by Westerners opening to the spiritual teachings found in native cultures.

family and/or tribe dictate, but has not yet developed her individual moral sensitivity.

For the child, an act of utter selfishness is apt to follow immediately after a gesture of spontaneous generosity, with no sense of inner contradiction. My daughter Pamela has always adored her cat Butterscotch and yet, at age six, she cut off his whiskers without a moment's hesitation because at that moment the cat was no more to her than one of her Barbie dolls, whose hair she cut regularly. Sensitive intuition about a beloved person may follow barbaric cruelty toward another (or even the same) person momentarily perceived as the "enemy." Sustained moral awareness of others depends on healthy ego development and the understanding of our separateness from, yet relatedness to, others.

The child is not yet differentiated or self-responsible in relationships with others. We can see the child self operating in us as adults whenever we unconsciously make our mates or those in positions of authority into "parent" figures from whom we demand and expect perfect love or unceasing emotional nourishment. An adult who is incapable of the give-and-take and essential equality demanded in a relationship between two adults is still living out a forgotten childhood script. A need for rigid rules and hierarchy is another indication of the child mind seeking a simpler world where Mommies and Daddies, or tribal leaders, were the ones who took responsibility and defined what was right.

In relation to God, the child/primitive in us is superstitious. We make God into an outer authority figure who will reward or punish our behavior, much as we expected our parents to do. In the child mentality, all inner psychological and spiritual currents are projected outward, and the world is peopled with devils and angels, good and bad spirits, which are thanked or blamed depending on the child's experience. The child makes the invisible world into tangible visible things and beings, and this is one of the things we love about children.

But the child does not understand that many of her fantasy beings are projections that originate in the self. Whenever we believe in our own superstitions, we are in our child mind. We all do this in secret attempts to make deals with God, make "sacrifices" so we will get what we want, or otherwise behave toward the divine as if it were a "big Daddy" in the sky.

The spiritual path requires that we uncover the undeveloped and negative inner child—in relation to self, others, and to God—so we can help mature the undeveloped aspects. If we are truly open to communicating with our inner child, she will speak to us and reveal where we are stuck. We must become like parents to our own inner child, encouraging her to grow and to become self-responsible and independent.

The child self, in its positive aspect, provides us access to our creative, spontaneous energies. The child self is our link to the deeper wisdom of primitive cultures as is shown in the following:

An older man, who worked as an organizational consultant, had the following dream during a three-day outdoor retreat on the land at Sevenoaks:

"I am supposed to be leading a group on organizational development, but it is going badly. A male child comes up to me and says, 'Nothing new is going on here. Everything happening here was already happening 2500 years ago.' I think 'He's right. Most of the group dynamics are really unresolved issues about disappointments these people had with their Mommies and Daddies, and most of the splits in the group have to do with tribal loyalties and territorial issues. Nothing is so modern after all about organizational development!'

"The boy then leads me out of the room and down into the basement of the building. From the basement we enter a cave and keep going down. Eventually he leads me into a dimly lit ceremonial room and points to something half-buried in the dirt. I go up to it and begin to uncover it. It is a large stone wheel, and I notice on it four sets of hand-prints, one set for each of the four 'spokes' of the wheel, corresponding to the four cardinal directions in the Medicine Wheel. One set is the hand-prints of a child."

The dreamer was led into a much deeper exploration of his inner child and its connections to his most primal self, the deep primitive inner wisdom that underlay his civilized veneer. Through uncovering more of his child and his "native" wisdom, he sensed he would also be led to be more of a "spokes" person for his new discoveries.

An exploration of the child in us can open us to the deeper energies of the universal or transpersonal levels of experience.

Adult Ego Self

Within each of us also lives an adult ego self, the self we normally identify with. The ego is capable of choice and follow-through, is able to bear frustration and to work hard toward a future goal. The ego allows us to be autonomous, responsible, orderly, and independent, to successfully negotiate our material/human realm as a separate self. But the ego is also calculating, materialistic, overly mental, enclosed in the rigid boundaries of narrow self-interest. By itself the ego is incapable of generating pleasure, joy, creativity, or love. It must be able to release to the larger self to experience the spontaneous streaming of the life force. But first the child mind must give up the demand for instant gratification and develop an ego capable of accepting the limitations of human life.

> You must accept your limitations as a human being
> before you can realize that you have an unlimited fount
> of power at your disposal. You have to accept your own
> imperfections, as well as life's imperfections, before you
> can experience that absolute perfection is your destiny
> that you must ultimately realize. But you can only com-
> prehend this after you have shed the childish distortion
> of this knowledge. You have to learn to let go of a
> desire for pleasure supreme and make do with limited
> pleasure before you can realize that absolute pleasure is
> your ultimate destiny. The doing with the lesser is an
> acceptance of the reality of the limitation of this dimen-
> sion. For that, the ego faculties are necessary. Only
> when your ego deals adequately with the realm in
> which your personality, your body, now lives, can you
> then deeply comprehend your real faculties, potentials,
> and possibilities. (PGL 132)

So long as the limitations of the human realm are not accepted, they cannot be transcended. So long as the ego is not sufficiently developed, it cannot be released. These may sound like contradictions, but they are essential steps on the spiritual path. "Only when the ego is healthy and strong, can we know that it is not the final answer, the final realm of being." (PGL132)

Positive and Negative Aspects of the Ego

As with the child self, the adult ego state is made up of both positive and negative aspects, of consciousness and energy stemming from both our higher and our lower selves. When we get lost in the belief that the ego is all there is, then our boundaries rigidify and a negative separateness sets in. Our perception narrows to outer appearances only, on what divides us from others rather than what unites us. This leads to competitiveness, envy, self-aggrandizement, pride, and self-will. The ego in its negative side promotes an exaggerated idea of the separate self, and a hostile view of others. When we identify exclusively with the adult ego, we enter the paranoid world of "me" vs. "them."

The positive aspects of the ego, on the other hand, include all those voluntary capacities that enable us to make positive choices and to stand by commitments, to differentiate from others, to accept frustration, and to make discernments. The positive ego includes the capacity for objective self-observation and growing self-awareness. It also has the ability to make connections between past, present and future, and to understand the operation of cause and effect in our own lives and in our collective human history. In its departure from the undifferentiated here-and-now world of the child self, the adult ego can extend its awareness backward and forward in time and can move sympathetically toward others perceived as discrete, separate beings rather than as extensions of himself. These capacities are bridges to the transpersonal higher self.

In itself the ego is neither good nor bad. The differentiation of the individual self from family and culture is simply a necessary stage of human development. It is the business of the growing entity to develop a distinct sense of self, to create his boundaries and accept his limitations. The spiritual potential of the ego depends entirely on which deeper aspect of the self it learns to align with—the higher or the lower self. If the ego function is aligned with the higher self, it will have the resiliency to do its work when that is appropriate, and to get out of the way and allow the spontaneous spiritual energies to come through when that is available.

> The ego must know that it is only a servant to the
> greater being within. Its main function is to deliber-
> ately seek contact with the greater self. It must know
> its position. It must know that its strength, possibility,
> and function are to seek contact, to decide for it, to
> request the help from the greater self to establish
> contact permanently with it. (PGL 158)

Ego in Relation to Others

The ego self is much more conscious and self-reflective than is the child self and is capable of self-responsibility and voluntary self-control. These capacities make it capable of mature interaction.

> As a person matures, he develops a sense of self. The more aware of himself he becomes, paradoxical as this may seem, the more concerned with others must he become. Just think of this great spiritual truth, my friends: lack of selfhood means self-centeredness. Full selfhood means concern for others, fairness in evaluating advantages and disadvantages of others and self. It does not mean annihilation of self for the sake of others in a distorted sense of martyrdom. But it does imply a sense of fairness in which one is capable of foregoing an advantage if it creates undue pain or unfair disadvantage for another.
>
> So, on one side of the scale, we have the infant who has no ego, no sense of selfhood, no awareness of itself, accompanied by utter self-centeredness and complete dependency on stronger beings. On the other side of the scale we have the mature person who has a sense of selfhood, an awareness of himself beyond the pleasure-pain principle. This results in a social sense, responsibility, concern for, understanding of, and feeling with others so that this person forms an harmonious whole with others around him in mutuality of purpose and interest. He is free and independent, not to be confused with omnipotent. He does not rule, nor is he ruled. Instead, a healthy interdependence exists between himself and his fellow creatures. (*PGL 120*)

An autonomous, responsible selfhood is a precondition for healthy mutuality. Without a differentiated ego, the person will re-create childhood relationships, tending to choose mates that represent a parent, and tending to surrender inappropriately to the expectations of the other, rather than to discover and stand by the self. Enmeshed families and overly dependent relationships are always the signs of insufficient ego differentiation.

On the other hand, if the ego is rigidly autonomous, it may be very difficult for the person to surrender to love or need for others, to admit when he is wrong, or to have the necessary resiliency for relationship.

The Ego in Relation to God

The pure ego self is atheistic and materialistic. The ego is suspicious of anything it cannot understand with the rational mind or see with the physical eyes. This kind of atheism is at least partly a rejection of the superstitious God-image of the child mind.

> This latter stage of atheism, erroneous in itself, still indicates a state of development beyond the superstitious belief in God. Such belief comes predominantly from fear, evasion, escapism, wishful thinking, and denial of self-responsibility. The second stage of spiritual growth—atheism—is often a necessary transitional period on the way to a more realistic and genuine experience of, and relationship to, God. During this stage of atheism, faculties of self-reliance are cultivated which are of the utmost importance for his individual growth. I do not advocate atheism any more than I advocate a childish, clinging belief in God. Both are stages. In each stage there is something important that the soul learns. (PGL 105)

When we first come back to ourselves out of our childhood enmeshment with family and culture, we are left with only ourselves. From this point of view and at this stage, we are confronted with our aloneness. We are born alone, and we will die alone. Our fate is in our own hands. No one will save us, and no one's damnation matters but our own.

Obviously the danger of the materialistic outlook is that it locks us in the belief that this is all there is. When the invisible worlds and deepest reality of spirit are denied, then the self must live in an arid desert without the life-giving waters of mystery, wonder, and spirit.

Need for a Healthy Ego

We need a healthy ego not only to negotiate our human world effectively, with a sense of autonomy and personal power. We also need a strong ego to do the work of the spiritual path.

The leap into the spiritual self requires much inner preparation. The negative self-centered child and the negative rigidified ego, both being aspects of the lower self, need re-education and re-alignment in order for the surrender to spirituality to be grounded and enduring.

This very process of re-education requires a strong positive ego. We need to be able to evoke and integrate the contents of the unconscious including childhood thoughts and feelings, cultural and mass archetypes, karmic imprints, and our primitive and spontaneous impulses. The ego must be strong enough not to be permanently overwhelmed by the expressions of these many selves. Ego strength is required to discriminate in order to actively encourage some aspects of self and to transform others. Thus the ego must have focus, discipline, and openness.

A healthy ego knows that there is something deep within the self which is much bigger than itself.

> To expand the consciousness of the limited mind
> represents a tremendous difficulty. For you have, at
> least at the beginning of your search, only this same
> limited mind at your disposal. Thus this limited mind
> must transcend itself in order to realize its unlimited
> power and scope. The path therefore constantly
> requires that the mind bridge the gap of its own
> limitations by considering new possibilities, making
> room for other alternatives for the self, for life, for
> expressing the self in life. (PGL 193)

The choices required for spiritual growth cannot be made by a weak ego. A weak ego constantly needs to be shored up and reassured of its value, so it has difficulty going beyond itself. When a weak ego structure dips into the pool of the unconscious, it may be swept away and left floating in a sea of other realities, before it has a sense of its own distinct and separate reality. With no clear definition of the outer self, the powerful energies of the unconscious can wreck the fragile personality.

Therefore spiritual work may need to focus first on the development of positive ego functioning.

Donald had a small inheritance which he had stretched through living frugally. After graduating from college, he had made only a marginal living for years. He had made frequent use of marijuana and other drugs for relaxation and for occasional spiritual insight.

Now he was ready for more serious work on himself and in the world. He realized that his ego strength—for focused, steady work and for sustaining his will power—had never been great and had been further sapped by his steady use of marijuana. He began a recovery program, and then started work as a journalist, a job he truly enjoyed, working for very low pay. After a year of work he knew it was time to ask for a raise, which made him apprehensive. He had the following dream:

"I am in a northeastern city. I have no money to get home to Virginia. I meet a very creepy guy who tries to con me out of money. Then a student appears, obviously wealthy, and the con-man starts bullying him for a handout. Then the con-man disappears with the student's money.

"I run off with the con-man and we stop in a residential district, entering a house there. I decide to hitch back to Virginia and the con-man says he will show me a shortcut to the highway. But when we get there, I see that the on-ramp begins in mid-air; there's no way to get on the highway from where we are. So we go back to the house.

"The con-man leaves to go get drunk. Then the student arrives. It turns out that we are in his house. I explain everything that has happened and the student believes me. Together we discover some of the money that had been taken buried under some plants in the garden.

"The thief returns. I explain to him that this is the student's house and that we must now talk with him. I start explaining to each of them what has happened in karmic terms. To the student I say that he needs this lesson in learning to stand up for himself. He understands. I'm more afraid of talking to the con man, but I tell him that his lesson is that he has to straighten out his life. At first he looks angry, but then he silently nods in tacit agreement. It's clear that my job is to mediate and teach the two of them."

Donald worked on the dream characters. He most easily identified with the student who had been robbed, as he was feeling ripped off by the low pay of his job. It was time for him to stand up and claim his worth at his work, rather than hide behind his inheritance.

As the con artist Donald could see that he indeed was still addicted—no longer to marijuana, but perhaps even more to his inheritance, which kept him from making his own way in the world. Thus in the dream he was unable to get on the road leading home because the on-ramp was too "high," ungrounded and disconnected.

Before he could get on the road home, he first had to be arbiter between these two sides of him—the student and the con-man. The responsibility of Donald's adult ego was clearly defined—to help these parts of him to grow up. He felt hopeful that his inner work would succeed, as the pile of money found in the garden seemed a good omen for his professional potential.

Some people try to make a spiritual virtue of out a weak ego, but this is an evasion which can lead only to more weakness. Anything that leads to abundance must come out of abundance. As long as the ego is weak, we lack some of the faculties of thought, discrimination, initiative, or follow through. Without all of these capacities we will not have the discipline and perseverance required for spiritual growth. In the dream above Donald affirms his need to stand strong in his confrontation of those parts of himself which do not want to grow up.

In contrast to those who put down the ego, some people claim that a strong ego is equivalent to self-fulfillment. But a strong ego is never enough to make us happy.

> Happiness, pleasure, love, and inner peace are all a result of tapping into the deeper, spontaneous inner being. When you identify exclusively with the ego, with the outer conscious willing self, you become completely imbalanced and your life becomes emptied of substance and meaning. . . . Substitute pleasures are then—often frantically—looked for, which are hollow and leave you exhausted and dissatisfied. The ego cannot produce deep feelings and a deep flavorful, pleasurable life. Nor can it produce profound and creative wisdom. (*PGL 158*)

A truly healthy ego, therefore, is one which is neither too big and strong (over-active, over-controlling, rigid, proud, or willful) nor too small and too weak (passive, helpless, wishy-washy, ashamed, unable to act). Strong and resilient, a healthy ego is open to change and new ideas. Above all, a healthy ego is aware of itself as being merely a fragment of consciousness within the whole, and therefore able to retain its humility. "When the ego becomes strong enough to take the risk to trust faculties other than its limited conscious one, it will find a new security, hitherto undreamed of." (*PGL 152*)

Soul/Transpersonal Level

The soul is without limits in time or space. It does not die because it was not born. It is eternally and everywhere available. While the spirit of God will manifest differently in each individual soul, depending on personal and cultural conditioning, its essence is identical with the eternal life force that permeates the entire universe.

The experience of the soul or transpersonal level of the self transcends and shatters the "container" of self created by the ego. Our experience of self "spreads out," as it were, to encompass more and more of who we are. When we open ourselves to this level, we leave the familiar boundaries of our present incarnation and personality, this time and space manifestation, and experience ourselves as larger, deeper, more inclusive, whole.

We may experience past lives and then know ourselves as an eternal soul, one who has traveled through many lifetimes gathering wisdom, seeking more and more wholeness. We may enter a shamanic reality, the hidden worlds of nature that exist on the inner planes and which we can contact in non-ordinary reality. We may come to know our angelic essence, as beings of light, or aspects of God who have manifested on earth for specific tasks. Or we may touch into universal archetypes—wise woman or mother, sage or king, and know ourselves as also existing at this level of the collective unconscious as it flows through all human cultures. We may experience our inner guides and gurus, moving beyond the normal human boundaries of interaction.

Barbara, whose story introduces this chapter, had frequent contact with a major personal guide whom she experienced as a Grandmother of the Earth. In her dying process she was often with the Grandmother, who also taught her to fly with the eagles. The following is an experience of mine, which came at a time when the teaching I needed about death might not have reached me any other way.

I am an impressionable person. Though grounded and competent in the normal adult ego world, I find it fairly easy to enter other realities. As a child I identified with characters in the many novels I read. Past lives are accessible to me. This can be a wonderful asset, as I can readily enter another person's "universe," but it can also be a liability, as I can sometimes lose myself in another's reality.

Movies are special challenges. On entering the fictional reality of a good film, I suspend disbelief, my ego lets go and "floats" for the duration. After the movie it takes me a while to "come back" to my ordinary sense of self. Occasionally, before returning, I will drop into some other reality or aspect of my unconscious. This altered state is often useful to illuminate some hidden aspect of myself which would not have been available in my normal ego state.

*One evening in the mid 1970s, after seeing the movie **Heaven Can Wait**, I had an extraordinary expansion of consciousness. The movie is a light comedy about a person who dies "by mistake," and then re-enters several other bodies until he finds the right one. While I was walking out of the movie theater with my husband Donovan, I began to have strange sensations at the back of my head and neck. As I paid attention to these sensations, I felt something pulling me back and out of my body.*

Out on the street with Donovan, I suddenly found myself standing about three feet behind and about one foot above my physical body. I was flooded with the strongest feelings of peace and well-being I had ever experienced. At that moment I knew myself to be eternal, incapable of ever not being. I just was, and would forever be, this being I now felt myself to be. The closest I could come to words burst out to my husband, "Do you know who I am, Donovan? Do you know who you are? We are devoted angels of God. That's who we really are! And we cannot die because we were never born, we just are."

As we crossed the street toward our parked car, I had an impulse to throw my body in front of an on-coming vehicle. Experiencing my body as a lifeless puppet dangling below and in front of me, I was perfectly confident that whether it lived or died made not a particle of difference to the existence of my real self, the being I now knew I was. But I also knew better; it was not my place to destroy this body, for I understood that I was called to inhabit the earth plane in order to purify myself and to serve God. It would be arrogant and selfish of me to destroy my body, however irrelevant it momentarily felt to my true identity.

By the time Donovan and I arrived at our car I was beginning to come back inside my more limited self. I felt and heard a gentle "whoosh" as I settled back into my body.

"It's about death," I kept repeating. "It's so important for us to understand about death. That it isn't what people fear; that it is just a passage from one smaller identity to another, larger one. We need to understand this. I think I was given this experience so I could understand better, and help people better. Oh, what a gift!"

I was quiet and thoughtful on the ride home. For a while I could feel the "larger" identity in back of me, and then awareness of that too faded, and I was again just Susan, back in my normal body and ego consciousness.

Only later did I realize the significance of the timing of this experience in my life. It was shortly after my spiritual teacher Eva Pierrakos became sick with cancer, and before she died. Even at the time I knew that to do this work with other people I would have to have confidence that death, including Eva's death, was not the end. Later on, of course, I still had to pass through deep grief and despair after her dying; but the knowing that came from my out-of-body experience sustained me.

By the time I worked with "Barbara," whose story begins this chapter, I knew the work of self-purification is the healing of the soul which lives beyond any particular lifetime. The imminent death of the person is not only no impediment to doing this work; it provides an added urgency.

The gentle "whoosh" of energy that I experienced as I came back into my body was the sudden contraction of my consciousness as it returned to the ego/body "container." We can often experience something similar on waking up from a dream in which we have expanded into a different, broader consciousness. And the reverse often happens when we are falling asleep, where we can feel ourselves slip out of the ego container and into other dimensions of reality.

Positive and Negative Aspects of the Transpersonal Level

At the transpersonal level we expand beyond the ego to the larger beings that we were before birth and will be again after death. We can open up a channel to other spiritual entities or energies that exist beyond our ordinary everyday reality. We can enter these other realities through meditation and other spiritual practices and know ourselves and reality to be so much more than we thought.

However, the transpersonal level is still in duality. We can tap levels that are evil, ignorant, or distorted on the transpersonal level just as we can on the child and ego levels. The lower self is made up of the impulses of the immature child, the negative ego, and the distortions of the transpersonal level.

The experience of archetypes and psychic abilities available on the transpersonal level is especially seductive, because we touch into powerful spiritual energies. But spiritual entities also have their shadow side; they may or may not be aligned with an ethical intention. The "glamour" and spiritual power of contacting this level should not distract us from our task of personal transformation and service to God.

As we deepen personal work on our distortions, we inevitably gain greater spiritual power. This brings with it a greater responsibility to handle this power well. We will experience temptations. We may contact the archetype of the black magician who uses his spiritual power for personal aggrandizement. Or, as we expand our capacity to affect others through our love, we may need to look at the distortion of using love as a way to control others. We may contact the archetype of the mother who devours her children. If our intention continues to be aligned with spiritual growth, contacting and transforming the negative archetypes in us can be a very powerful level of the work.

I once did an important piece of past-life work, entering a very ancient African male lifetime during which I had extraordinary shamanic gifts. I could readily enter the consciousness of others and effect changes in their energy which resulted in some extraordinary healings for which I became well known. However, I eventually abused those gifts by using them to seduce women and destroy my male competitors. I was finally thrown out of the tribe and shortly thereafter died in anguished isolation. Contacting this lifetime within me has made me extremely cautious about the potential for abuse of spiritual power and has increased my commitment to use my awakening gifts solely in service to all my brothers and sisters in our human family.

We long for contact with the transpersonal level within us; such experiences carry tremendous excitement and aliveness. We can open ourselves to hearing within us the voice of God, which may be experienced as that of Christ or our guardian angels, the Goddess or our spirit guides, or simply the "still, small voice." However, in the process we may also open ourselves to hearing the voices of unevolved non-incarnate entities, including the evil powers, sometimes called Satan, who would misuse the connection with us. Thus it is always essential to evaluate any experience of contact with spirit beings to make sure the messages are truthful, loving, and in service to all humanity and to the higher good. We should be especially wary of guidance that flatters or makes promises. Messages that challenge us to look at ourselves more deeply usually indicate the guidance is real. As we contact spirit entities, we must keep making the choice to align our ego and will with the divine, with service to God.

It is possible to delude ourselves about which level we are tapping. Evolution toward the unitive state is reliable and grounded only if we actively work with and commit to transform the lower self, the force for separation, whether it manifests through the inner child, the ego, or at transpersonal levels.

The Soul/Transpersonal Level Distinguished from Other Levels

When we are alive to the reality of our own soul, we live in a greatly expanded sense of self. We are open to all the unconscious levels that live in us, and know that they each manifest a "piece" of who we are. We know we are entirely responsible for the creation of our own lives, but also understand self-creation in the larger context of accepting our personal and collective karma. Self-understanding moves beyond what can be understood by the ego and into the realm of true inner knowing.

The experience of the transpersonal levels of the self is a letting go into involuntary processes and spontaneous feelings, but with greater awareness and capacity for discrimination than the child self possesses. Having gone through self-scrutiny in the process of clearing out our negativity, we recognize appropriate moments for surrender to the divine flow. And we can and will return to the ego boundaries when this is appropriate.

In relation to others, we can thin the boundaries of the self, entering into deep sympathy and compassion for the other, surrendering to the experience of inner communion. This intimate knowing of another differs from the fusion experience of the child, who lacks a mature awareness of being a separate self. Also unlike the child, the transpersonal self is capable of nourishing others, and thus moves beyond both the need of the child to be nourished and the self-nurturing task of the ego.

In relation to God, the transpersonal self knows the reality of invisible worlds, both inner and outer. In this stage we know that matter, or outer reality, is only a reflection or creation of the more inner world of spirit. Like the child, we sense the invisible; unlike the child, we do not simply personify the invisible, but also know it as subjective, inner, and essentially beyond form. God is not objectified, but realized as alive within us and all life.

Unitive Level

At the unitive level the experience of self is synonymous with the experience of Cosmic Consciousness. In the awareness of the absolute Oneness of all life, all distinctions among separate selves, even separate souls or different archetypes or kinds of angels, evaporate in the experience of the "Beingness" behind or within everything. Within what we normally think of as the self is an experience totally beyond the self. Because there is no duality at this level, there no "self" and no "not self." This level is experienced as good and true, but not the same kind of good or true that has an opposition in duality.

> Genuine God-experience is **being**. God is not perceived as acting—punishing or rewarding, or guiding along certain ways. You realize that God **is**. (*PGL 105*)

> In the state of cosmic feeling you experience the immediacy of the presence of God within. . . . This manifestation is then experienced as your eternal reality and state, as your true identity. (*PGL 200*)

The unitive level is the experience of the ground of being, the state of cosmic consciousness, an awareness that all of life is truly one, that there really is no separation. It is all one gigantic pulsating energy-consciousness. It is all God.

Surrender

Openings to the transpersonal self and to the unitive level come through grace; no amount of self-discipline or spiritual practice can guarantee such experience. We can, however, practice giving over to the experience of the present moment, without the judging, discriminating ego mind separating us from the rest of life. When the ego is sufficiently confident to negotiate the time-space limitations imposed on us through incarnation, then it can relax enough to allow the greater being to come through.

Such surrender may happen in deep relaxation, moments of creative ecstasy, prayer or meditation, dance, sexual union, or even in deep grief or pain as long as we do not separate from the experience. Whenever we are deeply open to allowing our inner reality to manifest, then we may be blessed by the rewards of surrender. To reach into, and gradually learn to live from, this source of eternal renewal is the goal of any spiritual path.

Stages Co-Exist

Each of the stages of inner child, adult ego, transpersonal self, and unitive level co-exist at the same time in any adult person, whether or not they have been made conscious. The process of spiritual growth involves learning to anchor in the higher self while also honestly and lovingly accepting the other aspects of the psyche. For example, we may call on the transpersonal archetypes of Divine Mother and Divine Father to help the adult ego love the wounded inner child. Or we may activate the positive ego in order to restrain and limit the negative inner child who wants to act out destructive feelings. At another point, the positive child self may need to educate the over-controlling ego in how to play and have fun. The wounded child will often stay repressed until we have developed a sufficiently strong adult ego to be able to face the buried hurts and resulting misconceptions of childhood.

When the ego is sufficiently healthy and resilient, it will have the strength to release itself to the universal streaming of love and pleasure which go beyond ego. A healthy ego is often the "negotiator" which allows us to contact and to integrate experiences of both the inner child self and the transpersonal level, in both their positive and negative aspects. Our gradual awakening brings us access to all the different selves.

Spiritual growth is never neat or linear; instead, it constantly spirals inward, circling and re-circling the many inner selves at deeper and deeper levels of exploration and integration. Our inner child will reveal where our energy is stuck at some developmental phase that needs our attention. Similarly, our ego will reveal its immaturity in its manifestations of weakness or rigidity. Whenever we find stunted development, facing the truth about ourselves is the first step toward healing. Our weaknesses are nothing to be ashamed of; they show us the purpose of our incarnation. We are here to discover our shortcomings and mature into beings of greater capacity for love and truth.

The Paradox of Spiritual Evolution

Paradoxically, evolution is the impulse toward both differentiation and union. Our personal process of individuation brings us simultaneously into a greater sense of our distinct individual identity and a greater identification with the whole of life.

The evolutionary impulse toward differentiation can be seen in the gradual growth of individuality and complexity as life moves up the evolutionary scale. As humans, we are constantly being challenged to differentiate, to pull ourselves out of a regressive over-identification with family, tribe, religion, or nation. We need to be able to challenge the mass thinking that enthralls our consciousness, and instead find our own unique truth. We need to be willing to stand alone with our truth. The principal instrument for differentiation in humans is the ego function.

The evolutionary impulse also leads toward union. If an individual is constantly working against others of his species, he risks extinction. All of life is essentially one fabric, a web of intricately intertwined energies. Disturbing any part of the fabric affects us all. When we grasp that all of life is one in essence, though diverse in expression, we come close to the reality of evolution.

The thrust of the personal growth process is to gain enough individual ego strength to be able voluntarily to let go of our separateness and unify with the cosmic streaming of the Life Force pulsating through us—and, conversely, to allow the Universal Intelligence to express itself through us in a way that is focused, effective, and well-integrated. To the extent that we free our personalities of obstruction, we become agents of transformation, channels for bringing spiritual energy to the planet. We become co-creators in the joyful task of spiritualizing matter, and materializing spirit.

Exercises for Chapter 4:

1. Consider an area of difficulty in your current life. Ask to hear the voice of the inner child in relation to this difficulty. Be open to whatever you hear. Or it may be easier for you to see the inner child. Get a clear and concrete picture of him/her—what the child is wearing, where he/she is, whether or not alone, what expression is on the face. Or you may have a kinesthetic sense of the child in some part of your own body. However you can, tune into your inner child. Then let the adult part of you become the objective, compassionate observer so you can listen to the child. Then, as the child, express fully your thoughts and feelings about the area in which the adult you is having problems. Allow yourself free expression, however seemingly crazy, immature, or destructive are the thoughts and feelings of your inner child.

2. Bring the positive adult ego into dialogue with the inner child. The positive ego (including the capacity for objective, compassionate self-observation) may be likened to the good parent, caring yet confrontational, helping the child to mature in whatever area is still undeveloped. Write out the dialogue.

3. Focus on a disharmony you have written about in your daily review. Invite into awareness any negative inner voices—the cynical ego or rebellious child or whatever. Record what they say, listening to them objectively. Then use the positive ego to enter into dialogue with them.

4. Still focussing on the same disharmony, invoke the transpersonal level of the higher self and ask for its guidance, direction, or blessing. Listen within for its messages to the immature child and/or the negative adult ego. You may then engage in a three-way dialogue allowing each to speak to the other: 1) transpersonal higher self, 2) adult ego (positive and negative), 3) and child self (positive and negative). The positive ego is the negotiator or one in charge of keeping the inner characters clear.

CHAPTER 5

Seeing How We Re-Create the Past in the Present

"The child forms certain wrong conclusions about life, which sink into the unconscious, and then mold the life of the adult."

—paraphrased from Pathwork Guide Lecture 38, *"Images"*

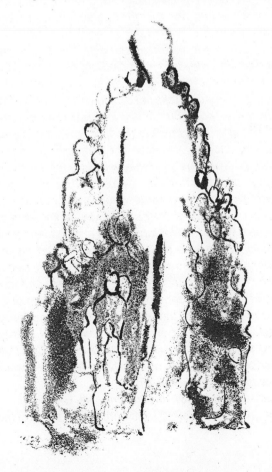

Bill and Joanne: Untangling the
Sexual Knots in Relationship

"We want help with our sex life," Bill announced for himself and his wife Joanne at the first session of their week-long couples intensive. *"We love each other, but our interest in expressing our love sexually has dropped off a lot in the last few years, and we want to reawaken it,"* Joanne added.

Bill and Joanne shared the sexual pattern which most troubled and frustrated them over the ten years of their marriage. Bill would initiate sexual interaction, often with great urgency in his desire. At some point Joanne would feel scared by the intensity of his masculine energy coming toward her, and would communicate her fear to Bill, asking for his loving reassurance. Though Bill would sometimes attempt to comfort Joanne, Bill's sexual energy would deflate, and he would start to withdraw from her, feeling defeated. Often then Joanne would feel bad and attempt to turn Bill on again. Sometimes this would work and the sexual exchange would complete itself, but with a loss of the original intensity. More often, Bill would be resistant and sullen, and Joanne would feel frustrated.

Both Bill and Joanne felt frustrated and defeated in their efforts to be physically intimate. After they had each discharged feelings of anger and blame toward the other for the sexual stagnation in their relationship, we began to explore their mutual stake in keeping their sexuality frozen. They began to see that they had both settled into a no-risk pattern of withdrawal and blame rather than feeling the fear, vulnerability, and potential disappointment that lay beneath the surface. At the end of an evening's session, I asked, *"Are you really willing to resolve the problem?"*

After thinking about this question overnight, they each came into the next session with a commitment to do whatever work was necessary to open up their sexual feelings with the other. Bill acknowledged that he was easily frustrated when the woman did not respond immediately to his initiating lovemaking; this was a pattern that preceded his relationship with Joanne. Joanne could also acknowledge that she felt easily threatened by any man's sexual aggression, and was more comfortable when she was in control as the initiator. Both could feel their wanting to be the one in control, and their fear of surrendering to the other. More deeply felt was an unconscious fear of their own involuntary sexual energy, a dread which reinforced their control struggles with one another. Their willingness to consider taking personal responsibility for their sexual patterns opened the door to their mutual healing.

In the next sessions, both Joanne and Bill brought in significant dream material. Joanne's dream: *"I am with Bill in the basement of the house where I lived as a teenager, and where I first experimented with boys sexually. In the dream I find a scorpion and try to hand it to Bill, because I am scared of it. But Bill won't take the scorpion. He is instead clutching to his chest a black widow spider."*

Joanne saw the scorpion as her passionate sexual nature which she kept disowning, attributing to Bill the erotic intensity she did not admit in herself. But the dream told her clearly that it was her scorpion, not his. The dream also revealed what she had known unconsciously, that Bill had his own fear of feminine sexuality, represented by his clutching the female spider who kills the male after mating. Joanne could then acknowledge more fully her fear of her sexual life force, and cease rationalizing this as fear of her mate's sexuality. Glimpsing Bill's fears softened her feelings toward him.

Bill's dream: "I am in my mother's house and I pee into the crack between the pages of an open book. I know my mother will be mad about this, and to appease her, I break off the end of my cigarette." For the first time Bill had a deeper glimpse that he himself was breaking off the intensity of his sexual sensations in some long-forgotten penance associated with his mother.

The dream revealed the suppressed world of his inner child. He had for a time as a young boy believed that sex happened when a boy urinated on a girl, in her "crack," and that this was a very bad thing to do. His mother had always felt to Bill like a stern moral authority who preached to little Billy against sex, though she herself had been very seductive with her son; Bill had hated her moralism and her hypocrisy. As an adolescent and young man he had rebelled by being defiantly sexual. Yet through his dream, Bill saw that he also judged himself as "bad," and had capitulated to his mother by a kind of self-castration.

I then asked both Bill and Joanne: "Are you each willing to take 100% responsibility for your own sexual fulfillment in this relationship?" By now Bill could see that the difficulty he had in sustaining interest after experiencing rejection by Joanne originated in his deep ambivalence about his sexuality. Whatever its origins, the resolution would come by opening to the buried material within him, not by any way in which Joanne would change. Joanne also knew that her fear of her sexual energy and of Bill's masculine intensity was an ancient issue that could only be met within her own psyche. As she took more responsibility for herself, she stopped displacing her anxiety and need for reassurance onto Bill and released her demand that he do it just right.

The two commitments that Bill and Joanne had now made—being willing to resolve the difficulty between them and being willing to take

*individual responsibility for that resolution by looking deep into them-
selves to the source of their own inner problems—laid the groundwork for
a successful couples intensive.*

*Such commitments are not easy; the temptation to blame is very pro-
nounced in couples. And in this couple, as in most, their individual difficulties were exactly matched by the other. Where Bill expected to be
rejected sexually, Joanne's fearful response gave him the opportunity to
keep re-experiencing that rejection. Where Joanne expected to be
assaulted sexually and to find receptivity unsafe, Bill's initial sexual
urgency and difficulty in giving her loving reassurance gave her the opportunity to keep re-experiencing her fear of sexuality. They expressed hope
that their selection of each other as mate had as its basis a desire for profound self-healing in the sexual arena.*

*We created a ritual in which they each symbolically let the other off
the hook of blame and dependency. They made commitments to one
another to take responsibility for their own sexual healing, and to forgive
the other. Their love began to flow during the ritual, as each began to see
the other as friend and helpmate, not the cause of their unfulfillment.
Now the work could begin in earnest.*

*Joanne explored her associations with the basement in her dream.
She remembered it as a dangerous place, where her budding sexuality
had threatened to get out of control. Her family had been very repressed
sexually; what she remembered was a climate of fear, and a hushed
warning about not getting out of control or hurt by boys, who wanted
only sex from girls. She dialogued with pillows representing her parents,
protesting and feeling the pain of the chronic anxiety in her family. Later
she spoke as a sexually enlightened parent to the adolescent Joanne she
once was, re-educating her inner child to a new, safe reality about sex to
replace the old fearful one.*

*Bill worked on his intense ambivalence about sex. As a Catholic boy he
had been taught by nuns who stressed how bad sex was, and, until
adolescence, Bill had tried very hard to live up to unrealistic standards of
purity and goodness. When the sexual force was awakened in him as a
teenager, he gave in to its demands, but only by accepting a negative self-
judgment which made it impossible for him to connect sex which was "bad"
with love which was "good." Further, since the hormonal demands of adolescence were so urgent, he abandoned his desire to get to know and love
a girl and instead, furtively and guiltily, tried to live out a loveless script of
sexual conquest with any girl who would let him. In the course of his work
in the couples intensive, Bill felt his intense guilt and sorrow for his
mistreatment of girls and women and for his betrayal of his own desire to love.*

Bill remembered a dream he had first had as a high school student, when he had just begun smoking cigarettes: "I am walking through the front yard toward our house and I am carrying a lighted cigar. Halfway to the front door, I realize that I don't want my mother to see me smoking, so I start to shred the cigar and stuff some of it in my mouth. I start chewing it up, including parts of it that are still burning. I am puffing out the smoke and my mouth is burning with intense heat as I try desperately to make the smoke disappear." The similarity of this dream image to his earlier one of breaking off his cigarette made it clear to Bill that he was the one responsible for cutting off his passion, his smoking cigar. And once again Bill learned that he expected the woman, originally his mother and the Catholic nuns, to reject his sexual passion.

Both Joanne and Bill uncovered pivotal events with their parent of the opposite sex that had solidified their misconceptions about sex.

Bill was led into his childhood through another dream: "I am standing on a New York City street watching women walk by and feeling sexually attracted to a number of them. Nearby is a rectangular patch of fresh tar. I step in it and sink all the way down to a subway platform. On the platform, my teeth start feeling funny; three teeth loosen and fall into the palm of my hand." Bill saw again that in his unconscious (the subway), he was punishing himself for his sexual thoughts by losing his teeth, his "bite," his potency.

This led Bill back to reliving a formative event when he was seven years old. As a little boy, he had been very close to his mother, and yet he was also terrified of her. He recalled, "I am running around the kitchen, being normally rambunctious, maybe also slamming the kitchen screen door as I run in and out. My mother, who is working in the kitchen, tries to get me to be quieter, but I continue my childish high spirits. But then, as I am running toward the sink where she is, she yells at me and lifts something high over her head, maybe a knife. I duck, overreacting, and bring my head down hard on a white porcelain sink. I break off my two new, permanent front teeth." In this traumatic event Bill concluded that he had unconsciously "sacrificed" his teeth to appease his mother who was threatened by his aliveness. In just such a way Bill had "sacrificed" his sexuality with Joanne, with whom his loving intimacy had raised fears similar to those he had had with his mother.

Here was a pivotal experience of self-suppression in reaction to his mother's perceived rejection, a pattern which he had been re-creating ever since. Bill talked to his inner child, and prayed for the help of his higher self to re-enliven his spontaneity and deepen his trust in his God-given sexual nature.

Joanne's work on her inner basement led her to re-experience a formative event that occurred with her father when she was at home for the summer before college, and before she was sexually active. During that year her father had contracted cancer and had undergone a series of surgical procedures. During the course of his surgeries and illness, he had been given painkillers and had eventually gotten dependent on them. His performance at work had been affected, and his boss was suggesting an early retirement. Her father knew he had to do something. So, on a summer weekend when Joanne's mother and other siblings were away at the beach, and Joanne was staying home alone with her father, he announced to her that he intended to stop all his medications that weekend, and needed her help to go "cold turkey."

Joanne had not clearly known of her father's addiction to painkillers and his announcement had overwhelmed her. On reliving the moment at the kitchen table when her father had shared his decision, Joanne trembled and cried, screaming her fears and squirming with how inadequate she had felt as a seventeen-year-old trying to meet her father's needs. Only now could she realize the full intensity of his adult need that was directed toward her at that time. She remembered his vomiting and his depression that weekend, and her own contracted state, trying her best to support him and cook for him while inwardly denying her own terror. Although her father had not been sexual with Joanne, she suspected that her own budding sexuality had gotten mixed into her fear of his need. For Joanne this moment in which her father's urgency and intensity were directed at her was what she had re-created in her sexual relationship with Bill. Now she had the opportunity to experience her fear at its source. She felt her terror and outrage at his inappropriately asking her for a level of reassurance and support that was beyond her years to give. She also felt her love and longing toward her father, including her wish that she could have given him what he needed.

Joanne's adolescent self had not been big enough to contain her father's intensity, nor to allow her own true reactions, and so she had split off from herself, but had then re-created the feelings with Bill until they could be met at the source. Eventually, Joanne would be able to release the fear that had gripped her as a seventeen-year-old. She realized that she was now a bigger person with a much larger capacity to receive the feelings and desires of a man. She no longer needed to stay stuck in recycling an old fear.

Bill and Joanne deepened their love and respect for one another enormously as they observed each other struggle to reclaim their vibrant and safe sexual self-expression. They were no longer so caught in projecting *their own parent of the opposite sex onto their mate, and this brought enormous clarity into their perception of each other. Their lovemaking became a tender time for connecting more deeply with each other, moving slowly and sensitively, taking time for communicating their feelings moment by moment.*

Seeing How We Re-Create the Past in the Present

Spiritual evolution is the process of gradually expanding and integrating our experience of what it means to be human. As adults, we live most of the time within a very limited idea of who we are. Our minds are narrowed; our energy is held and compacted, or diffuse and unfocused. Our experience of life is constricted. In order to expand beyond our limited experience, we must first know how we constrict ourselves. In order to escape from our prison, we must first see clearly what it is and how it has been built.

The baby at birth is a wide open system with free flowing breath and an undefended responsiveness to the world. The separate self is not yet formed, though there are certain predispositions and tendencies inherent in the soul at birth. During the course of our birth, infancy, and childhood we have experiences which seem to teach us that certain aspects of ourselves and of life are unsafe, wrong, and painful, and, on the basis of this negative learning, we shut down the full flow of life through our bodies.

From the soul level, we come into incarnation with a plan to face and resolve certain issues in this lifetime. From this point of view, our parents and the difficult circumstances of our childhood are the conditions we have set up for ourselves in order to illuminate our areas of difficulty so that they can be brought to the foreground in our childhood and, later on, faced and transformed.

During our early years, we instinctively recoil from the negative side of life's inevitable dualities. We retreat from the pains and disappointments of our childhood, and we conclude that certain parts of ourselves and/or certain kinds of feelings are unacceptable. We thereby deny parts of our experience, thus limiting our idea of who we are and what we can handle. From the soul level, the pre-existing "dents" or distortions in the soul become manifest in the early life of the child.

Bill and Joanne worked in their couples intensive to discover that they had individually and together constricted their adult sexual relationship out of fear, in an attempt to avoid the pain of unmet traumas from their childhood.

As children, after we experience some of life's disappoint-ments, we attempt to ward off future pain by making certain generalizations about life, forming conclusions based on our par-ticular experience and our specific interactions with our unique parents. For example, on the basis of his mother's behavior toward him, reinforced by the Catholic nuns, Bill had concluded that having his full sexual energy would result in rejection by the woman. Joanne, on the basis of her adolescent experience with her father, concluded that male sexuality was overpowering, more than she could handle. Both of them had unconsciously concluded that sex is dangerous, and that it was safer to avoid sex or to keep it low-key.

These conclusions, based on unhappy childhood and ado-lescent experiences, went into the unconscious and became the lens through which they viewed sexuality and which then con-ditioned what they experienced. Whenever Bill's positive mas-culine sexuality was not met perfectly by the woman, it confirmed his expectation of rejection and made him feel defeated. Over time he risked less, and more often felt rejected, thus having his wrong conclusion confirmed. Similarly, Joanne expected to be overwhelmed and so, if the man was not per-fectly loving and reassuring ahead of time, she easily became frightened. Over time, her fear was more quickly triggered, thus confirming her wrong conclusion that male sexuality was not to be trusted. Their negative expectations created negative experi-ences; and their negative experiences then confirmed their negative expectations.

We all unconsciously impose on the outer world our limited ideas about how we think life works and how we expect to be treated, based largely on our earliest experiences of how we were treated by our parents when we were children. More often than not our expectations get fulfilled by our experience since that inner reality we have created is so persuasive. We will tend to ignore whatever does not fit into our preconceptions and we will attract to us whatever does fit. Furthermore, our defensive reac-tions and behavior, formed to support our expectations, usually guarantee the result we expect. Thus our limited reality becomes self-reinforcing, a vicious circle. We expect a certain negative response from life and behave in accordance with that expectation. When the expected response comes, it reinforces our original wrong conclusion.

Since our self-limitations have been created by us, usually in response to childhood pain and the limitations of our own parents and family, the process of reclaiming all of our selves must include re-visiting our childhood. By feeling our childhood hurts, we strengthen our adult capacity for embracing the opposites within—the good and bad aspects of our parents, the good and bad aspects of our own inner child, the pain and the pleasures experienced by our open, undefended child-self. And we discover that we have a much greater capacity now to tolerate feelings and realizations that might have seemed intolerable to our fragile child-selves. We learn to go back and re-experience what was incompletely felt or denied or inwardly split off from. In this process we uncover the limiting and negative beliefs and ideas we have about life, and learn to replace them with expansive, positive, open-ended attitudes. This then creates a benign circle of positive expectation, fulfilled by benign experience, which reinforces our optimism and openness toward life.

When we dissolve our personal limitations, our expansion has an impact on everyone around us, in a ripple effect. Whenever any one of us makes the leap of expanding his personal boundaries, deepening his sense of inner security and safety to include more of life, then all of humankind expands. The evolutionary process of the species is furthered.

An Image Defined

In the Pathwork we call our false and limiting beliefs about life "images." This wrong belief creates cramped energy in the body, resulting in constricted emotions and defensive attitudes that further support the misconception. Thus images define and limit our reality. Images become a set of blinders or dark glasses which inhibit and circumscribe our vision and experience of life, and prevent us from embracing life directly and wholly as it is.

The Guide uses the word "image" because this false idea about life is something that is overlaid on top of pure life experience, a "picture" through which we view life. Additionally, this superimposed picture is something which can be seen on the spiritual level. From the spiritual vantage point, thoughts and emotions are "things" which can be seen. An image is a compact configuration of thoughts and emotions which have become a rigid mass in the soul substance, a stuck place in the energy of our bodymind, which then blinds us from a clear perception of reality.

> We spirits see the whole thought process as a spiritual form—or an image. Thoughts, feelings, and attitudes that are unconnected with an image flow harmoniously with the divine forces and currents, adapting themselves spontaneously to the immediate need, subject to change according to the current necessities. All such thoughts and feelings are fluctuating, dynamic, and relaxed; they are flexible. But the thought-and-feeling forms emanating from wrong beliefs or images are static and congested. They do not "give" in accordance with different circumstances. Thus they create disorder and disharmony. I might say that a short circuit is established. This is the way **we** see it. The way you see and feel it is through unhappiness, anxiety, and puzzlement over many apparently inexplicable things in your life. The fact that you cannot change what you wish to change, or that certain happenings in your life seem to repeat regularly, are two examples. (*PGL 38*)

Origin of Images

An image springs from the dualistic belief that some aspects of life are unsafe and must be defended against. The child we once were encountered a specific disappointment and pain and made a generalization about life based on his unique experience. For example, Bill found his exuberant sexuality both aroused and harshly judged by his mother during his vulnerable childhood. He did not then have the ego strength to feel the shock and pain of her rejection all the way through, and had instead suppressed his reaction and turned against himself.

The child has nothing to compare his experience with; he knows only the reality presented to him in his family. So he naturally concludes that this must be the way life is for everyone. Bill concluded that his sexuality was unacceptable not just to his mother in that instance but, in his attempt to make sense of his life experience, he generalized to all women an expectation of rejection of his sexuality. The child then further concludes that he should respond in a certain way in order to prevent future pain. Bill unconsciously resolved that if he himself shut down his sexual feelings he wouldn't have to feel the pain of rejection by the woman.

It is at first quite a shock to discover how the immature "thinking" of childhood still dominates much of our adult mind and behavior. But it is also quite illuminating to see how our present difficulties are often rooted in unconscious childhood logic. Once this childish thinking is revealed, we have an opportunity to undo the pattern. Until then, we will keep unconsciously enacting the inexorable pattern of re-creating our childhood experience in our adult lives.

A bicyclist, born and raised in Ohio, had a dream about being on a bicycle trip. He was traveling through the Virginia countryside where he lives, but was not achieving his destination. When he finally pulled out the map to check his location, he discovered that he had been following a map of Ohio, not the Virginia map! The dreamer awoke knowing that he was still following the map of life which he had created in childhood rather than the map that would be appropriate for his life as an adult.

Origin of Images at the Soul Level

Many images originate in this lifetime's infancy and childhood, a time of the soul's heightened and continuous vulnerability. More often, images pre-exist in a person's soul prior to this incarnation. For pre-existing images, the experiences in this lifetime during infancy and childhood usually solidify or draw out the deeper misconceptions or soul dents which are magnets for certain kinds of negative experience in childhood. Past-life work will sometimes reveal the origin of these deeper images. However, since the soul undertakes the task of incarnation precisely to bring the distortions into manifestation, most of the unraveling of our images can be accomplished by a deep exploration of the issues presented by this life.

We each respond to negative childhood experiences quite differently depending on the predisposition of our soul. Some childhood experiences are genuinely threatening to the child's mental, emotional, or physical well-being. But many which are not will be perceived as life-threatening due to the pre-existing soul dents of the child. An event such as parental divorce may be perceived as much more devastating than it is in reality.

Though most of our work has to do with unraveling images as they appear in this life, having the perspective of the deep soul origin of some images often helps us to understand their peculiar hold over our emotions. And if we do get in touch with specific material from other lives, it can lend depth and vitality to our present struggles. Naturally, whatever images we do not dissolve in this lifetime will be carried over to another.

Kinds of Images

The child thinks in absolutes and generalities. Such conclusions help the child to try to understand and hence defend against being overwhelmed by her painful experiences. As an adult, with a stronger ego, she is able to open up her unconscious assumptions about life and investigate these generalities more closely. She can search to find the specific truthful personal experiences behind them. And then, with her stronger ego, she can experience and integrate the unfelt childhood pain behind the false generalization.

Images may be simple generalizations: On the basis of experiences with a cruel father, we conclude: "All men are cruel." On the basis of a family's many fights about money, we conclude: "Money just causes trouble."

Whenever we use generalizations, especially toward someone with whom we are in close relationship, such as: "Men always __" or "Men never __" or even "You always __" or "You never __," we are in the territory of our own childhood images rather than responding accurately to the present situation. We are seeing the present through the generalizations we made based on our past unhappy experiences, which we are using to defend against the pain of the present situation.

Another wrong conclusion takes the form of, "**Since** (men/women/authorities/etc.) are __, **then** I should behave in such and such a way." We base our current emotional responses on this conclusion from the distant past.

Our images also take the form of false connections between cause and effect: "**If** __ (some stimulus happens), **then** __ (we expect a certain result)." "If I behave in a certain way, Mommy will punish me. Therefore it is dangerous to express that part of myself." Eventually the part that has been deemed unacceptable goes underground and is disowned by the child. Only the adult can go back and correct the child's wrong cause-and-effect conclusion by affirming that just because Mommy punished me for expressing myself in a certain way does not mean that part is unacceptable.

The child lives in an instinctively dualistic world in which things and people, attitudes and feelings, are either good or bad, either o.k. or not o.k. Images always reinforce dualistic beliefs of either/or. For example, if mother punished us in some way that feels unfair, we conclude either that "I am good and Mommy is bad" or, more likely, "I am bad and Mommy is good." Only the adult we now are can correct these conclusions and expand the thinking to both/and. "Both Mommy and I are right. Mommy was justified in responding to what I did, but she overreacted badly because of her own unresolved issues."

The "thinking" involved in the process of creating an image is non-rational, yet has an emotional logic of its own. We need to enter the mind of our own inner child to understand how these wrong beliefs get solidified as the basis for our emotional responses to others, even though our adult intelligence tells us that these conclusions do not make rational sense.

We are often ashamed of the child who lives in us. We may no longer remember the childish thinking processes, and we may have long since forgotten the experiences or impressions that led to our wrong conclusions. But the sense of shame stays with us. We must "realize that a guilt feeling is nothing but the rejection of the state in which you find yourself at this time, indicating that you are unwilling to accept yourself as you are now." (*PGL 40*) All growth begins with accepting what is now true about us, including our irrational self-limiting emotions and behavior and the underlying images that dictate such a misguided or constricted response to life.

More Examples of Images at Work

A young boy playing happily in the snow stays out in the cold longer than he should and later contracts pneumonia. The mind of the child could properly learn: "If I stay out in the cold too long, I risk getting sick." This would be a reasonable conclusion to draw from the experience.

However, his conclusion may go further: "If I go out in the cold, I will get sick. Cold weather is scary. It is much safer to play inside." Or if the experience met a pre-existing soul dent about fear of physical existence, it might lodge even deeper in his psyche: "My body is not to be trusted because it makes me sick." Or "The outdoors is not to be trusted because it made me sick." Such conclusions might result in a withdrawal from the body or from nature. If the child was left outside by a neglectful parent, the conclusions will be even more serious: "My Mommy let me get sick, therefore women are not to be trusted." How deep the experience goes depends both on the parental context and on the child's predisposition.

An attractive young woman, Beatrice, had an absorbing career, good friends, and many interests. After an unsuccessful early marriage, she could not find the "right" man for another relationship. At first she ascribed this to the scarcity of eligible men her age, but eventually she began to look within for the causes of her unfulfillment. In her daily review she observed her reactions with men, and discovered a consistent pattern: she was fearful of being rejected by men she considered desirable, and had contempt for those who admired her.

Beatrice and I began to look for the images underneath this pattern. Her unconscious assumption apparently was: "Any worthwhile man will reject me; only undesirable men will love me." And further: "If I want to avoid being rejected, I must not show that I want a man; I must pretend to be cool and aloof. Only then will I have a chance of attracting someone."

Beatrice explored how these images, rooted in childish unconscious thinking, set in motion a vicious circle. When she was around desirable men, she anticipated rejection and became anxious, suspicious, and fearful. She covered her insecurity and desire by becoming haughty, aloof, and arrogant. Naturally this behavior produced real rejection from men, thus apparently confirming her original conviction that all valuable men would reject her.

Beatrice remembered that, as an only child, she had little experience of intimate peership with males. Her father was severe and authoritarian, giving her much criticism and little praise or encouragement. She grew up with the impression that she would lose his love if she did not please and obey him. She unconsciously resented this, but she also loved and admired him, felt protected by his strength, and greatly desired his approval. This atmosphere caused a deep imprint on her soul, and solidi-fied an image that all desirable strong men, like her father, would disapprove of her. She also made the unconscious equation that only men who rejected her were desirable.

Her mother was very loving and accepting, but unable to protect Beatrice from her father's severity. In fact, her mother was also intimi-dated by her husband and was therefore unassertive and submissive.

Thus Beatrice developed an unconscious tendency to see all potential partners as either strong, rejecting, and desirable like her father, or lov-ing, weak, and too easily available, like her mother. Thus Beatrice was dis-satisfied with all the men she met.

Compulsion to Re-Create Childhood Hurts

Beatrice's difficulties, and the opening story of Bill and Joanne, illustrate another aspect of childhood images as they operate in our intimate relationships: unconsciously we are attracted to and choose partners who remind us, however subtly, of the parent(s) from whom we still desire missing love. We then try, by force of will, to make them give to us and make up for what we didn't get when we were young. It is as though we suf-fered a defeat then, and are trying to "win" this time around.

> As long as you are unaware of your longing for perfect love from your parents, and of the hurts and resentments you have suffered, **you are bound to try remedying the situation in your later years**. You attempt to reproduce the childhood situation so as to correct it. This unconscious compulsion is a very strong factor, but is usually deeply hidden from your conscious understanding. . . .

> This entire procedure is utterly destructive. In the first place, it is an illusion that you were defeated. Therefore, it is an illusion that you can be victorious. Moreover, it is an illusion that, sad as the lack of love may have been when you were a child, it represents the tragedy that your subconscious still feels it to be. The only tragedy lies in the fact that you obstruct your future happiness by continuing to repro-duce, and then attempting to master, the situation. (*PGL 73*)

So Beatrice continues to attract men who remind her of her father (authoritarian and strong) and then tries to "force" them to be loving and kind. And yet, in her attempt to be desirable to these men, she unconsciously mimics her father whose aloofness and inaccessibility she associates with desirability. Her aloofness, of course, does not invite the warmth and affection she craves.

Once Beatrice understands her childhood images about men, and once she sees her pattern of trying to re-create the childhood situation in order to force a different conclusion, then the illusory nature of her efforts becomes clear, and she can make different choices.

Beneath the negative compulsion to re-create childhood hurts, there is also a higher purpose. Sooner or later we will be brought face to face with our pattern and we will be able to take responsibility for it. When Bill and Joanne were willing to see their sexual difficulties as their own, and to search within for the childhood origins of their patterns, they could for the first time change what had, until that time, felt like a closed prison door to which only the other partner held the key. Because we re-create our present lives in response to past hurts we will sooner or later come back to ourselves to find the root causes.

How to Find an Image

The regular use of daily review of our disharmonious experiences will eventually lead us to the common denominators of these events. Behind every such pattern of unfulfillment, where we seem stuck and unable to change, there is an image working in us. Whenever we seem to attract certain kinds of events or people that are consistently troublesome or unsatisfying, an image is dominating our behavior.

The common denominators of such patterns always point the way to some false ideas we are cherishing, usually unconsciously. These ideas then need to be crystallized into clear, concise expressions, however irrational they may seem. Such expressions may begin with generalizations like: "All men are __" or "Love is __" or "Work is __." Other false conclusions about cause-and-effect begin, "**If** __, **then** something terrible will happen." Our images often convince us that situations that are painful or merely unpleasant are actually life-threatening. Anytime we feel threatened, we are caught in the defenses which support a misconception that our lives are in some way at stake here. We must learn to put these misconceptions into precise words—what exactly do we believe is at stake. To get the image in clear words will both illuminate its irrationality and reduce its power over us.

Often we can sense the working of an image after a particularly unpleasant experience or relationship when we feel a peculiar, bitter kind of "satisfaction": "That's what I expected all along," or "I always knew (wo)men were sadistic," or "Kids will only bring you grief," or "People are not to be trusted," and so on. Our disappointment corroborates a negative belief, and there is a kind of perverse comfort found in that confirmation.

Each time we have this experience of glimpsing our inner negative preconceptions, we also have an opportunity to see how our images shape our reality. Do we set up unrealistic standards to serve our expectation of disappointment? Do we believe our needs will not be met, so we do not ask? Do we assume we are undeserving, so we do not create abundance?

Often we are more attached to disappointment and failure than we are to happiness and success. Such an image about not deserving fulfillment will attract negative experience which confirms our expectations, leading into a vicious circle of self-defeat.

When we feel especially hopeless about a personal situation, we can know that a deeply entrenched image is at work. Such an image may be handed down from generation to generation in a particular family, and thus be particularly difficult to dislodge in any one lifetime. Every family perpetuates certain illusions common to all members of that family system; bringing these misconceptions to awareness greatly loosens their hold on us.

Beyond our family's false beliefs, we all share images common to our culture and historic time, as well as images common to all humankind, which the Guide calls mass images. The principal mass image of humankind is a fundamental belief in our species's separateness from and superiority to the rest of the web of life.

Shame Indicates an Image

A primary indicator of an image is a pervasive sense of shame about ourselves, a feeling of not being worthy or deserving.

A specific shame lives in the inner child of all of us, stemming from the time we discovered, with a great shock, that our parents and our world were not perfect. The child has a great need to believe that her parents are perfect, since they are all that stand between her and chaos or death. When the child first discovers that she is not loved perfectly or is even treated badly, she assumes it must be her fault, because she usually does not know any other family intimately enough to compare with her situation. She will then be deeply ashamed of whatever in her deserves, as she falsely believes, to be punished or abandoned. By the time the growing child understands that parents and other adults are themselves imperfect and troubled, the shame is already deeply rooted, the self-esteem already damaged.

We now know that such a process goes on in cases of child abuse. Children are generally unable to perceive the real source of the destructive behavior of people who are also their protectors and caregivers, and so they conclude that whatever harm is coming to them must be their own fault. Building defenses against being hurt again while harboring a growing secret shame, children find it very difficult to bring the truth out into the open.

Thus the whole process—discovering that something is wrong in the family, believing that one has caused this wrong oneself, while also generalizing that people are not to be trusted, and building defenses against the hurts and indignities suffered—goes underground. And, like a plant that is perpetually kept in the dark, a large part of the personality cannot grow. The light of awareness must penetrate the fear, resentment, and shame of the child, in order to uncover the images that have become buried in the unconscious mind. We must be willing to see the truth of our mistreatment as children, including our parents' flaws, without having to eradicate the good that may also have been present.

As adults, we can be led by feelings of shame or disappointment arising from present-day situations back to hidden childhood traumas. The present-day feelings are synonymous with the childhood ones. If we fully feel our present pain, it will lead us back to the early, formative experiences. We can learn to ask ourselves what in the past we may be reacting to when we find a persistent negative pattern or a deep inner shame. Every time we "discover" the imperfections of partners, bosses, or of life itself, we re-experience the original shocks of childhood. Every time we feel shame, or blame ourselves for the faults of others, we can be sure we are reacting from a childhood image.

Bringing the original disappointments to awareness, we can then face the reality of the imperfection in our parents, and consciously pass through the inevitable hurt, anger, and resentment that are part of the universal human experience. Until we make this deliberate passage, we will go on trying to force others to be our "perfect parents" in our adult life situations—and we will be disappointed time and time again. In fact, no one is ever perfect, or will love us perfectly, and that is just the way it is. It is not our fault, and there is nothing we can do to force others to be more perfect. Everyone is imperfect. . . and everyone is forgivable.

The Main Image or Soul Splits

Eventually we find that, after unearthing our misconceptions in such diverse areas as love relationships, friendship, work, play, sexuality, and creativity, there will be certain common denominators to our images. Our work will circle around certain kinds of issues and we can begin to identify these issues as our main images. The main images will define our central character issues or primary dualistic soul splits. We will keep meeting these same distortions as we circle ever deeper on the spiral path of spiritual growth.

The main image is usually some central false conclusion about the nature of life itself and about who we are in life, such as "life is unsafe and I will never feel secure," or "life is a battle and I have to stay armored and ready to attack or I will be destroyed," or "life always disappoints, so I will never try to fulfill my dreams," and so on.[1]

Our main image is our primary way of splitting from the totality of life. Life in its essence is one interconnected flow of energy and consciousness, but when we reject some life experience, we separate from the unity of that flow. How we separate, what we consider dangerous or unacceptable in life, defines our soul split or main image.

The main image is the core of our soul's life plan for this

---

[1] Our main images correspond to the belief underlying our particular character structure. See John Pierrakos's *Core Energetics* and Chapters 12 and 13 of Barbara Brennan's *Hands of Light*. *A Summary of Character Structures* by Susan Thesenga and Alan Hill is available through Sevenoaks Pathwork Center.

incarnation—what dualistic splits we hope and expect to transform this time around. Sometimes we can discover this by looking at our choice of parents and life circumstances from the perspective of the soul. It is useful to ask: how are the splits in our own soul represented by our choice of these particular parents?

Beatrice, whose story was given earlier in this chapter, had a main image that vulnerability, need, and femininity were unacceptable. Her soul's choice of a weak mother brought out her contempt for the feminine, and her choice of a distant father confirmed her self-rejection as a woman. She defended against her vulnerability by emulating her father's aloofness.

Bill, whose story introduced this chapter, had a main image that sexuality and aggression—essential aspects of his manhood—were shameful and unacceptable. He found this confirmed by a mother who could not accept her son's sexuality nor set proper boundaries for its expression. Bill defended against rejection by holding back his true masculine power in the world. Joanne had a main image that receptivity was dangerous and would annihilate her; she developed a compensatory controllingness.

Our main image includes the central misconceptions we hold about life and ourselves, along with the resulting emotions and defenses which support those false beliefs. The main image is the linchpin in our character structure, or principal pattern of personality defenses. It is the nuclear point of our wrong attitudes and our particular dualities. Once we uncover our main image, we no longer take our defenses so seriously nor hold on to our beliefs about reality so adamantly.

We then have the key to unlocking the prison of our limited consciousness. Whether or not we are able at any particular moment to transcend our limitations, we cannot, from that point on, take our negative beliefs and anxieties quite so seriously, and life becomes lighter and more joyful.

How to Dissolve Images and Resulting Vicious Circles

The first step in dissolving an image is to open our minds to the possibility that the way we individually experience life is not the only way, or the right way, but instead is rather the way derived from our particular history. We, and hence our life experience, could be otherwise. We could challenge the false conclusions we have made about life which create our negative experiences of life. We could open to the deeper reality already alive in us which is free of our self-imposed limitations.

> Thoughts and thought processes that are directed into an erroneous channel affect all other levels of will, feelings, and physical expression. They always create vicious circles. These vicious circles entrap you, they put you into a situation that feels hopeless. But the moment the vicious circle is broken, you are free from the entrapment.
>
> It is therefore imperative to clearly see, understand, and give up these components of attitude and behavior that create the vicious circle. This always means to basically change a concept, a thought process, an approach to reality. The misconception must be recognized as such: why it is one, how it exists and in what way it leads into a vicious circle. How does the vicious circle proceed? What is the corresponding true concept? How would living according to it lead into a wide open world, into a benign sequence of creative self-expression? All this must be clearly perceived, understood, made conscious, and eventually emotionally experienced.
>
> Only through the emotional experience can the misconception be replaced by a true concept. Only then will truth take root in the psyche and open up new channels of functioning, of spontaneous behavior— as opposed to behavior based on conditioned reflexes— and of creative expression of feelings. (*PGL 193*)

As we discover the common denominators behind our negative life experience, we are led to discover the underlying and not yet conscious generalizations we harbor about many aspects of life. When we find these generalizations, we put them into words such as "women are __". When we discover our specific beliefs about cause and effect, we put these into words such as "If __, then __". Then we look for the common denominators of our beliefs in order to discern our main image, which may be put into words such as, "Life is unsafe because __" or "I am unlovable because __". We then see how our principal defenses have been formed to support this belief.

Childhood, or occasionally even past life, origins need to be explored and the original emotions re-experienced. When we can allow ourselves to experience the pain we fought against as a child, it no longer holds its early terror. We can expand our sense of what is safe to experience by remembering that we now have the adult ego resources to tolerate the feelings that threatened to devastate the inner child's still unformed ego. By facing these painful and negative feelings, we no longer need the erroneous generalization we forced on life to avoid pain.

Both a cause and an effect of our willingness to face our childhood hurts is our ability to face our present feelings. If we do not fight the painful or scary side of life, we can let go of the defenses that consume so much energy and prevent a direct, open-hearted experience of life.

At any stage of the work on our images, their hold on the unconscious can immediately be lessened by our willingness to take responsibility for our lives. Even if we do not know exactly what in us causes the disharmony or unhappiness, assuming responsibility for our own unhappiness loosens parts of the inner puzzle of which we may not yet be aware. It frees us of the feeling of victimization which is part of the origin of all images. As children we felt genuinely helpless and therefore tried to gain control of our environment as best we could by drawing conclusions from our experience which we hoped would make us invulnerable to pain in the future. But in our adult lives we will feel only as victimized by life as we believe we are. As we take responsibility for ourselves, we no longer need to constantly re-create our childhood sense of total helplessness.

Another important step in the healing of images comes after we have fully exposed the false belief. We then activate the truth through imprinting the soul substance with truthful concepts. Where we have discovered a misconception that "sex is dangerous" we can affirm a new reality: "With my husband whom I love and trust, sex is a safe, pleasurable expression of our closeness." We replace the untruth of the closed image with the truth of the open, benign universe. Such affirmations can go deep in imprinting the soul only after we have done the work of identifying and releasing the misconceptions.

Throughout the process we activate our higher self through prayer and meditation—asking to live in truth and to align with love.

A significant step in the process of relinquishing the image is to fall into the emptiness of not knowing. Since the image was an effort of our child self to make sense of the world through drawing a false conclusion and, in that way, trying to get control over life, especially the painful aspects of life, in the process of releasing the image, we must temporarily fall into the state of unknowing before we drew our wrong conclusions. The Path-work calls this process falling into the "abyss of illusion," and that is just the way it feels. When we let go of the prop of an image and its related defenses, we fear falling into the abyss; but at the end of such a fall we are always on healthier, truer ground.

Harriet, whose story was begun in Chapter 1, had suffered the death of her father when she was only six years old and had approached her life as though it were a terribly bumpy road, full of potholes. No passage was smooth. She often crouched inwardly while engaging with other people, in fear of the dangers she believed lurked around every corner, especially in intimate relationships. Harriet knew that her main image about life's unsafety had been formed at the time of her father's death, when her mother had become unable to provide consistent care-taking.

Harriet had spent much of her life searching nostalgically for substitute fathers who could once again return her to the security of her earliest years. But she was unable to form a committed relationship because of her terror of being left by a man. Instead, she created fantasy relationships with men who were unavailable to her.

She was feeling ready to give up this pattern, ready to replace the false security of nostalgia with the true foundation of security within herself. But Harriet knew she would have to face again the feared oblivion inherent in her family tragedy. In an extended visualization, she imagined coming to the edge of the cozy, innocent road of her first six years of childhood, looking over the edge where everything dropped off into nothingness. In the visualization Harriet finally jumped into the abyss. Unexpectedly, she found herself floating down, as if held by angelic arms, even as waves of pain wracked her body. She screamed out her fear and then felt herself floating again, gently downward, onto a new road, far beneath the idyllic path of childhood.

For many days thereafter Harriet felt empty, living with the loss of both her fantasy security and her underlying negativity about the dangers of life. Life was new and disorienting, but also exciting and full of promise. It would take a while to learn to walk this new road.

The emptiness and even temporary depression we feel on releasing an image is the crisis that comes from surrendering a false belief that had seemed to make our lives understandable. An image creates a "false unity" of belief and experience which gives us a kind of security because it seems to make our lives coherent and our experiences familiar. But it is a closed system, a familiar vicious circle, in which we are imprisoned. Addicted to our negative patterns, we are like the abused child who clings to his abusive mother even when the gentle matron comes to lead him to a more benign environment. Spiritual growth requires that we release our familiar belief systems so as to make room for a larger truth.

Letting go is always a vulnerable time, sometimes accompanied by disorientation and depression, and needs to be met with gentle self-acceptance. The feeling of emptiness is a necessary step in letting go. A new, deeper unity, based on our surrender to love and truth, comes slowly and cannot be forced, but it comes surely and can be trusted.

The Benign Circle

Just as an image creates a closed circle of self-reinforcing negative experience, an attitude of truth and openness creates an ever-expanding circle of benign experience and belief.

> The human soul contains all wisdom, all truth, deep down. But the wrong conclusions, or images, cover it up. By making them conscious, both emotionally and intellectually, you must finally reach the goal of unfolding your inner voice of wisdom that guides you according to the divine conscience, according to your personal plan. (*PGL 50*)

All of life moves in circles: day and night flow into each other; the moon waxes and wanes; the seasons of the year move into each other endlessly; all life forms are born, grow, die, and then new forms are born anew.

The spiritual path also progresses in circles that create an ever-deepening spiral of growth: we dissolve images and learn new ways of being, then we go deeper and see the errors in the ways we now follow, and we dissolve those blockages. Facing a particular issue, we work something through only to circle around at a later time and face the same issue at a deeper or more subtle level of its manifestation in our lives. We work until we eventually dissolve the image at its nuclear point in our soul.

Gradually we learn to live life without expectations. In the unfolding of each real moment we are fulfilled. As we learn to approach life with gratitude for what has been given to us, with a readiness to open to truth and to love in a spirit of trust, life will give us back many generous surprises. We learn that giving and receiving are one. Thus we become one with the circle of life, receiving the in-breath and giving back the out-breath that animates us all.

Exercises for Chapter 5:

1. Keep a daily review of disharmonious events in one area of your life, e.g., relationships with the opposite sex, relationships with the same sex, or your work life. Find the common denominators of your problems in this area, and from that begin to deduce your images, as follows:

a. Look for and write out the misconceptions that operate in this area. These can be expressed as:

"Men are_____." (Complete this sentence with as many endings as you spontaneously find within.)

or: "Women are_____."

or: "Work is_____."

Then also write out the false conclusions you drew about yourself. E.g., "Since men are_____, then I need to be/act_____in relation to them."

Then also write out the false chain of cause and effect you created for yourself. E.g., "If I act in a certain way, then_____." and "If I don't act this way, (or act the opposite way), then_____."

b. Trace out the vicious circle that results from one of your images and resulting conclusions. Discover how you create apparent "justification" for your image, "proof" that your limiting idea is true.

2. Explore your main image, around which your particular images cluster, by looking for the common denominators of the images you explored in exercise 1. This will be easier if you complete sentences on more than one subject. The main image will usually appear by completing a sentence like:
"Life is dangerous and cannot be trusted because _____. Therefore I need to defend myself by _____."

or: "I am unlovable because_____. Therefore I expect to be treated_____."

3. Explore your main image by looking from the perspective of your soul. Look at your parents, childhood situation, and principal childhood traumas as if you had chosen these to illustrate basic soul distortions of yours.

a. How do your two parents represent your basic distortions about the masculine and the feminine?

b. How do your two parents represent your split in approaching life? Does one represent one "conclusion" about life and how it should be approached or defended against, and the other represent another conclusion and generalization?

c. What in your childhood circumstances seemed to substantiate your main image, your basic negative view of life?

d. Was there some particular event or trauma that seemed to solidify a negative generalization about life? Can you remember the exact moment, or situation, in which you drew this false conclusion about life?

4.   a. Go back to the images you exposed in exercise 1. Write an affirmation of the truth in this particular area, to replace your misconception. Meditate with this affirmation, and invite your higher self to work with the inner voices which want to pull you back into your old false beliefs.

b. Write out the affirmations which contradict the main image you uncovered in exercises 2 and 3. Such affirmations might say: "Life is safe" and "I am lovable just as I am." Meditate with these affirmations; impress your soul substance with the possibility of experiencing reality in this new way.

CHAPTER 6

Understanding the Mask Self

"When you muster the courage to become your real self,
even though it would seem much less than the
idealized self, you will find that it is much more."

—Pathwork Guide Lecture 83, *"The Idealized Self Image"*

Connie's Mask: Dropping the Idealized Self-Image

Connie came to an introductory Pathwork weekend in a spiritual crisis. A devout Episcopalian, she served on church boards and committees, and had authored a book for women on how to live the Christ-centered life. She was a devoted wife and mother to four children, and had given much to others, as she felt required to do by all her roles of service as Christian wife, mother, and church leader. But now she felt given out, depleted, dried up. Her energy had collapsed and she was becoming less functional in her many roles. In a state of bleak depression, approaching despair, she had recently begun attending religious retreats and workshops in search of spiritual renewal.

Tall and overweight, Connie was a great bulwark of a woman whose grim demeanor showed that she felt the weight of the world on her back. But for all her ample body and strong will, she slowly revealed just how thoroughly empty she felt inside. Her mask of good Christian wife and mother was threatening to annihilate her inner spark, and she was immensely burdened by her own expectations for herself and the demands she perceived from others. The more she talked about how much others wanted from her, the angrier she became, until it was clear that her greatest burden was her repressed rage.

Connie needed a lot of encouragement for self-expression, but finally she cut loose with some of her anger and stormed around the room, shaking the floorboards as she stomped and shouted. She blamed her parents and she blamed the church; she raged at her husband and she raged at God. As her energy quieted for a moment, she reflected, "My God, I've taken on everybody's expectations for me. I've tried to win everybody's approval by being so damn perfect all the time. I'm suffocating from my goodness!"

To help Connie get all the expectations of perfection and devotion "off her back," we had her sit on the floor as we piled pillows onto her shoulders, each representing one of the many demands she had accepted or placed upon herself. She then flung them off joyfully, tossing each one as far away as she could.

Then, when the metaphorical burdens were all thrown off, she was quiet for a moment before rising to her feet again. "You know, I really am just plain furious at how I've bought this role for so long. I'm so angry I feel like I could kill someone right now. Or maybe I should kill myself for being so stupid." I encouraged her to bring out her killing rage, to express her fury. Again she started stamping and yelling, not even bothering to make sense, releasing the energy of her lethal fury.

In the midst of one tirade, Connie halted. "My God, I am a destroyer. I really feel right now like I could kill everyone around me. This is terrible.

I must be a terrible person!" The group reassured her that her behavior was not terrible. To give vent to such feelings in a safe and supportive environment is, in fact, much healthier than her recent depression and dysfunction, through which she had been acting out a covert destructiveness toward herself and her family. Her exhaustion and collapse had been a hostile and guilt–provoking message to those she had served for so long. Her unconscious passive negativity had been much more destructive to everyone, including herself, than was her active expression of anger in the safety of the group. We assured her that her life force was being liberated though the willingness to risk her rage. As Connie dropped her mask of required "goodness," she was finding a new reservoir of authentic energy by no longer denying the fury within her. Only through opening up these real feelings could she find her way back to her real self, the inexhaustible source within.

"Oh, so my exhaustion was hiding this anger. This terrible feeling was in me all the time! Still, doesn't this make me a terrible person?"

"No, it just makes you more real," I explained. "Your mask of the perfectly loving Christian had to break sooner or later. It was made up of unreal expectations, and the price you've been paying to hold up that mask was depleting your energy. Now instead of the victimized Christian martyr, we're seeing the power of the real you!"

After this exchange, Connie plunged back into the vivid expression of her anger. Her large body shook all over, and she began to enjoy the energy pulsations that moved her. The power that came out of her now was glorious. I suggested that everyone get up on their feet and join Connie. She then led the group in a powerful expression of pure aggressive energy. As Connie shook and stamped, leading the others, the grim heaviness she had exhibited before began to give way to a new and joyful radiance.

Then I encouraged Connie to turn her aggressive energy into a dance, in celebration of the primal power and creative energy of God that was moving so fully through her and everyone now. Soon the whole room was vibrating with Connie's primitive dance to the power of life. We all experienced the pure energy liberated by releasing our feared rage. The effect was exhilarating for everyone present, and we thanked Connie for her leadership in the dance.

As the dance quieted down, Connie reflected on her new-found power and realized that her rage was not something to be feared as "anti-Christian" but could be welcomed as an avenue into her own power and energy. Having felt a glimmer of the potential that was in her to lead and to heal others, Connie ended her work with a commitment to claim her own energy, take better care of herself, and use her power to follow her own feelings, trusting that they would lead her into sincere, not resented, service to God.

Understanding the Mask Self

The mask self is the outer layer of the personality, the self we superficially identify with, the face we show to the world. It is the self we think we ought to be, or wish we could be, based on idealized mental images. Connie tried to live up to the idealized image of a "good, loving Christian woman," a forced identity which kept vast parts of herself suppressed. The pretense of the mask keeps us from the reality of all that we are, moment to moment.

All of us were psychically wounded as children; we were imperfectly seen and loved. The mask is the self we constructed to hide the vulnerable, wounded child we once were. By putting a false self between other people and our inner vulnerability, we try to prevent ourselves from getting so close to others that we can again be hurt the way we were as children. It is our way to try to control life.

Created in reaction to pain and rejection, the mask is designed to try to please, fend off, or control others. When we are in the mask self we are focused on reacting to others, and are thus cut off from our own inner source. The mask self separates us from the energy of our real, spontaneous selves, both negative and positive. When we are in the mask self we blame others for our miseries, rather than being responsible for our own feelings. Thus the mask entails belief in our victimization, the misconception that someone else is responsible for our happiness or unhappiness.

Beneath the mask is the lower self—the source of negativity and destructiveness within us. Our own negativity is the true cause of our unhappiness. The lower self is usually unconscious, in whole or in part, because it is hard to admit our negativity to ourselves. As children we were made to feel ashamed of the lower self, and we feared that being honest about our negative feelings would cause us to be rejected by our parents. So we covered them with a mask that we hoped would insure our lovability.

The mask is in some ways like the Pharisee of Christ's time—putting on a show of goodness or power or respectability that is inauthentic. Christ felt so much more attracted to the sinners because he sensed their genuineness. Their negativity was neither denied nor justified; their flaws and their pain were much more apparent and thus their hearts were more accessible. Christ knew that the lower self, or sinner, must be acknowledged before its creative potential can be transformed. Our own higher self, our Christ-consciousness, will also learn to embrace the inner "sinner" after shedding the hypocritical Pharisee mask.

The higher self is the place in us where the stream of universal life energy flows freely. The higher self is our true nature as individualized expressions of God. Yet, in the human realm, the layers which hide the higher self—the layers of the mask and lower self—are also real and must first be penetrated.

> When people are emotionally sick, it is always in one way or another that a mask self has been created. They do not realize that they are living a lie. They have built a layer of unreality that has nothing to do with their real being; thus, they are not true to their real personality. Being true to oneself does not mean that you should give in to your lower self, but that you should be aware of it. . . . Underneath the layers of your lower self lives your higher self, your ultimate and absolute reality which you must eventually reach. And, to reach it, you must first face your lower self, your temporary reality, instead of covering it up, because that puts an even greater distance between you and Absolute Reality, or your own higher self. In order to face the lower self, you must at all costs tear down the pretenses of the mask self. (PGL 14)

Here is a visualization of the three selves with principal aspects of each self listed:

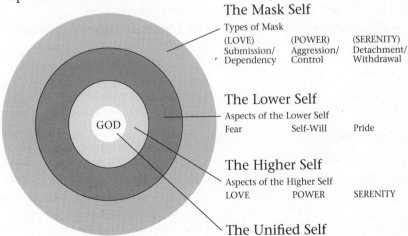

The Mask Self
Types of Mask

(LOVE)	(POWER)	(SERENITY)
Submission/ Dependency	Aggression/ Control	Detachment/ Withdrawal

The Lower Self
Aspects of the Lower Self

Fear	Self-Will	Pride

The Higher Self
Aspects of the Higher Self

LOVE	POWER	SERENITY

GOD

The Unified Self

In reality the three layers are not so self-contained as pictured in the above illustration. If we view the outer circumference of the circle as the outer boundary of the personality, where it meets the world, an actual picture of the three selves might look more like this:

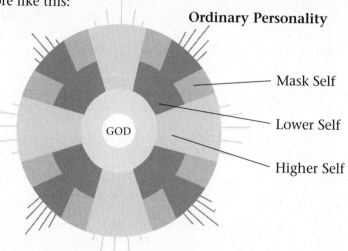

Ordinary Personality

Mask Self

Lower Self

Higher Self

GOD

This picture portrays the reality that in every personality there are places where the higher self shines through, and other places where the lower self has not been covered over, and undiluted negativity may be seen on the surface. In yet other places, both lower self and higher self are masked. The mask and lower self may be present to a greater or lesser degree than pictured, depending on the degree of purification of this soul.

We might ask what an evolved personality would look like. My guess is that it would look something like the following:

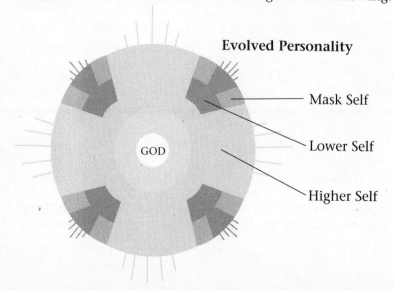

Evolved Personality

Mask Self

Lower Self

Higher Self

GOD

In the picture of the evolved personality, most of the mask has been eliminated, most of the lower self has been released, and the remaining areas of mask and lower self have been more infused with consciousness (and are hence less dense). However, as long as the personality still exists, that is, as long as we are still in human incarnation, all three aspects of the self will be present to some degree. We learn to shift our self-identification to our higher self center, to know who we really are, and to channel this energy out in service to others. But we also learn not to deny the remaining mask and lower self whenever they appear. We learn to gently welcome into consciousness all aspects still in need of healing.

The Mask and the Journey of Transformation

The mask is the first layer of the personality which must be penetrated, accepted, and released on the transformation journey. Yet the fact that we must come to grips first with the mask does not mean that we can dispense with it easily or once and for all. We will continue to have a mask until we are ready to reveal and take responsibility for our lower self, and are simultaneously able to identify with our higher self. Only then will the defenses of the mask no longer be needed. In the meantime, as with all our other human limitations, our task is simply to identify our mask selves without guilt and without self-denigration.

The transformation journey requires that we constantly penetrate one after another of the three selves—mask, lower self, and higher self—at each of the different developmental levels of consciousness. How the three selves intersect the different levels of consciousness—child, adult ego, soul/transpersonal, and unitive consciousness—is described and outlined in the chart on page 71 of Chapter Four.

We usually start with working on our adult ego personality—learning to drop the ego mask and be more authentic, to strengthen the positive ego, and understand and release the negative ego—before we move on to work with the inner child, and then descend to the soul, or the universal consciousness. We need to ground ourselves in identification with the objective, compassionate observer of the positive ego self before we can explore the deeper recesses of either the wounded inner child or the transpersonal level.

However, the inner path has its own trustworthy rhythm that alternates work on different levels with different selves. At one point we may need to make contact with the soul level of the higher self, or listen to our spirit guides, in order to have the strength, dignity, and courage to continue our self-exploration. At another point we will go deeply into the distortions of the lower-self child. And then again we will be led to another aspect of the ego mask that needs exploring. It is a continuous journey, an ever-deepening spiral of self-awareness.

What Is the Mask?

The mask stems from our often frantic and always doomed attempts to live up to a "perfect" ideal, an idealized self image. The effort to force ourselves to conform to a perfect picture of who we think we ought to be keeps us agitated and distant from the peace of self-acceptance. Perfectionism is a central block to happiness, preventing our ability to relax and accept the imperfections of the here and now.

> The more you accept imperfection, the more joy you
> will give and receive. Your capacity for joy and happi-
> ness depends on your capacity to accept imperfection,
> not just intellectually, but as an emotional experience.
> . . . An important step is to allow yourself to know that
> you resent the imperfections in yourself and your life,
> that you do **not** accept them. Only when you fully
> realize your resentment against imperfection can you
> begin to accept it. And only as you accept imperfection
> can you lead a joyful life and derive enjoyment out
> of your relationships, all of which are bound to be
> imperfect. (*PGL 97*)

We have to work a long time at accepting ourselves as we are, and others as they are. The first step is to see clearly our resistance to self-acceptance: to some degree, we each feel that we are not enough just as we are. So we create a false self. But investing energy in creating and maintaining this idealized self-image is like building a robot rather than living the life of a human being. Tottering on stilts high above the real self, the mask self stays artificially in place at the price of a great strain on the soul.

That is why the mask self is always the first part of ourselves to collapse in a crisis. Crisis often brings with it the feeling of a loss of identity; in fact crisis is often nature's way of helping us to come off the shaky pedestal of trying to be someone we are not. Crisis stirs up the stagnant soul matter trapped in an idealized version of ourselves and forces us to come into a truer, deeper, more flowing, and more vulnerable human identity. As we learn to claim more of our reality as it appears moment to moment, we cannot collapse because there is no place to go but where we already are.

Living each moment with self-acceptance is the antidote to the mask. But that does not mean that we should not have ideals, or the desire for self-betterment. Having ideals, however, is very different from having an idealized self image.

> The genuine desire to better oneself accepts the
> personality as it is now, as the basic premise. Then
> any discovery of where you fall short of legitimate
> goals for self-betterment will not throw you into
> depression, anxiety, and guilt. It will rather strengthen
> you. You will not need to exaggerate the "badness" of
> the trend in question; nor will you defend yourself
> against it with the excuse that it is the fault of others,
> or life, or fate. You will gain an objective view of your-
> self in this respect and this view will liberate you. You
> will fully assume responsibility for the faulty attitude,
> being willing to take the consequences on yourself.
> Taking responsibility for your faults is the clearest
> way to say, "I am not my Idealized Self." (PGL 83)

We can often uncover the mask by asking, "What impression of myself do I want to create and why?" If our motives are to create an appearance that is other than exactly what is inwardly true for us at that moment, then we can know we are putting on our mask.

When we are quick to judge self or others, or when we are secretive and afraid of exposure, then we know the mask is present. If we frequently experience shame, anxiety, or guilt because we fail to meet the standards we set for ourselves, then we can be sure the mask is at work. Whenever we live solely in the mask, our lives will feel shallow and meaningless.

Origin of the Idealized Self Image

The mask is rooted in the dilemma of human duality. Every human life includes pain as well as pleasure, disappointment as well as fulfillment, unhappiness as well as happiness. As infants and children, we were extremely vulnerable to the experience of disappointment, rejection, and misunderstanding—both real and imagined. It is an instinctive human response to look for ways to escape these pains and to protect ourselves from further hurts.

Most painful to the child is the experience of being rejected or unseen by the parents. This may be a harsh specific rejection or a prolonged but persistent unloving or unseeing attitude on the part of the parents. Or it may be only a temporary punishment and distancing. Or it may be a situation which in reality has little or nothing to do with the child, such as divorce. But the child will always blame himself for any parental rejection, punishment, or withdrawal. He assumes that the parent "goes away" because of his "badness." The child then desperately tries to deny or repress whatever in him seems to contribute to the withdrawal of parental love and concern.

The child carries the further misconception that his parents' approval is crucial to his survival. So he comes to believe that it is safer to deny whatever in him seems to cause parental rejection and disapproval. Instead the child takes on a role that he hopes will bring him the desired approval or at least invulnerability. The idealized self image then becomes the pseudo-solution to the problem of his supposed "badness."

No adult, and therefore no parent, is capable of perfect love. So there is always some basis for the child's feeling of rejection. But the unhappiness and lack of security and self-esteem that the child feels can never be measured objectively. The predisposition, or inherited karma, of the child plays an important part. What one personality may be able to cope with quite well in the parental environment may be devastating for another temperament.

Sometimes we can actually recall the moment in which we decided that something in our environment was intolerable, just too painful to be felt. We decided from then on to deny our real feelings. Such a decision, renewed and amplified many times in the course of a life, solidifies the construction of the mask.

Elizabeth remembered the moment at which she decided to close her heart and adopt a mask of being always powerful, in control.

As a child she had adored her romantic father but always felt frozen out by her mother, a cold, efficient, dutiful woman. Furthermore, her mother had blocked the full tender relationship Elizabeth had wanted with her father. She had also felt a buried resentment that her father had not fought more fully for their relationship, and instead had let his wife control his interaction with Elizabeth. She had consciously endured this pain throughout her childhood.

As a young teenager, Elizabeth had fallen in love with Andrew, the boy next door. They would take long, romantic walks together talking about everything, emptying the contents of their hearts to each other. They were young, innocent, and in love. When the boy's family moved to the suburbs of a distant city, Elizabeth and Andrew wrote faithfully to each other for a year, unable to visit but maintaining their feelings for one another.

The following year Elizabeth moved near to the city where Andrew lived, to attend college. Often homesick and confused, Elizabeth felt an intense craving for Andrew's attention, and decided one day to visit him without calling ahead. The result was disastrous. Andrew's mother answered the door with the hostile greeting, "You are not welcome here. We did not expect you. What do you mean showing up here unannounced!" Remaining silent in the background was Andrew, obviously overwhelmed by his mother and unable to come to Elizabeth's rescue. She left immediately, and then spent the night crying—feeling not only the pain of rejection and isolation from Andrew, but also the powerful echo of her frustrated relationship with her father.

Thus she re-experienced the pain of early rejection more intensely than ever before. And that night she made the commitment, "Never again." Never again would she be vulnerable to a man like that, never again would she need anyone so much.

By the time Andrew came to visit her two weeks later, Elizabeth's mask was already in place. She was no longer in love with Andrew. She was already dating another man, whom she would eventually marry. She had begun a life of calculated relationships, in which power and control in all situations became the goal. She constructed a poised façade—the sophisticated, artistic, competent and self-sufficient woman of the world. Neither in her marriage nor in any subsequent relationships did she truly and totally risk her heart. Having constructed a mask of queenly invulnerability, Elizabeth lost sight of its origins and came to believe that this was who she was.

Only much later in life did she realize that this self-constructed ideal-ized image was much like that of her mother—cold and calculating, con-trolling rather than admitting the flow of life and feelings. And it took even longer to realize the terrible price she had paid by trading in her spontaneous feelings of warmth, love, and even pain for the half-life of the frozen façade.

Connection Between an Image and the Mask

An image is a false conclusion or generalization about life. The idealized self-image (or mask) is a false front, or attempt to portray a perfect generalized picture of who we think we ought to be. Both the image and the mask are motivated by the attempt to avoid in the future certain specific, real hurts of the past. Thus the real feelings of the present, and the real and particular people and circumstances of the present, are replaced with an unreal, generalized picture of reality derived from mental conclusions or generalizations based on the past. When we are caught in our images we live in our ideas about the past, rather than in the reality of our present.

The mask is the defense we create in response to our main image or principal negative conclusion about life. Elizabeth's main image was that expressing her need, love, and vulnerabil-ity would create intolerable pain. This led directly to her mask—idealized self-images of power and withdrawal—which might be stated as "I must always pretend to be strong, aloof and inde-pendent, so no one will ever know I need or want them." The image is the child's attempt to make sense of the situation of imperfect love from the parents. And the mask is a false solution to the problem of how to prevent further pain and rejection because of parental imperfection. The mask is an attempt to become invulnerable in order to avoid being hurt.

Often, as in Elizabeth's case, the mask is also modeled after the parent who was least accepting since, unconsciously, this is also equated with what is most desirable. Since the child desired most that parent who gave less love, she connects that parent's qualities with desirability.

The basic image behind the creation of any mask is the false belief: "I am not acceptable/desirable/lovable just as I am." Since the natural self is believed to be unacceptable, a mask is created with the hope that **it** will win the longed-for acceptance and love, or will at least help us avoid rejection and pain. Even though the idealized self-image is often made up of true and positive aspects of the personality, its intent to cover up the real self is just as false as the mistaken idea that we are inherently unlovable. We need to challenge this negative belief about the self again and again. And we need to risk our real self in the present reality, not acting out of the generalizations made from the past.

In Elizabeth's case, she believed that her need for the woman's support was not acceptable, so she created an idealized self-image that denied her true need. The result for her, as for all of us, was emotional starvation. Because the real feelings and needs are not acknowledged, they can never be met. Because the real self is not accepted and expressed, it can never attract the love and respect of others.

The Defense

Human beings, like animals, are equipped with a natural defense system which serves us well in the face of immediate danger. Faced with a threat to our physical survival, our bodies generate a rush of adrenalin that heightens our senses and focuses our perception on the source of danger. Thinking is restricted to strategies for escape from the situation at hand— what is called the "fight or flight" reaction—and our emotions are restricted to fear or anger as additional defenses. Even our spirit is cramped, as all our resources are focused on the survival of the body, rather than on spiritual connection. In the face of immediate physical danger, all of these responses are appropriate and help us deal with the genuine threat of the moment.

Unlike animals in the wild, human beings tend to extend and pervert this natural defense capability. Not only do we try to fight the reality of physical pain, and the inevitability of physical death, we also try to defend ourselves against emotional pain, and against blows to our ego as well as blows to our bodies. Instead of reserving the all-out natural defense reaction for situations of genuine physical danger, we call up our defenses whenever our self-esteem feels threatened. A slightly critical remark, a cool reception from a friend, or even an opposing opinion can trigger our defenses, make us ready to fight or to flee. Our minds shut down, our emotions narrow, and excessive amounts of adrenalin shoot into our system, poisoning the body because no dramatic physical response is actually required.

But who or what is really endangered? Our real, spiritual self can never be threatened because it can never die. Our physical well-being is not endangered by words or opinions, no matter how hostile. The threat we perceive is thus against our ego, to which we are as attached as to our bodies. Most easily threatened is the mask of the ego, a fragile identity resting on our idea of who we think we ought to be. Something threatens to expose us, to make us once again vulnerable to buried pains, and to topple our shaky, limited, idealized version of ourselves.

> When you are more or less permanently defensive due to the erroneous belief that any hurt or frustration, any criticism, any rejection, is a danger you must guard against, you limit the range of your feelings, the potentials of your love and creativity, the ability to reach out into life and communicate with others, to love and to understand, to feel and to express yourself. In short, your spiritual life is gravely impaired. . . .

> Whenever you are on the defensive, your primary aim cannot be truth. When it comes to real dangers, this real danger is the truth of the moment. But when it comes to unreal dangers, the truth lies somewhere else. . . . In this moment, it subtly becomes more important for you to prove that the other is wrong or unjustified, and that you are right, rather than to find the elements of truth in whatever comes to you. Therefore, in your defensiveness, you run away from truth, from yourself, and from life. . . . All this is due to a completely erroneous concept of perfectionism in which you believe your value and acceptability to be at stake because of your imperfection.

> If people would probe within to find and eliminate this defensive wall, so much hardship could be avoided. Having a mask which must be defended creates the constant fear of being inadequate. The feeling or fear of inadequacy is itself so much more painful than the simple pain if someone says or does something hurtful to you, or challenges how you see things, or does not respond to your wishes. . . .

> Let go and receive whatever comes to you. Look at it quietly with the dominant aim not to ward it off, but instead to seek and see the truth. (PGL 101)

Secondary Defense Reactions

When we are afraid or ashamed of our feelings we work hard to deny and cover them up, thus creating defenses. However, each time a feeling is denied and a defense created, secondary reactions set in which further deny feelings and perpetuate defenses. Initially, as children, we experienced fear or anger. Then, when these feelings were deemed unacceptable, we rejected them. We became afraid of our fear, and angry at our anger.

> A denied feeling compounds itself, so that it multiplies. Denied fear creates fear of fear, and then the fear of feeling the fear of the fear, and so on and on. Denied anger creates anger at being angry. Then when this is denied, one becomes even angrier for being unable to accept the anger, and on and on. Frustration itself is bearable when you fully go into it. But when you are frustrated because you "ought not" to be frustrated and then are even more frustrated because you deny it, the pain extends on and on. Understanding this process points to the necessity of feeling directly, no matter how undesirable the feelings may be. If you compound the pain because you deny feeling your pain, this secondary pain must become bitter, twisted, unbearable.
>
> If you accept and **feel** the pain, a dissolving process begins automatically. Many of you have experienced this truth a number of times in your pathwork. Thus, when you feel the fear of your fear and can then let yourself drop into the fear itself, this fear will very quickly give way to another denied feeling. The denied feeling—whatever it may be—will become easier to bear than the fear of it, and its subsequent denial. Fighting your feelings, defending against them, creates a whole extra layer of experience that is alienated from the core and therefore **artificial and more painful than the original it fights against.** (PGL 190)

A major reason for our reactive defenses is that many of us still unconsciously identify ourselves as children and those around us as grown-ups—parent figures—who could devastate us with their rejection and whose protection is necessary for survival.

In the process of personal growth, we must choose to face, feel, and release childhood hurts. We gradually learn that **we are** the grown-ups and **there are no more Mommies and Daddies**. As adults, we are now capable of absorbing the hurts of life without feeling annihilated. No one can now hurt us the way we were hurt as children and no one can take care of us the way we needed to be cared for as children.

As our attitudes mature, we relax our attachment to perfectionism. We learn to experience others' confrontation or criticism of us as either useful feedback, that we can evaluate objectively, or as unwarranted hurtfulness, that we can witness without being wounded. The pain of not being seen, though never pleasant, need not be devastating to our self-esteem. If we are devastated, we can be sure that there is some part of us clinging to our childhood identity and thus re-experiencing childhood pain. We must be patient with ourselves, remembering that it is neither quick nor easy to grow up into emotional and spiritual adulthood.

The Mask and the Re-Creation of Childhood Hurts

Until the adult re-experiences and releases the original childhood hurts which gave rise to the mask, these hurts remain frozen in the personality and continue to be re-enacted in present-day reality. If we expect rejection or disapproval from others for being ourselves, this is just what we will create in our relationships. We attract disapproving or rejecting people, thus confirming our worst fears.

Since the inauthentic behavior of the mask is instinctively disquieting, others often avoid it. The rejection of our mask, however, rather than convincing us to be more real, more often reinforces the apparent need for a more perfect mask, so that the pain of rejection can be forever avoided. Thus we create more phoniness and strain in struggling toward an even greater idealization. A vicious circle begins to operate, not only in our interactions with others, but within ourselves as well. We internalize a "top dog" voice that demands that we be more perfect. This is the "parent" voice, the tyrannical, moralizing super-ego, that constantly berates and chastises the beleaguered inner child. Self-alienation deepens progressively as we raise the stakes after every inevitable failure.

By age forty, when Elizabeth began to work on herself and her mask of power and competency, she was aware of her defenses against open-ing her heart. Furthermore, she could see that her defensive mask had re-created rejection or apparent rejection from others. For years her husband Max had tried to penetrate the wall of his wife's apparent coldhearted-ness, but had finally given up. She felt keenly her isolation from him, because beneath the queenly mask she knew she was still needy, insecure, and vulnerable.

She wanted his affection back, but knew she could not achieve this without risking her own heart more fully in loving him. She could see the vicious circle: to the extent that she froze him out, he would withhold his warmth and caring, and to the extent that she experienced this as rejec-tion, she would entrench her commitment to her defensive coldness.

Thus, the idealized self (or mask) actually creates a much greater feeling of failure and disappointment, loss of self-esteem and painful rejection, than it was originally designed to prevent.

Three Types of Mask

The pseudo-solution of the mask is usually based on a dis-tortion of one of the three divine principles of **love**, **power**, or **serenity**. In the unified state these principles operate in har-mony. Steeped as we are, however, in duality and ignorance, we tend to see these principles in opposition to one another. We unconsciously choose **one** of these divine attributes to emulate in an attempt to appear perfect—perfectly loving, or completely powerful, or entirely serene.

However, because we are attempting to create an impenetra-ble, invulnerable perfection as a defense against the vulnerable imperfections of human life, these attributes turn into their dis-tortions. Love becomes dependency and submission, power becomes control and aggression, and serenity becomes with-drawal. In the distorted state, these attributes do contradict one another.

1) The Mask of Love

The mask of love is an attempt to extract love from others by always appearing to be loving. The personality becomes submis-sive, dependent, appeasing, and self-denying in the hope of guar-anteeing, controlling, and buying love and approval from others.

The false belief of such a mask self is that it must be loved at all costs, and therefore the personality is deliberately made weaker, more helpless, or subservient, than it really is. Security and self-esteem are then imagined to rest on securing and possessing the love and approval of others.

> The need for protective love has a certain validity for the child, but if this attitude is maintained into adult-hood, it is no longer valid. Since he does not cultivate the faculty of self-responsibility and independence, his need for love and his dependency can actually make the person helpless. He uses his entire psychic strength in order to live up to his ideal of himself so as to force others to comply with his needs. He complies with others so they will have to comply with him. His helplessness is the weapon. (*PGL 84*)

Such a mask self complies with the real or imagined demands of others in order to receive their approval, sympathy, help, and love. He may use his subservience as a weapon to create guilt in others in order to force their protection and caretaking of him. Or, he may use his mask of virtue to feel superior and contemp-tuous of others. All these are, of course, distorted ways of trying to get his needs for self-worth met.

The person with the love mask may see the world as full of benign protectors ("big Daddies" or "big Mommies") from whom he needs to seek protection. Or he may be a disappointed idealist, viewing himself as one of the few good people left in an uncaring world. The love mask will always project being "good" or "nice." Often, along with that will go a significant streak of moral superiority, feeling better than other people. He is weak and needy, or he is a nice guy, but he is taken advantage of by the bad bullies of the world.

The effect on the personality of such unconscious self-crippling is a deep resentment and bitterness. Others are blamed for his lack of fulfillment, and the secret resentment of others creates a double hiding. In order to stay "true" to the idealized self image, he must suppress his resentment and bitterness, along with hiding his original imperfections (and strengths). The love mask then carries a double guilt. He feels guilty about his real faults, and then adds to that the guilt for pretending to be more loving or nicer than he is. Such an inner climate is unable to generate authentic love, which can only thrive in an atmosphere that is open, spontaneous, and guilt-free. To revive the capacity for true love, the person must admit his negative feelings, including resentment and bitterness, and learn to take responsibility for both his needs and his limitations.

Connie, whose story introduced this chapter, tried hard to be the perfectly loving mother and Christian woman. In order to conform to the expectations of her idealized self image, she had suppressed her resentment and settled for silent suffering. Connie often betrayed her own needs in order to sell out to others with the intent of earning their love and respect. She was trying to be whoever she imagined they wanted her to be. Naturally this never worked, and she eventually had to discharge the accumulated resentment and also learn how to ask directly for what she wanted.

2) The Mask of Power

The mask of power is an attempt to get control of life and others by always appearing completely independent, aggressive, competent, domineering. Falsely reducing life to a struggle for domination, the power mask is attempting to escape from the vulnerability experienced as a child. Security and self-esteem rest on winning in all situations and becoming free of human needs and weaknesses. The power drive is idealized, and love and contact are rejected.

Denial of the real needs for warmth, comfort, affection, caring, and communication results in a frantic drivenness, an inability to relax and accept life and self as they are. Unable to admit mistakes or weaknesses, the power mask is obsessed with competition and the drive to win. He tends toward a pessimistic and cynical view of human nature which justifies his idealization of selfishness and domination. He also places a great value on self-control, but may act out his negative feelings while justifying them as the "way of the world." And he is often plagued by a secret sense of shame and failure, precisely because it is impossible to surpass everyone in all respects, or to win and dominate universally. He compensates for this by striving yet harder to dominate, and by blaming others for his failures.

Elizabeth, whose story was introduced earlier in this chapter, began to see what a terrible price she had paid for her apparent invulnerability as she explored her power mask. She had cut herself off from her own heart and felt isolated from others. Careful self-honesty meant learning to share any and all feelings, especially vulnerable feelings. Though it was hard for her, she began sharing with her husband Max every time she felt hurt and every time she felt needy.

The first temptation was to dramatize all her feelings into something so extreme that Max would have to respond to her. But then she realized that her over-dramatization was yet another means to try to control others, to get them to do her bidding, rather than a candid expression of her feelings for the sake of honesty alone. She had to accept that there was no guarantee anyone would be able to fulfill her needs and she began to risk feeling the inevitable disappointments in life which she had defended with the power mask.

As Elizabeth worked with her images, she was able to feel more fully her past hurts, her fear of rejection, and her real needs. She saw where she had betrayed her love for her father and her need for her mother, and had denied her own softness and femininity. She learned that she could risk being more vulnerable with her husband, to which he reacted with more of his own vulnerability, thus setting in motion a benign circle of love between them. Of course all of these changes did not happen overnight, nor without much pain and struggle. But the growth toward reality, and away from dependence on the idealized self image and the false beliefs that underlie it, is steady and sure, and carries its own positive momentum.

3) The Mask of Serenity

The mask of serenity is an attempt to escape the difficulties and vulnerabilities of human life by always appearing completely serene and detached. In fact what the person really pursues is the distortion of serenity which is withdrawal, indifference, evasion of life, non-commitment, cynical worldly detachment, or false spiritual detachment.

Very often this pseudo-solution is chosen because the child was unable to make either of the "love" or "power" masks work for him. Unable to gain the needed love through submission, or the needed self-assertion through aggression, he withdrew altogether from the problems inside and outside himself. Underneath the withdrawal, he is still torn and insecure, believing that neither self-assertion nor love is available to him. But all of this is effectively denied by an attempt to withdraw to a vantage point above his inner storm.

The misconception of the serenity mask is that problems will go away if we can effectively deny them. Security and self-esteem are believed to be achieved by rising above all difficulties, being "cool" and unaffected by life. The person with a serenity mask idealizes aloofness and detachment, and may have contempt for the struggles of other "mere mortals." The effect on the personality of such massive denial is numbness and secret despair, often covered over by either a cynical view of life or an ungrounded spirituality. The life force gets shut down and the energy flows slowly. The capacity to engage in meaningful work or in fulfilled relationship is often impaired.

Harriet, whose story was begun in Chapter 1, had frozen her self-identity at age six when her father died. She had withdrawn from life and put on a mask of serenity pretending that nothing affected her. Whenever any feelings—good or bad—came too close, her inner sentinel would force her back inside the wall of her fear so as not to have to face the emotional devastation she had suffered as a child.

She had become very quiet, a good student, but non-communicative. Her life-long withdrawal had left her living a gray reality, which eliminated all extremes of feeling. No sunshine; but no blackness either. She knew that to reclaim her life she would have to come out of her mask of serenity and begin to talk about and tolerate her feelings.

The emotional self-betrayal of the withdrawal mask is almost complete. The feelings of the real self are trusted so little that only a small degree of engagement with life and others can be tolerated. Often the person withdraws into the intellect or into an inner spiritual life. Unlike the love or power mask where feelings are often exaggerated or manipulated to serve a purpose or create an impression, the serenity mask has feelings that are still intact and undistorted but hidden, and need a lot of encouragement in order to be revealed. The transformation of the serenity mask is a step-by-step process of risking the real self, of stepping out into life.

4) A Combination Mask

Sometimes the masks of love, power, and serenity are mixed in the same person, which causes tremendous inner confusion since they pursue contradictory goals and idealizations. Whereas the love mask pretends to be all-loving, and to deny strength and independence, the power mask denies the need for love, pretending to be all-powerful. Preferring to be "above it all," the serenity mask engages in neither the struggle to love nor the battle to dominate, regarding both with contempt. While the love and power masks go in different directions, they are equally false, rigid, unrealistic, and unrealizable. Nor is the combination of these masks any closer to reality.

Many people do have contradictory personality ideals. Their lives may be compartmentalized, such that the power mask rules their lives in the business world, for example, while the love mask runs their lives in intimate relationships, or vice versa. A woman who plays a submissive and dependent role with men may be viciously competitive in her relationships with other women. Or a man may be submissive with women, but dominating in relation to men. Such a combination mask always adds confusion to the falsehood of the mask level of the personality.

> Even if it were possible never to fail, or to love everyone, or to be entirely independent of others, it becomes even more of an impossibility when the dictates of a person's idealized self image simultaneously demand of him to love and be loved by everyone, **and** to conquer them and be invulnerable to them. Such an idealized self image may simultaneously demand of a person to be always unselfish, so as to gain love; to be always selfish so as to gain power; and to be completely indifferent and aloof from all human emotions so as not to be disturbed. Can you picture what a conflict is in this soul? How torn the soul must be! Whatever he does is wrong and induces guilt, shame, inadequacy, and therefore, frustration and self-contempt. (*PGL 84*)

Transformation of the Mask Self

The mask is doomed to fail and to create more misery than it was designed to prevent, because it is based on the essential misconception that we can avoid the imperfections, disappointments, and rejections characteristic of the human realm. When we recognize these inevitabilities, and assent to feeling our human pains, flaws, and struggles, we begin to lessen the attachment we have to the mask.

Transformation of the mask includes the process of grieving the death of our idealized self, realizing that this false self is actually already dead. It is a lifeless, non-vital version of ourselves that must be let go if we are to become who we really are. To release the mask also requires that we re-experience the childhood hurts that gave rise to the mask.

How can you manage to re-experience the hurts of so long ago? Take a current problem. Strip it of all the superimposed layers of your reactions. The first and most handy layer is that of rationalization, that of "proving" that others, or situations, are at fault, not your innermost conflicts which make you adopt the wrong attitude to the actual problem that confronts you. The next layer might be anger, resentment, anxiety, frustration. Behind all these reactions you will find the hurt of not being loved. When you experience the hurt of not being loved in your current dilemma, it will serve to reawaken the childhood hurt.

With the present hurt, think back, try to re-evaluate the situation with your parents—what they gave you, how you really felt about them. You will become aware that in many ways you lacked something you never clearly saw before—you did not want to see it. You will find that this must have hurt you when you were a child, but you may have forgotten this hurt on a conscious level. Yet it is not forgotten at all. **The hurt of your current problem is the very same hurt**. . . . Once you can synchronize these two pains and realize that they are one and the same, the next step will be much easier. Then, by looking over the repetitious pattern in your various problems, you will learn to recognize where the similarities exist between your parents and the people who have caused you hurt or are causing you pain now. When you feel the similarities, at the same time experiencing the pain of now and the pain of then, you will slowly come to understand how you re-created the childhood hurt out of a mistaken notion that you had to choose the current situation in a misguided effort to 'win' love in a situation in which you originally, as a child, felt 'defeated.' (*PGL 73*)

When Marcie began a serious relationship with a man, she at first felt her almost fanatic attention to her man's needs was both romantic and natural.

Only after about two months of being the perfect caretaker to him did she begin to realize that she was resenting him for not taking equally good care of her.

She was waking up to the fact that she was putting on her sweet "good girl" love mask with this man out of an unconscious belief that she would only be lovable if she placated him, put him first, and catered to his needs. She began to realize that she was not taking very good care of herself, expecting him to second-guess her needs even though she was not sharing them.

As she started to work on her love mask, it felt to her like taffy—sticky sweet stuff that stuck to her and anyone she touched. She could feel that this mask was created very early on in her life, in imitation of her mother and who she thought her mother wanted her to be. She learned to never say "no," to be always cheerful, to manage everything that might cause anyone else anxiety, to control as much as possible, and never to allow feelings of fear, anger, or incompetence. She was supposed to keep it together, be quiet, and serve others. Her mother had even once said, "You are here for me. You must help keep me together." Realizing that her love mask was full of made-up feelings, Marcie began to get sick of it.

In a Pathwork session she externalized her mask by putting it out on a pillow and talking to it. "I want to be free of you. You're suffocating me." Immediately, however, she began to feel the taffy pulling her in, entangling her in its stickiness.

As the mask, she rejoined, "How can you say such mean things? I'm your best friend. I keep you safe. As long as you are sweet, no one will hurt you the way you were hurt as a child. Better listen to me and keep playing the love game." Her mask was entangling Marcie in its sweet, sticky stuff, and it felt fruitless to try to fight free.

Marcie then asked her higher self, which she symbolized by another pillow, what to do about this situation. As she sat on the higher self pillow, the words came suddenly. "Eat it," said the higher self, "the sticky stuff is medicine. If you eat it, accept it, ingest it, it will dissolve and turn into its essential nature, pure sugar, out of which you can create yourself anew." This visualization and exchange helped Marcie accept and incorporate her mask more fully. She realized that its essence was composed of the same ingredients as her higher self. She was in truth a loving, caring person and, once she could release the fear of her unlovableness which held the mask in place, she could reclaim her true sweetness.

The Mask as a Distortion of the Higher Self

The mask is always a distortion of genuine higher-self qualities of the personality. We draw on our real strengths—love, power, or serenity—in order to fashion an imitation which keeps people away from the intense vulnerability of our true higher self. Out of fear of our vulnerability we depend on the lower self and mask to "protect" us.

The true qualities of the higher self are then distorted by the lower self into an "imitation" of the higher self which we hope will make us both invulnerable and acceptable to others. The fear in the lower self distorts a true capacity for love into submission and dependency (the mask of love). The self-will of the little ego of the lower self distorts true power into aggression and control (the mask of power). The pride of the lower self, which seeks to rise above the ordinariness of being human, distorts serenity into detachment and withdrawal (the mask of serenity).

The fear that our true selves are unacceptable is what made us create the mask in the first place. And yet we learn that the mask—because it is phony and hence unattractive—actually brings about the very rejection from others that we most fear, thus recreating our original childhood hurts. When we are caught in the vicious circle, this rejection makes us re-double the effort to have a more perfect mask, thus creating yet more rejection, and so on. The principal antidote to the mask is to learn to accept and love ourselves as we are; then we can finally release the fear of not being loved and accepted by others. And then the genuine higher self qualities can be reclaimed in their original form. When we emanate our true higher self, we find that people are attracted to us, thus setting in motion a benign circle of reinforcement for being our true selves.

1) Once Connie was able to give up the "perfect Christian" mask of submission and acknowledge her anger and her power, she could also reclaim her great and generous capacity to love and care for others. She only needed to stop co-opting this energy into the construction of her martyr mask, a state in which she tended to care for others as a way to be seen as "good," superior to them, and/or to force others to pay attention to her.

2) Behind her power mask, Elizabeth was highly capable and powerful in the world. Her genuine sophistication, good taste, and competence were real qualities which could be nurtured as long as they were not used in service to her self-will, as a way to try to control others. She learned slowly to separate her competence from her hardness, her good taste from her judgment of others as inferior. And then her real artistic discernment and her business acumen could serve her well without getting in the way of opening her inner being in intimacy with others.

3) Behind the mask of serenity, Harriet's capacity for detachment became her ally when she started serious emotional work. When the waves of feeling became too threatening, she could retreat to the top of her inner wall, allowing herself to observe her feelings objectively and compassionately. She learned gradually to expand the wall enclosing her self-concept so that her identity could include all of her previously denied feelings. Her capacity for serene detachment became part of her spiritual strength, rather than a defense against being fully human.

When we penetrate the mask, we come face to face with both our lower and higher selves. When we stop trying to avoid our faults or our greatness, our evil or our true goodness, then we can see ourselves more truly as we are. Honest self-acceptance creates the basis for genuine self-respect, which replaces the false self-esteem built on the idealized self image.

> When you muster the courage of becoming your real
> self, even though it would seem so much less than the
> idealized self, you will find out that it is much more.
> And then you will have the peace of being at home
> within yourself. Then you will have security.
> Then you will function as a whole human being.
> Then you will have eliminated the iron whip of a
> taskmaster whom it is impossible to obey. Then
> will you know what peace and security really mean.
> You will cease to seek them by false means. (*PGL 83*)

Exercises for Chapter 6:

1. Name and explore five perfectionistic demands you have of yourself. Where do these demands come from? Whom are you trying to please, or at least prevent from hurting or rejecting you, by making these demands on yourself? Do these demands conform to either your mother's or father's demands on you? What demands do you see as coming to you from the larger society?

2. Pick an issue or disharmony in your life now, perhaps one that you have been exploring in your daily review. Write out a dialogue between your "top dog" superego perfectionist and your flawed human self about this issue. Then write out what you learned about the demands of your perfectionism. What seems to be its source? What do you imagine is its function?

3. In five days of your daily review, note instances of the appearance of the mask or idealized self image in your interaction with others. Note also your reactions when the idealized self feels threatened with exposure or penetration by others. Note the vulnerability you feel at these moments.

4. Decide which is your predominant mask—love, power, or serenity. Support your assessment through discussing examples from your life.

5. See how your primary mask is a pseudo-solution to the problem of childhood pain. Connect your main image (principal misconception about life) to your mask.

6. Refer to the quote from Lecture #73 that is presented on page 141. Do the exercise outlined there, beginning with "Take a current problem." Strip it down to the basic feeling of not being loved. Then see if you can find where the original childhood hurt with your parents is the same as or similar to the present-day feeling of not being loved.

Facing the Lower Self

"The manifestation of evil is not something intrinsically
different from pure consciousness and energy.
It has only changed its characteristics."

—Pathwork Guide Lecture 197, *"Energy and Consciousness in Distortion: Evil"*

Albert's Ghosts: Meeting the Lower Self

Albert loved women. Or at least he had always been in love with one, and sometimes more than one. At age 46, he still regarded himself as a chivalrous romantic. From childhood sexplay with a favorite girl cousin to his most recent temptation—an attractive client in his psychotherapeutic practice—women were of paramount importance in Albert's life.

But his first love was his mother, whom he always called Anna. Only sixteen years old when Albert was born, Anna never acted like a mother. The caregiver of his childhood home was Albert's grandmother, while Anna was more like a needy and neurotic big sister to him. Albert's father was much older and an alcoholic—a distant figure. So Anna had frequently turned to her son when she had problems, and showered him with hugs and kisses. Looking back, Albert was suspicious that there might have been sexual play between himself and his mother; he could remember intense sexual fantasies about Anna during his teen years.

But Albert did not come to the Pathwork because of his obsession with women. Lately he had been experiencing strange "hauntings," the presence of dark and menacing spirits which would come to him, especially in the night. Feeling frightened and insecure, Albert had been entertaining thoughts of suicide. He assumed that the hauntings were projections, but he was afraid to approach the region of his own inner darkness. Having grown up in a rural Southern culture that allowed occult superstitions to flourish in the midst of Christian fundamentalism, Albert now found himself more sympathetic to his young mother's beliefs in ghosts and evil curses. The dark spirits around him certainly felt real; he knew he needed a spiritual perspective to exorcise these evil presences.

Soon after undertaking a Pathwork retreat for intensive personal work with me, Albert awakened one night with a terrible anxiety in his stomach. He spontaneously began recalling very early sexual interactions with his mother. He felt tiny, and Anna was immense. Her large breasts and exciting presence overwhelmed him with powerful, contradictory feelings: shame and eagerness, terror and excitement, disgust and fascination. He huddled under the covers, until at last his stomach settled and he fell asleep, feeling very young and vulnerable.

In subsequent sessions, Albert remembered more of the sexual bond with his mother, all the way back to his toddler years. He remembered Anna bathing him and touching him sexually, and how she snuggled with him in bed, inviting him to suck her breasts. He could feel again her heavy breathing and excitement.

Regressing fully into these incestuous scenes, Albert called out to Anna, "What are you doing Mommy?. . . Where are you? Mommy, I'm scared, come back." He screamed out the agony of his memories, and his body shook with fear. As the shaking subsided, he felt ashamed—a hot, white shame that made him pull away from contact. As he sat with the shame, he began to feel his own excitement in having been sexual with his mother, along with the sense of specialness this intense relationship had evoked.

That night Albert felt the presence of the dark spirits. I prayed with him, and then suggested he speak to the presences.

He asked, "Who are you and what do you want from me?"

First Albert felt the presence of his grandmother, dressed as usual in black, beckoning to him to join her in death. "Die now," she called, "and you will never have to face the terrible things you have done."

"I don't want to die," replied Albert in dialogue with the presence. "I want to face whatever is so terrible." Suddenly, the grandmother ghost seemed to disappear.

But another presence came forth, more menacing and accusing than the first. I asked Albert to identify the ghost, and he reported, "It's my father." Albert's father had killed himself many years ago. The ghost-father now brought his son a message so terrifying that for a while Albert could only tremble without speaking. Then he started to pray out loud for Christ's help, and eventually his prayers and my reassuring presence steadied him enough to convey his "father's" message: "You are bad and deserve to be killed."

At first Albert did not have the strength to disagree. "Yes, I know," he blurted, beginning to shake all over again. "I did things with her I never should have done—bad things, very bad things."

I intervened now, speaking in the gentle voice one would use with a young child, "Remember, Albert, it was Mommy who started those games. She was responsible. You were only a little boy who wanted to please Mommy Anna and do what she asked you to do."

Curled up and quivering on the sofa, Albert whispered, "But you don't understand, you don't understand."

"What don't I understand, Albert?"

In a barely audible hiss, Albert replied, "But I liked it. I liked the games, the excitement. I liked being special." His voice trailing off, Albert whispered, "My Daddy. . . ."

"Yes?" I queried, in a reassuring tone, "What about your Daddy? What did you feel toward him?"

"I was her number one. I was better than my Dad. I didn't want him to be with her. I wanted him gone. I wanted him dead!"

Albert started coughing, crying, and clutching his belly. Gripped by anxiety, he rolled on the sofa gasping and spitting out his choked sobs. Eventually he quieted enough to whisper, "Now I know. I killed him with my badness."

"Oh, I see," I spoke softly, "You think you killed your Daddy because of the bad things you did with your Mommy, the games with her that you liked and that put you in his place. And you think all that makes you so bad you deserve to be killed?"

A nervous nod of Albert's head let me know that this was indeed the belief of the terrified child inside him. "Now we can understand why little Albert felt so bad about himself that he wanted to die," I explained. "Now we know why the ghosts of your grandmother and your father came to visit you. They came to show you your beliefs about your badness. Let's see what they have to say now that you have heard the things you most feared hearing about yourself."

Sitting up and holding my hand, Albert invited the ghosts to speak to him again. But the ghosts were not so dark now. He felt instead the benign presence of his grandmother, warm and maternal. She merged into the forgiving presence of Christ, light and comforting. I urged Albert to talk to this new Christ-like presence.

"I feel so bad, not little-boy bad, but really bad. I actually did want to replace my father and be special to my mother. I was not just her victim. I participated in her neurosis, even as a child. I want to know if this can be forgiven. I want to know how to be forgiven."

As I sat with Albert, we both experienced a deepening calm. The room seemed to fill with the light of the Christ presence, a warm radiance that was deeply comforting. Attuning to this feeling of universal, unconditional love, I felt my heart opening to reassurance and faith. Albert interpreted aloud the message he heard from this presence:

"All is forgivable, all is already forgiven. There is nothing so dark, even in the most despairing part of your soul, that it cannot be welcomed into awareness. And in awareness is redemption. All is well; all will be well."

Facing the Lower Self

While we do not all have such dramatic manifestations of the lower self as Albert's ghosts, most of us are gripped by the power of our unconscious ghosts and demons at some time in our lives. We all have secret places of shame, childish beliefs in our "badness." And we all have real adult guilt for our sins of omission or commission. We all have times when we find ourselves doing, thinking, and feeling things that we know are unkind or even vicious. We are usually disconnected from the source of this evil within us, and are often tempted either to disown or to justify our negativity.

Sooner or later, however, we are led to recognize that we ourselves are the source of the dark stains that discolor our world; the darkness emanates from us. Evil lives in every human being in the form of what the Pathwork calls the lower self. The moment at which we acknowledge our own lower self is a sacred moment that marks a turning point in our spiritual healing. We take back inside us our unkind and hostile projections of evil onto others and simply, humbly embrace the darkness as our own. "Yes," we say, "you belong to me. I accept you as mine." Our pride yields, our heart opens. When we consciously embrace the evil that lives within us, our truthful acknowledgment heals our unhappiness at its source: our spiritual alienation from God.

Like Albert, we find it hard to believe we can have a lower self and still be lovable, that we can be both bad and good. Also like Albert, we choose to act out the agenda of our lower selves unconsciously as a defense against feeling the deep hurts of our imperfect childhood, the inevitable pain of our adult life, and the existential despair of our separation from God. We too would like to be above our intense vulnerability, to control life and other people, to hide from feeling both our early and our existential helplessness. While we may not have been as actively abused as Albert was, we all harbor feelings of victimization which we use to justify our negativity. We resist looking squarely at our own evil and calling it by its rightful name.

What is the Lower Self?

The lower self is the creative center of our negative attitudes and feelings toward self and others, arising out of our egocentric separateness from the totality of life. It is our defense against pain, our numbness to feeling, our disconnection from ourselves and from other people. And it is the negativity we act out as a result of this numbness.

We project onto others the role of "enemy," thus enabling us to treat them badly, forcing them to play a part in our own secret melodramas rather than respecting their God-given integrity. The lower self stems from the false belief that our separate body-mind can live a life severed from the fabric made up of all other living beings and of which we are, in fact, but a single, interwoven strand. The essence of the lower self is the negative intention to stand apart from the whole of life, and then to aggrandize that separateness.

The lower self manifests at different levels of consciousness. At the ego level, we have certain chronic personality faults—such as competitiveness, or a tendency to gossip, or to be critical. At the level of our inner child, we have misconceptions and defensive negativity that resulted from our childhood wounding. As we explore more deeply, we find negative soul directions—toward revenge, or bitterness, or despair, for example—that manifest through entrenched negative life issues. These are aspects of the lower self that we brought with us into this incarnation for the purpose of purification. Deeper still, the lower self mainfests as our collective attachment to control and separateness. Ultimately, the lower self is whatever in us obstructs the free and focused flow of divine energy—love and truth—through our being.

Every human being living in the duality of the earth plane resists, to one degree or another, total surrender to God. We resist fully identifying with our own God-essence, the flow of divine energy which is our true nature. The choice to identify with our resistance and our separated ego creates our capacity for evil.

What is Evil?

In the Lord's Prayer, we ask God to "deliver us from evil." This is usually taken to mean that we should turn our backs on evil, shunning it in all its manifestations. The unfortunate result is that we end up delivering ourselves from **awareness** of evil in ourselves and in the world we have created. By denying the evil in ourselves, we push it underground where it grows like a cancer in the recesses of the unconscious. Only when we meet it face-to-face, bringing it out into the light of awareness, can this energy be transformed into its original true nature. Only through the work of becoming more self-aware can we truly deliver ourselves from the evil that has taken root in our unconscious. The time has come in our evolutionary process to face the lower self and, through integrating this awareness, to re-claim both our true humility as a part of the whole of life and our true power as an individualized expression of the universal Life Force.

We normally reserve the word "evil" for negativity that is extreme and/or consciously chosen. While moral distinctions can appropriately be drawn between different degrees of evil, there is nonetheless a continuum between the actions of a geno-cidal mass murderer like Hitler and the egotistical separateness in every one of us that unconsciously chooses to align with nega-tivity and fear, rather than surrender to love and truth. Hitler's blindness and viciousness were rooted in the same negative forces that exist in every human being.

When we repress our awareness of our own capacity for evil, we remain split within ourselves. The Guide explains:

> Mutuality between you and yourself will be absent if you reject your own evil. By rejecting evil, you ignore and deny the vital original creative energy that is con-tained in all evil. This energy must be made available in order for you to become whole. The energy can only be transformed when you are aware of its distorted form. When you reject its present distorted manifesta-tion, how can you convert it back? Hence you remain split within yourself, and when this is not conscious, the split mirrors itself in your relationships with other people or in the lack of them. No matter how evil and unacceptable any specific traits may be in you, no matter how undesirable and destructive, the energy and substance they consist of is vital force. (PGL 185)

The lower self is the dark side of the life force, whether manifesting as a Hitler or as a minor act of thoughtlessness in an otherwise evolved personality. Yet the lower self is also essen-tial, potent, creative energy. When we repress awareness of this part of ourselves, we end up repressing much of our creativity and vitality as well. Everyone carries distortions in their sexual and aggressive functioning. The more afraid we are of these distortions, the more we limit the energy available for these vital self-expressions. Everyone creates negative life experience from their unconscious lower self impulses. The more we deny the power of our own lower selves to create negatively, the weaker we will feel in life, and the more we will tend to blame others or fate for our misfortune.

The lower self has the power to create all the suffering and negativity we experience in our lives. It is a powerful and creative force. When we face and acknowledge its full destructive power in us, then we re-claim the creative power to shape our lives in more positive directions.

Denial of the Lower Self

The denial of the lower self in human beings is at least as powerful a force as the denial of death; sometimes it is even stronger. People have chosen death through suicide rather than face some truthful but negative revelations about themselves that have become public, threatening their reputations and self-esteem. We often feel our self-worth is so dependent on our being "good"—or at least appearing that way to others—that acknowledgment of our badness is tantamount to annihilation.

> The price you pay for recognizing and accepting the destructive, evil aspect in the self seems so high. It **seems** that way. It really is not. On the contrary, the price of denying it is enormous. . . . To the degree that evil is properly faced, self-acceptance, self-liking, new energy and deeper love and pleasure feelings ensue.
> (*PGL 184*)

As we deepen our commitment to our spiritual path, we develop the taste for truth and the understanding that, however temporarily painful, honesty is always better for us than self-flattery and denial. The most important tool for building our tolerance of our negativity is the development of the objective, compassionate observer self, an aspect of the higher self. As we name what is true without denial, we shift our identity from that which is being named to the namer. We become the observer, not that which is being observed; we become awareness, not the contents of our awareness. This gradual shift of self-identification lets us be less attached to and ashamed of the lower self and builds our grounding in the higher self.

But the need to work with the lower self does not disappear as we become more identified with the higher self. In fact, the stronger our experience of the higher self, the more important the purification of the lower self becomes.

> Many spiritual practices genuinely bring out the real, higher self, yet leave the undeveloped aspects of consciousness intact. Many entities have such an intense longing to realize their divine, inherent nature that they forget, while in the body, that they came to fulfill a mission in the universal plan. This mission is the purification and growth of undeveloped "cosmic matter." (PGL 193)

Three Aspects of the Lower Self: Pride, Self-Will and Fear

Pride, self-will, and fear are the crux of the lower self. Each of these attitudes is a different form of denial and therefore even more dangerous to the soul than more overt forms of evil. Pride says we are better than others so we have a right to our self-importance and specialness. Fear says we must protect ourselves so anything we feel we need to do for our own defense is justified. Self-will says we must get what we want when we want it, thereby justifying our egotism.

> Where there is pride, where there is self-will, where there is fear, there must be a state of contraction. The ego-structuring becomes tight and rigid. Self-will says, "me, me, me," the little me, the little self, the self that puts its stake only into the outer, conscious ego personality and that completely disregards, ignores, and rejects the greater consciousness, the universal consciousness, of which you are an expression. Unless the total person is unified with this greater consciousness that transcends the ego, holding on to the ego becomes imperative.
> The ego would not be so emphasized if the false belief would not exist that the self is annihilated the moment the ego is not the sole ruler of human life. Hence, when you identify exclusively with the ego, you cannot identify with the greater consciousness, nor with the feelings in your body, for they go hand in hand. If you identify with the ego you create a tightness in the ego structure that says, in effect, "It is my ego world that counts. This is all there is to me and therefore I cannot give it up, otherwise I cease to exist." (PGL 177)

The attitude of pride says, "I am better than others," or "I insist that I am my idealized image rather than my flawed real self." Pride keeps us elevated above our humanness and constantly seduces us by the fear that if we do not stay "above" ourselves, we will be plunged into unbearable worthlessness. Pride is the principal feature of the little separated ego-self that believes that to survive it must be elevated above others and be made special.

In a dramatic statement about the nature of pride in the human condition, the Guide says, "He who feels the humiliation of another person less than his own still has too much pride." (PGL 30) Our personal, racial, ethnic, or gender self-importance are often the justification for cruelty and superiority toward others. The antidotes to pride are honest self-confrontation and humble self-acceptance out of which real self-esteem comes.

> Pride says, "I am better than you." This means sepa-
> rateness, it means one-upmanship, it means everything
> that is opposed to a state of love. By the same token,
> pride may also manifest as, "I am worse than others,
> I am worthless, I have no value. But I must hide this
> fact, so I must pretend that I am more." Of course,
> these thoughts are not articulate, but they may not
> be altogether unconscious. This distorted pride, as
> opposed to healthy dignity, is always comparing and
> measuring the self with others and is thus perpetually
> in illusion. For no true evaluation can ever come from
> this. It is a hopeless and endless chase for an illusory
> goal that leaves the personality not only exhausted, but
> also more and more frustrated. The chasm between the
> self and others widens forever more, love becomes less
> possible and hence pleasure further removed. It does
> not matter whether you actually think you are more
> than others, or only pretend in order to hide your
> feelings of worthlessness, it is all the same.
> This cannot produce love. (PGL 177)

The attitude of self-will says, "I want what I want when I want it." Self-will is distinct from free will, which is simply the capacity of the entity to choose, to direct, to activate. Self-will occurs when free will is used in the service of the little self, the limited ego consciousness, in an attempt to control others and life. Because we have free will we have the choice, moment to moment, of aligning with our limited self-will or with God's will.

We can learn to recognize our self-will by watching our-selves when we are impatient, demanding, uncompromising, and tense. Self-will may or may not be conscious. In most of us it is no longer acted out so overtly as it would be in the child, the primitive, or the criminal. But it operates nonetheless in our insistence to have our own way, however justified or rationalized this demand might be.

The attitude of fear says, "I will not trust," and often also, "If I am not special, or do not get my way, then something terrible will happen." Fear both supports and results from the attitudes of pride and self-will. Fear keeps us restricted within the narrow boundaries of the little ego-self.

> Fear cannot trust anyone. Therefore the self that is in
> fear cannot let go of itself. Pleasure is unrealizable
> when the personality is bound to the ego, bound in
> self-will, pride, and fear, bound in the negative
> creations, bound in the struggle within itself that
> denies its own negativity. Hence it does not know the
> nature of its own suffering. The self denies its responsi-
> bility for suffering and lack, and renders others respon-
> sible for the lack, which, in turn, elicits resentments,
> bitterness, anger, defiance. The resulting confusion is
> a torment for the soul. (PGL 177)

The attitude of fear often makes us justify negative thoughts and acts which we never face directly because we are lost in the disorientation caused by fear. We need to bring the attitude of fear to the surface and understand its refusal to trust.

When we unearth the defenses of pride, self-will, and fear, they lose their destructive power. We allow our objective, com-passionate self-observer to name them, without justification or excuse, and also without self-judgment. However provocative an outside situation may be, we learn to be responsible for our own negative reactions.

My father called on the phone this morning. I felt a quick flash of hostility, I wish he were dead, so I could inherit his money.
   Ah. . . here's my self-will and greed.

My husband drank too much last night. He can be so crude. I am so far superior to him spiritually.
   Ah. . . here's my pride.

My daughter wants yet another party dress. I will never let her have it. She's already got more boyfriends than I had at her age, and she doesn't deserve it.
Ah. . . here's my competitiveness.

I wish my husband would say he loved me more often. I feel lonely and it's his fault.
Ah. . . here's my victimization masking my demand and self-will.

I don't trust my daughter is going to turn out all right. I better make stricter rules for her.
Ah. . . here's my fear and desire to control.

What the Lower Self is Not

Anger is not, by itself, an aspect of the lower self. Anger is a natural human emotion. It is an alarm bell in our psyche that signals that something is wrong in ourselves or in our environment. Anger helps us act, move, change. Without it we might stagnate in situations that are unhealthy for us. Without it we would lack the willingness to stand up for ourselves and for others who are being treated badly.

If anger is owned as a feeling clearly coming from the self, it need not be destructive. **It is always healthier to feel our anger than to repress it.** Repressed anger will always be acted out in some indirect and inevitably more negative way. Anger becomes an expression of the lower self only when it is used to hurt or destroy.

Janet had very high standards for how she ought to act as a mother: to be reasonable, loving and fair, and above all, not to impose her own problems on her four children. She maintained this idealized self image most of the time, but felt terribly burdened by motherhood and would occasionally fly into unexplained irrational rages, for which she would then feel extremely guilty.

In a Pathwork group Janet expressed her frustration at not living up to her high ideals. I suggested she might need to feel her resentment about the burden her idealized self image created. With Janet assenting to the psychodrama, we all pointed fingers at her and articulated the demands she constantly made on herself. As her resentment toward us built up, she realized that she was also angry at her children's incessant demands on her. In fact, she was furious with them—a feeling she had never previously acknowledged. I probed further into what lay behind her refusal to experience her anger in the actual moment when it might be an appropriate response to her children.

"I'm afraid," she whispered, "I'm afraid if I ever felt angry consciously, I might want to kill them." Here was the lower-self thought which she had been trying to hide from herself by repressing her anger. I encouraged Janet to allow the forbidden thought and, in the safety of our group, where no one would be hurt, to allow herself to develop that thought. This time she said loudly and clearly, "I want to kill them." She then allowed herself a full-scale visualization of killing all four of her children—marching them up to a platform where a huge cauldron of boiling oil stood. She saw herself dumping each one into the pot and watching them die.

She was very shaken by the visualization, but also very relieved. At last it was out, her worst secret, her buried killer, the opposite of her "perfect mother" mask. No longer did she have to bear the burden of her false guilt which was really a distortion of pride, trying to pretend to be better than she sometimes felt inside.

That night Janet had the following dream: "I come into a house where a very moralistic and strict stepmother, now dead, had been in charge. I go up to the attic and find there an old hamper. Inside it is a little girl who had been punished by the stepmother for her 'badness' by being cramped up inside the hamper and left to die. I let her out and the little girl is very grateful. She immediately goes outside and begins to play and run, and I feel very happy."

Janet felt that the "stepmother" was the idealized demands of her mask. And the "little girl" was her own spontaneous energy, including her natural anger, which had been so cramped up inside her that it was almost dead. Now that the "secret" of her killer was out, she was free, the "bad girl" could run and play free, and she could reclaim her life energy. This work allowed Janet to accept her anger with less harsh judgment and more consciousness.

The feeling of anger is always useful, because it is the simple emotional truth of the moment and can, therefore, lead us more deeply into ourselves. Expressing our anger, however, needs to be done consciously, with attention to how and where and with whom it is appropriate. In a safe context for self-work, in individual counseling or groups, we can feel and express our anger fully. Outside of such a context, we have to decide whether and how to express our anger, depending mostly on the degree of trust and the willingness to explore feelings that exist in relationship to the person with whom we are angry.

If there is no contract for intimacy and we sense there is no ability on the part of the other to hear our feelings, we may choose not to express our anger at all, or only to do so in a controlled expression or specific protest that is careful not to blame or humiliate the other. In every case, we need to explore the anger ourselves, preferably with some outside objective perspective, and eventually see if we need to take some appropriate action about the situation that disturbs us.

The agreement to express anger openly and directly is vital to any relationship where real intimacy is a goal. In such a situation a simple, clear "I'm angry at you" will often clear the air. This initiates the process of taking responsibility for our anger, sharing the provocation, and then working to discover whether the source was a genuine present-day offense by the other or the reactivation of a past hurt within ourselves, or a combination of both.

Lower-Self Anger

The clean expression of "I'm angry" is so much healthier than the usual alternatives spoken, or more often secretly felt, such as, "I hate you," "You so-and-so, see what you did to me" or "I'll pay you back for this." Hatred, blame, self-righteousness, and revenge are infinitely more hurtful to our relationships than simple admission of our anger.

Anger is an expression of the lower self only when its intent turns from simple self-assertion to a desire to hurt, punish, or destroy. Anger that is expressed violently or allowed to fester into hatred or revenge is always an expression of the lower self. If anger is not expressed until after many hurts or resentments have been accumulated, it will almost always be hurtful and revengeful. This kind of anger can be usefully experienced in the safe environment of spiritual counseling or therapy. Then we consciously go deeper to explore our negative feelings for clues as to their deepest origins.

We must realize, however, that perfect orderliness in the expression of anger is an unrealistic goal. Even the most spiritually aware person will sometimes blow up with an expression of long-simmering or semi-conscious anger. Such an explosion can alert us to the ways in which our masks of love or serenity may still be operating as defenses against our negativity. Our job is always the same in these instances: accept and forgive ourselves our flaws, and then go on to the exploration of their origins.

Uncovering the Lower Self

The lower self is a dangerous, exciting, and scary terrain for most of us. It is both repellent and attractive. While we find violence repugnant, it nonetheless fascinates us. Newspaper sales and violent movies and TV shows depend largely on our fascination with those who have acted out their lower selves, as we recognize the secret potential for evil that exists within every one of us. Instinctively we know that the lower self contains vital life energy, and so we are vicariously drawn to the manifestations of this energy in real-life crimes and cruelty, as well as in fictional stories and film. There is a positive potential in our attraction to these kinds of entertainment, for we can use our particular fascinations with evil as clues which we can follow into our own private "lower-self land."

For further clues we need to examine our own behavior. Some of us will act out verbally with strangers when we think we have been aggrieved. The rest of us usually act out only in intimate behavior; we are usually most cruel with those closest to us. We feel wounded or threatened and we strike back or withhold. Or if we restrain our behavior, our thoughts may be steeped in hostility. Or we may find we project our worst thoughts onto others, imagining their hostility toward us, when it is really our own.

The lower self operates in our lives through our images that distort reality and justify our negativity. The defenses of pride, self-will, and fear keep us trapped within a narrowly egotistic self-definition that further rationalizes our disconnection from others.

Even if we are not aware of how the lower self operates in our outer lives, our dream life will almost always reveal our shadow side.

A man who had worked as a cab driver in a big city dreamed: "I'm in the porno district of an anonymous big city. Everywhere I look there are desperate characters: junkies, pushers, whores, pimps. It's beginning to feel dangerous and I want to get out. However, every street I go down is a dead end. Finally, while my car is stopped at a light, two prostitutes jump in. They tell me they will show me the way out. We continue to drive through yet more filthy streets filled with low-life characters, while they both start telling me their life stories. Even in the dream I realize I am in 'lower-self land' and I probably won't be able to get out until I hear their stories all the way through."

Further, we can always throw light on the lower self by examining our sexual behavior and our secret sexual fantasies. Almost everyone has some sexual fantasy in which sexuality is divorced from love, involving degrading or forcing oneself or others, or being degraded or forced. If these fantasies were examined thoroughly they would reveal all our major distortions. Albert, whose story opened this chapter, was constantly drawn to "forbidden" women both in reality and in fantasy. Thus he re-created the original incest taboo, compelled by the attachment of his sexual energy to the original negative situation.

> It is often the case that a human being functions eroti-
> cally and/or sexually only in connection with fear and
> pain. ... Every one of you, at least to some degree, will
> find that your erotic response occurs only when there
> is at least a slight element of rejection, fearfulness,
> uncertainty, insecurity, or pain. (*PGL 119*)

We will examine the connection between sexuality and the lower self more fully in Chapter Nine, where we explore the attachment of the pleasurable life force to negative life situations.

The Creative Power of the Lower Self

As long as "lower-self land" is unexplored territory for us, it will seem overwhelming and fearsome. We fear that the ego-self which we ordinarily identify with will get lost in the thickets of our distortions. We are afraid of the monsters of the negative unconscious which lurk in the forests of these unknown lands.

And yet, since evil is an intrinsic part of our human nature, if we are to follow the path of truth, we have no choice but to enter the dark mysteries of our nature. Otherwise we will live on the surface of life, in the mask of denial.

We need to keep remembering that evil is not a separate force in the universe. On the ordinary, dualistic level, evil can appear to be an equal and opposing force to good. In reality, evil is merely a distortion of the one great creative force of the universe. Meeting and embracing evil is the only way to redirect its "energy current" back to its pure origin.

> When evil is understood to be intrinsically a divine
> energy flow, momentarily distorted due to specific
> wrong ideas, concepts, and imperfections, then it is
> no longer rejected in its essence. (*PGL 184*)

Transformation of the lower self is essentially the release of an ugly, congealed mass of soul substance back into its flowing essence. Just as solid matter will, through the application of certain physical processes, dissolve into gaseous energy, so does the lower self—through the application of the spiritual practices of investigation, acceptance, confession, and forgiveness—dissolve into divine energy. Sexual cruelty becomes sexual exuberance. Hostile aggression becomes positive assertion. Passive stagnation becomes relaxed acceptance. And so on. With each transformation we become open to more and more beneficial energy, gaining the unobstructed vitality of the undefended self.

The integration of our own darkness makes life more real and interesting. In the following dream, a young woman who had been battling her suicidal urges recognizes her self-destructive shadow as a friend:

Her dream: "I am sitting with my mother in a movie theater, just before the film has begun. We're about to see a mediocre light comedy. Down near the front of the theater, I see a menacing but attractive black man, and I start to go down to see him. My mother chastises me that the movie is about to begin, and adds a dire warning about something bad happening if I leave her. Frightened, I go to see the man anyway.

"As I approach the black man, he stares at me seductively and I'm afraid I'll be lost in his power. But the closer I get, the less scared I am. Finally I sit next to him and reach for his hand. We look into each other's eyes and seem to merge for a moment—I feel stronger and more grounded than I ever have. Then I know I will not go back to my

mother, and that the movie coming up is actually serious, exciting, and life-changing." [1]

The dreamer summarized: "My mother is like my idealized self, which pretends I don't have a shadow side. I leave her to face my own dark nature and I'm stronger for it. The movie of my life is now much more real."

Origins of the Lower Self

In any particular lifetime the lower self is activated by negative experiences in childhood, especially with the parents. Both the lower self and the mask are brought into existence by the soul's attempt to resist or escape painful experience, which is inherent in the duality of the human condition. When we encounter a painful situation, we spontaneously either feel pain and express grief, or react with anger. These are natural feelings, not yet the lower self.

However, often neither the expression of grief nor the expression of anger is accepted by our parents. Hence we learn to suppress our spontaneous feelings. And then we try to figure out a more acceptable way to act which will avoid future pain. Thus we construct a mask and cut off our natural feelings. Eventually, we become numb to our real feelings. And we vow—often without being aware that we have done so—to hurt others in revenge, often with our own misery as the weapon.

> The child who feels hurt, rejected, helplessly exposed to pain and deprivation, often finds numbing of his feelings the only protection against suffering. This is often, quite realistically, a useful protective device. Also, when the child experiences contradictory and conflicting emotions in his own psyche, he cannot cope with this, and becomes numb. Under some circumstances, this may be a kind of salvation for the child. But when the numbness is maintained long after the circumstances have changed, and when the personality is no longer a helpless child, this is the beginning of evil.

> Numbness and insensitivity toward one's own pain and inner conflicts turn into numbness and insensitivity

---

[1] This white woman's dream in which her shadow-self is represented by a black man is an example of the cultural symbolism underlying racism. The disowned lower self is projected onto the "other," whether blacks or Jews or any other group, which then gives the mask, or Pharisee in us, the excuse to oppress other human beings. Reclaiming our projections, as is being done by this dreamer, is the solution to personal and collective racism.

toward others. . . . It enables one to see others suffer
without the discomfort of any pangs of conscience.
Much of the world's evil is caused by this state of soul.
Passive indifference may not be as actively evil as committed cruelty, but it is as harmful in the long run.

. . . .

The next stage is one of actively inflicting cruelty.
This comes about due to fear of others from whom one
expects such acts; or due to an inability to cope with
pent-up rages; or due to a subtle process of strengthening the protective device of numbness. You will find
that a person may occasionally, almost consciously,
stand on the brink of a decision: "Either I allow my
feelings to reach out in participation with the other,
or, in order to refuse this strong influx of warm feelings, I have to behave in the exact opposite way."
The next moment such reasoning is gone, the conscious decision forgotten, and what remains is a compelling force toward cruel acts. . . . This then increases
the numbing process, prohibiting not only the influx
of spontaneous positive feelings, but also to ward off
fear and guilt. The active deed of inflicting pain on
others simultaneously kills off one's own ability to feel.
Hence it is a stronger device to attain numbness.

In all these instances, it can be seen, again and again,
how all harm, all destructiveness, all evil, result from
the denial of the feelings of the spontaneous real self.
(PGL 134)

As children we were intensely vulnerable and helpless. When
we experienced spontaneous but painful emotions of the real self,
we learned to shut them off because we believed them to be intolerable. That is why opening now to that long-suppressed childhood
pain is such an important part of healing the lower self. When we
can feel our own pain, we can be open to the suffering of others.
Hence we are much less likely to inflict cruelty on others.

The Innate Lower Self of the Child

In addition to the reactive evil resulting from specific childhood hurts, we are all born with a lower self. It might be considered the innate capacity of human beings to be destructively

self-centered, cruel, and possessive. This universal distortion first emerges as the child starts to differentiate into a separate self. If the real needs of the infant are met, this usually happens around age two.

At that time, the child first begins to differentiate herself from her parents, and to exercise her separate power. The lower self then shows itself in the form of unreasonable demands to be the constant center of attention, to have all needs met immediately, and to try to control others and her environment at all times.

The Pathwork Guide calls this the "mass image of self-importance," which is a universal human expression of the lower self. The mass image is that my self-worth depends on being special to and getting approval and goodies from other people. While this stage of dependent narcissism and demanding self-importance is natural in the evolving ego development of the child, if it is not met with both loving confrontation and good humor, this universal human distortion will be prolonged into adulthood.

> We, in our world, can hear your souls shrieking for attention. . . . When we approach your plane, all souls send forth this loud calling and clamoring, inaudible to your ears. But you can imagine how noisy it is for us. (PGL 57)

Because most souls do not outgrow childish self-centeredness, the whole world sounds like an out-of-control preschool class to the more evolved spirits who visit our realm!

If fully met in childhood, the self-importance typical of this phase of development will evolve into healthy self-assertion along with a recognition of boundaries. By the proper setting of realistic limits by the parents, the child learns that the universe does not exist just to cater to her every fleeting desire. It is precisely in experiencing this frustration that the child learns to separate from her environment. Every child will resist parental limits and will express her dislike and frustration about limits. She will instinctively respond with fury, hate, and a desire for revenge. Healthy parents can meet these reactions firmly, but lightheartedly, not taking the child's self-importance too seriously. However, if the child's spontaneous lower-self reactions are heavily squelched by the parents, they will go underground where they remain unresolved, only to be acted out later on in life.

The child needs acceptance of her selfishness and encouragement of her real need to be autonomous and powerful. But she also needs clear limits for her behavior and a parental willingness to identify the negative behavior without being judgmental, even as the child's feelings and energy are affirmed. In this way she can begin to learn the appropriate attitude toward her lower self—of acceptance and forgiveness, without condoning acting out. She can learn to differentiate her real needs from her excessive demands. And she can begin to learn to identify her negativity for what it is, without justifying or indulging it.

However, the distorted attitudes of parents toward their own lower selves will be reflected in their children. If the parents reject the lower self, the child will repress her own natural self-ishness and hostility, and disown responsibility for her negativity. And if the parents indulge their negativity or fail to confront the child's lower self, the child will act out negatively without feeling responsible for her behavior.

Whether suppressed or indulged, the child will try to numb the pain of real guilt which accompanies the awareness of the lower self. And she will try to fit a mold that is acceptable to her parents' conscious or unconscious expectations, for she believes this will spare her future pain. Thus the mask is formed and the consciousness of the lower self is dimmed.

If repressed, the lower self goes underground only to erupt in later life, especially in times of stress or crisis. If acted out, the accumulated unfelt pain of guilt further alienates the person from herself and from the possibility of transformation. By adulthood, the childhood origins of the lower self are forgotten. Then the hate, selfishness, and desire for revenge are rationalized by outer events, so the ability to take responsibility for one's own inherent lower self is reduced. Thus evil perpetuates itself.

Karma and the Lower Self

We can also look at the origin of the lower self from the larger perspective of the soul's journey. From this viewpoint, each incarnation is only a fragment of the journey of the soul through many lifetimes. The lower self is then seen as a cumulative creation, resulting from every negative choice we have made in all the lifetimes we have lived on earth. Every time we have chosen fear or revenge or numbness over love and courage and connection, we have frozen a piece of our souls. This contracted life energy is the lower self of the soul. We carry it into each lifetime like a piece of compacted baggage, in order eventually to face and release it. The lower self of the soul can only be thawed and lightened by feeling the pain of the negative choices we have made and by making other, more positive, choices. The age-old ritual of confession and forgiveness works to transform the lower self at the soul level.

From this perspective, we choose our parents and early life situations in order to activate the "soul dents," or unresolved issues, brought into one incarnation from previous ones. Certain kinds of childhood pain or rejection echo familiarly in our souls and we re-create the situation we have come in to face and to heal. This helps explain why different children of the same parents often respond so differently to the same parental situation. Each child has different karma or inherent distortions that are activated in childhood, and has a different task with these parents.

Once our particular soul weaknesses and distortions are brought to the surface through the formative experiences of childhood, we have an opportunity to recognize and transform our chronic faults. Our spirit guides and our own higher self plan our early environment so that our faults can be made manifest, brought into concrete form, and also so our strengths can be tested and refined.

Understanding that certain negative defenses are imbedded in the soul from experiences in past lives gives us a broader perspective on our present life issues.

Eleanor was exploring her inner resistance in relationship, her "no" to sharing herself openly with others. Sometimes it felt like a real physical restriction, an inability to talk. Even when she had decided to share something vulnerable about herself, she could not get the words out. She felt imprisoned in her fear of what might come out if she let herself be real and open with others.

In the course of a guided meditation, she saw herself in a dungeon. She could see and smell the cold, clammy walls of green-gray stone, a tiny barred window high above her reach, and a wooden bench chained to the wall. She saw herself sitting on that bench, dressed in a long medieval gown. She knew herself to be someone important, a duchess perhaps, who had been put in the dungeon cell because she was a threat to the ruling powers. The dungeon keeper appeared as a kindly, concerned man *dressed in rough brown cloth with a rope around his waist, who expressed pity for her. But Eleanor would have none of his compassion. To herself she thought, "They think putting me here will bother me, but it doesn't. **I don't care.** There's no way they can touch me, nothing they can do to me. That is my victory. **My victory is in not caring. I will never let them know how hurt I am."***

The picture of her proud isolation and resistance to vulnerability in this medieval lifetime was a dramatic parallel to Eleanor's present state of feeling imprisoned in her own defenses. She felt great relief upon experiencing this ancient scene which so clearly portrayed her present difficulty. She began to work actively with the inner character of the imprisoned duchess and her choice in that lifetime to stay in pride and separateness. Eventually she allowed the defended pain and helplessness to flood through her; from then on the prison of her rigid defenses began to break apart.

Into each lifetime we bring the issues and images that reflect our distortions. Our early lives with parents crystallize these images so that we can see them clearly. As these "ancient" problems get re-enacted in our later lives, we can begin to effect resolution. Along the way we will learn how specific attitudes inexorably bring certain results: separateness causes isolation, love creates harmony; dependency causes disappointment, self-responsibility creates self-esteem; and so on. These laws of karma operate within our present lifetime, and over the span of many lifetimes as well.

The Origin of Evil

On a still deeper level, the origin of the lower self in the individual psyche is synonymous with the question of the origin of evil in humanity.

The Pathwork Guide sees human beings as part of the cosmic matter created when some of God chose to separate from the rest of God. Self-identification with its separateness led this part of God into duality and evil. We are on a journey of self-discovery toward conscious reunion with God, our true essence. Unlike the rest of nature, we are endowed with free will, which allows us the choice of egocentricity and belief in separateness.

Our lower self would have us remain proudly separate while our higher self yearns for humble reconnection, reunion, and resumption of our identity with the whole of creation. This yearning leads us on a journey of many lifetimes until every piece of human consciousness that has ever split itself off chooses, of its own free will, to return to the unitive state.

The Guide generally uses the personalized myths and metaphors of Western Christianity to describe the universal process of separation and return. But occasionally a more abstract language, reflective of Eastern mysticism, is used. For each individual, the cosmology that best resonates with personal experience will offer the most useful model. Ultimately, attention to our own experience of the limited nature of our negativity and the expansiveness of our divine essence is much more important than any belief structure.

The Christian Myth

The Christian story of the original separation from God is the tale of Lucifer, God's second angel after Christ, who chose to pull away from his Father and Creator. In his rebellion, Lucifer became Satan, identified with his separateness, pride, and self-will. Although he believed that he thereby created his own "kingdom," Satan is subject to the ultimate laws of God's universe.

The evil of Satan is not an equal and opposite force to the power of God, since God created Satan and endowed him with free will. Satan is bound by the laws of cause and effect, which means that sooner or later he suffers for every negative choice he makes. It is this suffering that eventually awakens Satan to the reality of the pain that separateness engenders, so that he can make a different decision.

Satan's opposite is Christ. As Christ personifies the eternal light of the divine, so does Satan personify the darkness of evil. All the dualities of our human reality result from this original division between Satan and Christ, darkness and light, evil and good. God is the unifying principle, the Father of it all. And within every human being all three "characters" coexist. At the dualistic level we are both Christ (the universal higher self) and Satan (the universal lower self); the battle between our positive and negative impulses. But beneath it all we are also God, the unitive principle beyond duality.

"Original sin" really means the imperfections inherent in our human nature as a result of the original choice to separate our consciousness from God consciousness. The awareness of original sin is simply awareness of our alienation from the whole. But this is **not** our most basic identity. Our most original nature is divinity; the distortions accrued later. The myth of Adam and Eve's choice to disobey God and follow Satan, thus resulting in expulsion from the primal Garden of Eden, is one way of trying to personify our original choice to leave unitive consciousness.

Christ's incarnation as Jesus marked the turning point in the evolution of our ability to realign with God's purpose—to know that we are already forgiven and totally loved despite the reality of our lower self, the actions of our flawed and partial ego consciousness. Since Jesus Christ showed us the way back to union with God, we are able to choose consciously to participate in the plan of salvation. But in the process we must struggle daily between choosing Christ's way of conscious reunion with God or Satan's way of egocentrism and separation from God.[2]

Non-Christian Perspectives

The same story of original wholeness, separation and reunion can be told in non-Christian, non-personified terms, more compatible with Buddhist cosmology.

> Picture, my friends, a consciousness, a state of being,
> in which there is only bliss and infinite—literally
> infinite—power to create with, through, and by one's
> consciousness. Consciousness thinks and wills, and lo,
> what is thought and willed, is. Life and light can be
> expanded into more and more possibilities. Only in the
> human ego existence are thought and will apparently
> separated from deed and form.
>
> Since the possibilities are endless, consciousness can
> also explore itself by confining itself, by fragmenting
> itself off—to "see what happens," as it were. It experiences itself by contracting instead of expanding.
> Instead of unfolding, it tries out how it feels to draw in;
> instead of exploring further light, it wants to see how it
> is to feel and experience darkness.

---

[2]The Christian allegory is retold by the Guide in Lectures #19-22, whose titles are "Jesus Christ," "God, the Creation," "The Fall," and "Salvation."

There may lie a special fascination and adventure just
to tentatively try out the limitation and fragmentation
of consciousness, to see what darkness, non-awareness
of the whole, would feel like. Then it begins to take on
a power of its own. For everything that is created has
energy invested in it and this energy is self-perpetuating.
It takes on its own momentum. At some point, the
consciousness which has created for so long these
channels and pathways cannot reverse the course.
It gets lost in its own momentum, and has lost touch
with how to recall itself.

At the deepest level, consciousness knows there is no
real danger, for whatever suffering you human beings
feel, it is truly illusory in the ultimate sense. Once
you find your true identity, you will know that. It is
all a play, a fascination, an experiment, from which
your real state of being can and will eventually be
recaptured. (*PGL 175*)

This view of the cosmic drama of separation and reunion
does not talk about evil, but does see the human ego as part of
that consciousness which has separated from the whole. It sug-
gests that we have chosen to explore separation or evil simply
because it exists as a possible choice. All possible choices will
eventually be chosen, just so that the whole of creation can be
explored consciously.

Both Eastern and Western religious perspectives can be distorted. The Eastern emphasis on the benign, unitive level of reality can be distorted into a denial of evil on the human level. And
the Christian drama of the struggle between Christ and Satan,
good and evil, can be exaggerated into a denial of our underlying wholeness and divinity.

The Pathwork Perspective

The Pathwork is simultaneously Eastern and Western, a syn-
thesis of the mystical traditions of both the East and the West,
which emphasize direct experience of self and God. Human life
is seen as a school of purification for the soul, as it journeys
through lifetimes creating and then freeing itself of karma, the
results of our negative, limited self-identifications, and learning
to re-identify with our divine essence.

Evil originates from God's benign willingness to allow aspects of its wholeness to incarnate separately and to explore that separated identity. The split-off fragments become more and more self-aware of their limited condition, with the result that we will all freely choose union again.

> The reality of evil, as manifested on this plane of devel-
> opment, must be accepted by each individual in order
> to learn to cope with it and thus to truly overcome it.
> Evil must be faced and overcome primarily within
> the self. Only then can evil be dealt with outside the
> self. . . . The human consciousness finds itself in a
> state of development where both the pure and the
> distorted, the good and the evil, Christ and the devil,
> exist. It is the task of every human being, on the long
> road of evolution—lifetime upon lifetime—to purify
> the soul and to overcome evil. (*PGL 197*)

It is not important what cosmology or explanation about the origin of evil is embraced. And it does not matter if you believe in reincarnation, or an evolutionary plan of salvation, or any-thing else. What is important is to learn to look within, to face the self truthfully and compassionately. In this way we learn to face our own evil, knowing it is not the ultimate reality, but is divinity in distortion.

In the story of "Albert's Ghosts" which introduced this chapter, I recounted how, in a personal intensive experience at Sevenoaks, Albert had met the feared "badness" of his little boy caught in an incestuous web spun by his immature and neurotic mother. He had felt his shame and his guilt. The sexual entanglement with his mother had been more fully faced and forgiven than ever before in his life.

What lay ahead was to look fully at the negative patterns of the adult man who had, without understanding why, misused women in an effort to avenge the central trauma of his childhood. Albert now needed to make sense of his endless round of affairs, and find out how he could reach for committed love instead of the sexual power games to which he was accustomed.

In time Albert came to see that his attraction for "forbidden" partners arose from the early excitement of the taboo relationship with his mother. Every time his relationship with a woman became "acceptable," as in marriage, he would lose interest.

As Albert explored the incestuous relationship with his mother more fully, he realized that, in addition to feeling shame and a secret desire, he was also very angry at her. She truly had treated him very badly, and he had a right to be angry. Still it was hard for Albert to get angry at Anna, even in fantasy. He had, instead, acted out that anger in his hostility toward other women. He had fallen in love, but had never really given his heart or made a true commitment. He had used his psychological knowledge to feel "one-up," to intimidate and control women.

Albert now needed to face the real adult guilt for his negative behavior with women, to acknowledge his own dark power—his cruelty and his intimidation—to feel the fear and vulnerability they defended, and to seek a new source of power in his capacity to love, not in his desire for revenge.

Albert reported a dream: "I am in the front room of my childhood home and I am frightened and lonely. I desperately need someone to care for and protect me. Then I hear someone enter through the broken back door which I have left open. At first I think it is a man, but it is not really a man; it is a thick black shadow, like an old comic book drawing of a shadow. The shadow is now lurking in the back rooms of the house, and talks to me from that distance. He tells me he has come to protect me, to be the father I am missing. But I do not believe him. I think maybe he is the devil and I wake up frightened that I have let him into my house."

As Albert began to work on the dream, he felt the dark clouds that had haunted him earlier. I suggested we pray. We invoked the presence of Christ and asked His help for Albert to get to the heart of his darkness, to meet what was haunting him. As we waited, I could see the dark energy again swirling around Albert's face.

I suggested he speak as the "shadow" character of his dream. Albert began, "I am your darkness. I entered through the back door, the broken heart of your shattered childhood. You invited me to protect you and now you are mine. I will scare you and make you do my bidding. I am committed to revenge and hatred. I will never give up. I will possess and destroy every woman I can."

As he spoke, Albert's face changed. His usual smile was replaced by a leer; his shoulders became tense and hunched, his jaw determined. The dark power was revealing itself through Albert's body.

"Feel your body now Albert," I suggested. "Can you feel the demon within you?"

Albert's shoulders slumped and his jaw went slack. "I can feel it," he answered, "but I reject it."

I encouraged him further, "This is a wonderful opportunity, Albert. You have the chance now to meet the demon who has haunted you for years. This is the darkness you chose as a defense against your childhood pain. But now you can make a different choice. If you reject it, the demon will go underground again. If you accept it, you can change it."

Albert was uncertain. "I don't see what good will come from this. I don't have much faith right now. I don't want to do this. I'm scared."

I leaned forward and held Albert's hands. "Feel my hands, feel my faith, Albert," I urged him. "Remember that Christ is with us to help you go toward what scares you. Go, Albert, go and meet the darkness. This is the place where you long ago committed to revenge instead of love. It is a great step that you can see it so clearly."

"It's hard," Albert winced, "to accept that this demon is really me, that I chose him. But I know that he is the cause of all my distress. I guess I'd better get to know him better if I'm ever going to get him off my back. It's hard to know he is me and yet believe I am not all bad and unredeemable."

"You are not all bad, Albert," I reminded him. "Remember that every human being is both bad and good. And remember that in Christ you are forgiven. Your badness is only a temporary state, and a part of your humanness, your misguided attempt to protect yourself from the pain of your terribly lonely childhood. When you meet this demon, you can transform it. What you are doing now is holy work, heroic work. You can do it, Albert," I reassured him, "You can meet your shadow."

Even as I was finishing my words, Albert dropped my hands, and his posture started to rigidify. He threw his shoulders back and stiffened his jaw. "I will never be hurt again," he said defiantly. "I will be in charge from now on. I will do whatever it takes to put those bitches in their place. Mine is the power and glory. I will share it with no one."

"That's it, Albert," I said quietly, "That's the lower self."

Albert looked at me with scorn and contempt. I met his hard gaze with love and acceptance. I looked deep into his eyes, past his hatred and fear, and into his hidden vulnerability. Slowly Albert's eyes softened, his body relaxed, and he began to weep.

Exercises for Chapter 7:

In all these exercises, remember to invoke the presence of the benign, objective observer who can record all aspects of the self with truth and compassion, with gentle love for the self. After you have completed writing out Part I, which helps you to meet some part of your lower self, then do Part II in which you are asked to see if you can become aware of the pure energy behind your lower self. You can write out Part II or complete it in silent meditative inquiry.

1. Part I: Write out several dreams that you have had that include lower self characters or some aspects of your "lower-self land." Or find such characters in your daydreams or in movies or real-life events—evil characters that you are in some way drawn to. Create a full-scale description of one or more of these characters. Then create a dialogue between your normal ego-self and this (these) character(s) further exploring: Who are you? How did you get this way? What do you want? What do you really want?

Part II: In choosing a lower-self character, see if you can divorce the negativity from the "pure" expression of power, or charisma, or sexiness which attracts you to this character. What part of yourself, distorted in this lower self character, might you need to claim more fully in its pure form? In an affirmation, claim your desire to have the energy and let go of the distortions.

2. Part I: Explore your sexual fantasies for elements of sadism or masochism. Without judgment, simply acknowledge what turns you on. Write out a sexual fantasy and then relate the content of the fantasy to a current life problem, sexual or otherwise.

Part II: In exploring your sexual fantasies, again see if you can imagine separating your sadism or masochism from your sexuality, and letting go only of the negative distortions, but not of the essential sexual energy.

3. Part I: Choose a relationship in your life in which you are aware of disharmony. Find and acknowledge in yourself negative attitudes that contribute to the disharmony—judgments, hostility, competitiveness, greed, fear. For the moment, entirely let go of all your justifications and reasons, your cases against the other

person. Write out clearly only what is your negativity and how it creates negative energy in the relationship.

Part II: After understanding your negative contribution to a disharmonious relationship, find and affirm your commitment to the truth of this relationship underneath the distortions which currently manifest between you.

4. Part I: Explore your pride, self-will, and fear. Make one true statement from each of these places in yourself. Then decide which of these three lower-self qualities is dominant for you. Relate your dominant lower-self quality to the dominant mask you wear.

Part II: Find and claim the higher-self expression behind your dominant lower-self defense. For example, is your pride covering a need to claim your true worth and dignity? See if you can feel the potential for transformation of your major lower-self defense into its hidden higher-self quality.

CHAPTER 8

Meeting the Higher Self

"He who consciously and deliberately makes the decision
and commits himself to living his life for the primary
purpose of activating the real, or higher self,
he alone can find genuine peace."

—Pathwork Guide Lecture 145, *"The Call of the Life Stream and Response to It"*

Susan's Heart: Opening to the Higher Self

The old deacon walks slowly to the pulpit of Shiloh Baptist Church, leans over to the microphone, bows his head, and starts to pray. Behind him sit the choir members, mostly women, mostly dressed in lavender, who a few minutes before had entered the congregation swaying and clapping as they sang. On the white-washed wall behind them hangs a large vivid portrayal of the Last Supper, bright colors on black velvet.

"I thank you, God, for my waking up this morning, in a clean bed in a dry house, for this body still breathing, still able to walk out the bedroom to the kitchen. I give thanks, dear Jesus, that I have food for breakfast, and a family to eat with." Tears start down my cheeks as I feel bathed by the rich well of gratitude that fills this man whom others, seeing only through economic eyes, might label impoverished.

But as I try to pray my own thanks to God, I feel a lump in my throat, and a tight band of grief around my heart. By all outward indicators, I am doing fine, but my spirit is weak and my gratitude is not forthcoming. I feel needy for God's grace, spiritually depleted. I am deeply disappointed that my vision for a residential spiritual community at Sevenoaks, where I live, is not manifesting. I do not understand why. Am I doing something wrong or do I need to surrender my will to some as yet unknown plan God has for our center? I need help.

I bow my head more deeply in prayer. Feeling my heart beat, my breathing deepen, I remember my dream about another old black man, similarly filled with Spirit, who has taught and guided me for almost thirty years. He first came to me in 1964 when I dreamed that I was a serene, deeply spiritual black man who had, some years before the time of the dream, witnessed his son being lynched by an angry mob of white men. My dream came at the height of the civil rights struggle with which I felt deeply identified. In therapy at that time I re-experienced the outrage and sense of helplessness this man's story evoked in me. After the burst of feelings in my therapy session, I asked the man of my dream how he could be so calm, so accepting of this horror. He told me that he had been graced by an experience of forgiveness which transcended understanding, which held every outrage in its arms, soothed every hurt, opened the heart to a peace beyond pain. I understood that it had something to do with opening to Christ, to the healing power of Love. At the time anything Christian was anathema to me, so I could only partly understand what he was trying to convey. But I did know then that this man was my inner teacher, and also that in some way I did not understand, he also was me. I first entertained the possibility of past lives as a result of this dream, even though reincarnation was a foreign concept to me at that time.

As the choir members of Shiloh Baptist Church sing their love of Jesus, sometimes softly, sometimes passionately, I reflect on my own complex relationship with the entity of Jesus Christ. Christ has become real for me in the years since I was a rebel against the pathetic emptiness of the Protestant church in which I was raised. He is the embodiment of the Love Force, a universal power of the heart to move and open and care for others, and to forgive and bear all manner of pain and travail. He is not, for me, limited to the Jesus of the Bible stories, and he is certainly not the person St. Paul and others made into the spokesman for a harshly dualistic and moralistic religion which has done such evil in his name. He is, instead, a light-filled Presence which, at those times when I am open to his love, brings me home to my deepest self. The Buddhist descriptions of the bodhisattvas of compassion perhaps come close to describing my Christ experiences. Since I experience Christ as the universal power of Divine Love, I cannot identify with any one church, and am today visiting Shiloh Baptist for the first time. All these reflections tumble around in my head as the service continues.

Rev. John Franklin, the pastor, comes to the microphone in his heavy black and red robes. He pleads with us to accept the gift of Jesus Christ into our hearts. The bright sweat glistens on his dark cheeks, especially after he grabs the microphone from its stand, paces up and down the raised pulpit platform, shouting and pleading, and in between the torrent of words, dabbing his face with his handkerchief. In an exhortation that might have been addressed to me, he queries, "Do you think you have to save people, make the world a better place, fix up this broken society? Do you think you have to be the savior?" His voice fills with scorn for the sheer audacity of such an inflated idea, a calling with which I do indeed identify. And then he pauses, the air still full of the question. His voice comes back, only now with the sweetest lilt, "You don't have to do that. You know why? It's already been done!" he proclaims triumphantly. Rev. Franklin's voice rises in intensity, "The savior has already come! All you need to do is let him into your heart." His voice comes to a crescendo of passionate entreaty, "Accept that your salvation has already been earned by the sacrifice of Jesus Christ on the cross! You don't have to do anything. Just accept Him as your Lord and Savior!"

My mind goes back to 1980, riding the train, all day, from London to Scotland, en route to Findhorn community where I would be meeting my husband Donovan. I had arrived in London the day before with a terrible headache, an unbearably tense body and an anxious, uptight mind to match. My spiritual teacher, Eva Pierrakos, was dead, and I feared that the Pathwork, which had been my whole life for eight years by then, was falling apart. I felt deeply self-doubting and uncentered; all I could do was pray. I prayed to know my spiritual self more deeply, and to find how I was meant to serve God. My prayers went on all through that night, just below the threshold of my conscious mind, as I thrashed around in an unfamiliar bed.

I felt exhausted when I boarded the train the next morning, but found my mind still engaged with my ongoing prayer. As I meditated and sank more fully into myself on the train, I saw another version of myself in a forbidding black nun's habit, on my knees in a cold stone medieval monastery, trying to learn what it meant to be a bride of Christ, to devote my life to His service. "My Lord and Master," I kept repeating to myself, as tears of yearning sprang to my eyes, and the English landscape blurred outside the train window. In that lifetime as a nun, I had left a very comfortable outer life to enter the search for the spirit within, to find and serve God. In spite of my failings, I knew I had, in that and many other lifetimes, surrendered to Christ, made the hard moral choices as best I understood them, and become convinced that the state of purity of my immortal soul, especially at the moment of death, was more important to me than any worldly accomplishment. At that moment on the train, I again knew Christ as my eternal "Lord and Master," the only guru I would ever need. The sense of His presence filled me; my mind and body at last relaxed so that I could enjoy the beauty of the passing English countryside.

About an hour later I became agitated again and heard a voice inside my head pressing for recognition. "I would speak with you," it said. And so I took out pen and paper and wrote down its words. "It is no longer enough to remember me as your Lord and Master. That is old, familiar. What you are called to do now is to **be me**. You are to embody the Love Force as it flows through you, just as it was my job to do that. Many will now be called to this task. This is the true meaning of the Second Coming. As more people awaken to their inner grounding in love, and come to know love as their true identity, the manifestation of love will spread throughout the world."

I felt nervous on hearing these words. "Who am I?" I protested to this voice, "I don't recognize myself in such an exalted identity. I only know deeply my flaws and distortions, my uptightness and lack of faith, my fears and compensatory controllingness. You are asking too much of me," I said fearfully. "Are you sure you're talking to the right person?" Even I could laugh at that. I knew that there was nothing being said that was meant to appeal to my pride nor of which I need be afraid; I was simply being invited to assent more deeply to an identification with my higher self, my inner Christ. To the best of my ability then, I said "yes" to that call. A suffusion of warmth, both sensual and spiritual, filled my body, and the landscape from there to Findhorn glowed, exuding the same inner light I had just found in myself.

Coming back from my reverie, I watch Rev. Franklin up at the pulpit, getting very excited as he is preaching about letting go, giving over to Jesus Christ. "Stop thinking you've got all the answers. Turn it all, all over to Jesus." I feel the area around my heart begin to warm up and start to ache. I feel a wave of pain now, as I struggle to let go of my cherished dreams for Sevenoaks, and to give it over to God. Letting go is never easy, and I am quietly crying now as I pray to release my fantasies of the future and allow the fullness of each moment, just as it is.

I watch Rev. Franklin's dark brown hands waving in the air, his strong arm muscles visible as the robe's sleeves fall back. I am moved by seeing all that masculine power being engaged in service to Love. Rev. Franklin, in his power and his dignity, reminds me of another past life experience in which I remembered myself as an African prince taken into slavery; a man sorely tempted to seek revenge on his masters but who, instead, maintained his moral integrity and sustained his capacity to love, even in the midst of a life of degradation and brutality.

This being is also me, an aspect of my animus, another personification of my higher self. He is alive in me now as I sit in this church in rural Virginia. He lives in me, as me, and is especially reassuring to me now, as my self-doubts as a spiritual teacher have been stirred again by my recent disappointments. I hear his voice gently reminding me, "Remember who you are." Yes, I assent, finding a new dignity entering me as my posture straightens ever so slightly. I am this young African prince of immense composure and great moral stature, even as I am also an anxious middle-aged white woman, struggling and uncertain as I try to discover what is right for my beloved Sevenoaks Pathwork community.

Rev. Franklin's preaching is over now; the clapping and shouts of "Hallelujah" and "Praise the Lord" are subsiding. Then he asks a woman from the congregation to come up and sing. She is big, with a huge squared-off chest, and she moves slowly to the microphone. Her voice is unexpectedly heavenly. Full-throated, yet immensely gentle, her singing pierces my heart and I again begin to cry. "I surrender," she sings, "I surrender all to you, my Lord." I bow my head and assent as fully as I can to my own surrender, letting go of the plans and designs of the little ego, fully releasing both disappointments of the past and ideas for the future. I hand it all over to God, to the mysterious yet immensely trustworthy design of the universe, which moves through me, as me, and yet is also *so much larger and more intelligent than the separate me I so often, and so mistakenly, identify with.*

My arms begin to feel very heavy, even as my heart is beating louder and stronger. I feel the pulsations of heartbeat intensify and extend all the way to the periphery of my body. I sense an immense internal pressure, as if the walls of my heart were being pushed out, enlarged, from the inside out, to make more room for something within me. Some larger divine presence, some Spirit, seeks to expand its lodging here. I do not consciously initiate this welling-up from within and yet it requires my assent. I sense that I could stop this involuntary movement if I tried, but instead I keep praying to align with what feels like a regeneration, a spontaneous expansion of my heart's capacity to feel and know God. I pray to release whatever in me restricts the free movement of the Power of Love to direct my life.

By the time the benediction is sung, the wave has passed and I feel a little more normal. My chest is aching, but it feels good—larger, with more empty space around my heart. I find I can tune in to this empty spaciousness and hear its messages. Mostly it is a non-verbal sweetness, a reassurance that all is well, all is very well. But there is also a message for me about pain, about not taking it too seriously, letting it flow without attachment, and especially about not trying to save others from their own pain, their own karma, which each must work out for him/herself. "You will learn," I hear, "to bear the pain you feel from others without having to do anything about it, without trying to change what cannot be changed except from inside of each human being. You will learn to dwell in the bliss of Love as the central unifying reality behind the apparent fragmentation of outer life." Thus the voice of my higher self speaks to me. My faith flows sweetly in me at this moment.

As the service concludes, I shake the warm, friendly hands of many who come to welcome me and urge me to share again their religious service. I give Rev. Franklin a big hug and head toward my car, still a little unsteady, but with immense fullness and gratitude for the continuing guidance of the Spirit of Love in my life.

Meeting the Higher Self

We all have moments in which we contact a deeper reality, when we feel especially expanded, centered, clear, compassionate, or connected. Such moments may occur while being in nature, making love, creating music or art, sitting in meditation, connecting to dreams, waking from a restful sleep, or even sitting in church or synagogue. We glimpse a larger version of ourselves, an expanded state of consciousness, an essence that is continuous with universal spiritual energy, a window into the cosmos. We hear the still, small voice within. We sense the presence of God within us.

In my experience, the higher self often presents itself to our awareness through personification of our inner divinity in the form of angelic or archetypal presences. The higher self may come to us personified as a figure in our dreams or inner journeys; it may speak in the voice of a guru, or appear as an animal ally, a god or goddess, or as an angel or Christ figure. Sometimes it is simply a wordless, peaceful silence that holds all experience in its depth. Such peak experiences reveal the existence of our personal divinity, our soul's essence, our higher self.

What is the Higher Self?

The higher self is our personal embodiment of and connection to the universal spirit that moves through all things. Meeting the higher self is an experience of ourselves as filled and flowing with spirit, the life force, or God. It is an experience usually accompanied by relief, as we feel we are coming home to our true identity, remembering who we really are. The parts of ourselves that have forgotten and are lost in separated ego, wounded child, or revengeful demon, are temporarily soothed, put into perspective, as we know ourselves to be larger and essentially whole, securely connected to the enduring consciousness of the earth and to the benign pulsation of life in the universe. In this expanded identity we find our center and ground.

The higher self exists at many levels of consciousness. It is a continuum that begins at the ego level and broadens, deepens, and expands into the transpersonal levels of awareness and to the unitive experience of God. Knowing our true identity as the higher self can begin with claiming those positive aspects of our personality which are aligned with truth, love, serenity, or beauty. Even when much of the personality lives in distortion, there is always some place, some moment, where the light of God shines through and we experience unity and harmony. We may express our personal divine "ray" in an area of artistic talent, or in a compassionate way of being with children, or in our integrity at work, or in our love of trees. However fleeting, these moments of awakening to the best in us can connect us to our deeper essence.

When we begin to work on ourselves, we awaken to the truthful and compassionate observer self, which is an expression of the higher self at the level of the positive ego. We can know the higher self at the level of the body as the pleasurable flow of energy, as the breath and blood which pulsate with divinely inspired, universal rhythms of life.

In a moment of intimacy with another person we can know that we are but a single expression of the one universal human consciousness. In ceremonies and worship services, we can know all humans as our brothers and sisters.

Often we can feel our oneness with non-human life while in nature. At such moments we may experience ourselves as but one expression of the universal Spirit of Earth, the Goddess worshipped in ancient times who calls out to us again to connect with the earth in a sacred manner. In meditation or moments of deep inspiration we can we know our higher self essence as archetypal beings of wisdom, love, serenity or beauty.

At a deeper level still, the sense of a separate higher self dissolves into unitive or cosmic consciousness where all separate identities disappear into the One.

The Experience of the Higher Self

Experiences of the higher self at any level, especially that of ultimate God-consciousness, permanently alter our understanding of reality and of our own identity. However, such moments of enlightenment do not remove the mask and the lower self.

> Many movements exist which have practices and teachings that help actively and effectively toward the end of bringing the inner divine potential into reality. . . . However, this does not necessarily mean that the other fragmentary levels of consciousness are thereby automatically eliminated and incorporated into the divine center. Often such practices genuinely bring out the real, higher self, yet leave the undeveloped aspects of consciousness intact. Many entities have such an intense longing to realize their divine, inherent nature that they forget, while in the body, that they came to fulfill a mission in the universal plan. This mission is the purification and growth of undeveloped "cosmic

matter." In order to do this, the light of conscious awareness and experience must be shed on the inner distortions, the ugliness, the darkness, the evil, the suffering, as well as on the inner truth, the beauty, the love, the goodness, the joy.

It requires a fine sensitivity, so that the organic rhythm and alternation that each individual path needs can be perceived: to know when to concentrate on the higher self, so as to strengthen its staying power and to make it possible for it to give further guidance; when to pay attention to the lower self with its hidden evil, its dishonesty and cheating, its camouflaged hate and malice; when to focus on the specific devices of the mask self and what defenses it uses to keep the lower self hidden. (*PGL 193*)

The spiritual path requires that we get to know intimately both the higher and lower self, which we can find within us, and which manifest in our life experience.

The Higher Self and the Lower Self

The higher self and the lower self are both creative, pro-active, centers of our consciousness. Both the higher and the lower selves are much more real and energized than is the mask. The mask is not creative, only reactive. Since its principal function is to cover over and deny the deepest fears and longings in our soul, it does not contain much vital energy; instead, it drains our energy.

All our life experiences are a creative manifestation of our higher and lower self energies which create our lives in opposite directions. The higher self leads us toward our divine center and the lower self leads us away, toward a false identification with our defenses, our separatist ego, and our unconscious demons.

An in-depth encounter with either the lower or the higher self will leave us permanently changed. We can no longer deny the presence of either evil or God within. The lower and higher selves make contrary claims on our souls. They represent the archetypal split or soul conflict in every human heart—the dualistic tension between our longing for God and our identification with the ego, our desire to do the right thing and our attraction to evil, our intention to unite and our will to separate, our desire to love and our fear of loving.

When we do the work of transforming the lower self, the energy that is released gives us a stronger connection with the higher self.

Joe had been working hard on his lower self, especially on that part of him which undermined his love for his wife. He had faced his violent need always to be right and superior, which kept him separate from her and frightened of surrendering to love. Just before going to sleep one night, Joe decided it was time to "bury" his fierce attachment to his differences with his wife, and instead seek his potential for loving union. He had the following dream:

"My wife and I have a dog which starts digging at the foot of a bush. Digging frantically, the dog uncovers a dead man's hand. I think, 'It's that guy we buried earlier.' When we get closer we discover that there is only a thin film of dirt over the hole, and the dirt is moving as though with the breath of a person buried beneath. I am freaked out that this person might have been buried alive. But then it appears that the 'breathing man' is an illusion, because when I look again the hole is empty. My wife and I are both astonished and filled with awe, recognizing that we are witnessing a kind of resurrection.

"As I look around, I realize we are in the yard of my family farm. Looking up in the sky, we see a huge barge, a flat-bottomed ark, cruising through the sky, with birds flying around on the bottom of the ark. On second viewing, I see a side view, like a building, with unfinished beams— a floating church in the sky. People are laughing and walking around on the deck. Even though the ark is tumbling like a space ship, they appear content and secure. I feel very joyful and my wife and I start laughing with a deep pleasure in sharing this vision."

Joe awoke feeling light-hearted and happy, knowing his higher self had indeed been resurrected from the burial of his lower self, and was giving him a vision of a happier, more loving life, on an "ark of safety."

Since the higher self encompasses a much larger reality than the lower self, its creative power is more enduring. The lower self is finite, an expression of limited, dualistic human consciousness, whereas the personal higher self expands beyond the human to the infinite, beyond all personal limitations to the All-Consciousness of God. The higher self, which partakes of the infinite, is thus the most expansive part of our identity. It is who we most truly are.

Denial and Shame of the Higher Self

Because we feel vulnerable when we go beyond the known confines of our usual identity, we resist claiming our higher selves just as we resist admitting our lower selves. We may reject our own compassion and wisdom just as fervently as we deny our darkness and cruelty. We all develop and then identify with our mask to avoid our inner extremes. But the inner journey requires that we penetrate the mask to reveal both the highs and lows of our total reality.

Shame of the higher self results from the childhood experience of having one's loving, sexual, assertive, spontaneous, or generous impulses rejected, abused, or subtly ridiculed by the parents and other authority figures. The child is often made to feel inferior or ashamed of her best qualities. When we choose to work on recovering the best in us, we commit to uncovering the innocent inner child who was rejected for the spontaneous expressions of her higher as well as her lower impulses. We must be willing to go through the temporary barriers of fear and shame, and feel the pain and anger at having had the best and most vulnerable parts of us rejected by parental authorities.

We also begin to understand that we have internalized parental voices of oppression, creating our own self-repression. Identifying with these parental judgments, we betray our own vulnerable love and longing, and judge others who show similar "weaknesses." As adults, our suffering is the result of our internal oppression, which can be reversed as we learn to replace the inner critical parent with an inner loving parent.

Often a child perceives one parent as more loving and accepting than the other, simultaneously feeling more rejected by the less loving parent. Working harder to "win" the love of the rejecting parent, the child begins to take for granted the other adult's "easier" love. Eventually, the child tends to betray or scorn the loving parent while seeking compulsively after the rejecting one. From such a pattern arises the common misconception that the qualities of loving and caring are weak and undesirable, whereas aloofness and distance are valuable and desirable. The child may grow ashamed of her spontaneous, loving nature.

Until we understand such origins of the shame of our higher self, we will be weighed down with conflict about loving. Since our love was apparently rejected in childhood, loving can seem a dangerous path in adulthood. The betrayal we felt when our innocent, spontaneous love was rejected is further aggravated by our subsequent rejection of the more loving parent, thus adding guilt on top of our grief about not having been loved. The feeling of hopelessness about love is then further intensified by our rejection of our own loving nature. This self-betrayal is the most painful.

> This betrayal weighs you down with guilt. It is the deepest of your guilts. . . . and is responsible for the deepest roots of your inferiority feelings. You do not trust yourself with this betrayal locked in your soul. Your psyche says, "How can I trust myself knowing that I am a traitor, knowing that I go on constantly betraying the best in me? If I cannot trust myself, I cannot trust anyone else." (PGL 66)

Ronald had few male friends and found it exceedingly difficult to express his need for friendship. He rarely showed his vulnerability around men, even though he knew this was the only way he could gain the level of friendship he longed for.

Ronald had been raised by a bitter, cold woman who controlled her husband through rejection of his affection and taught her son to do the same. When Ronald's father would scoop up his little boy for a hug, his mother would show contempt for them both. Whenever Ronald cried or expressed a need for his father, his mother would call him a sissy. Later, when Ronald's father would invite him to ballgames and Ronald would say "No!" his mother would compliment his independence. Gradually his father stopped seeking contact with his son, and Ronald was left alone with his mother who gave him little warmth.

Only as an adult did Ronald realize that he had rejected his father's warmth by choosing to emulate the cold pseudo-strength (the power mask) of his mother instead. Ronald had to work very hard at opening his heart with men because he had shut it down so early.

The Higher Self and the Mask

The mask hides and disguises both the higher and lower selves. When we have been made to feel ashamed of our need and love, we may hide them behind a mask of power, expressing pseudo-strength in our rejection of others. Or we may create a serenity mask, expressing pseudo-detachment in our aloofness and withdrawal from life. When we have been made to feel ashamed of our power or anger, we may hide behind a love mask of pleasing others. Or we may create a love mask to overdramatize our affections because we are ashamed to show our simple real need to love and be loved.

Exploring the character flaws in the adult personality will reveal roots in childhood shame. Someone with a love mask will be deeply ashamed of their personal power and effectiveness, as if that were somehow "not nice." Someone with a power mask is more apt to be ashamed of his love and need, and to see them as a weakness. The person with a mask of serenity is usually powerfully ashamed of any strong feelings and passions which would expose him again to his childhood vulnerability.

But the mask will often also show our real higher-self strengths in distorted or caricatured form. Beneath the love mask is a strong connection with true loving feelings. Beneath the power mask is a genuine desire to be effective and responsible in the world. And beneath the serenity mask is a profound ability to detach from personal melodramas. The mask results when our innate higher self qualities are covered over by fear and shame.

> In all cases, you have to remove this layer of the
> mask and look where your real self is. Allow it to step
> out, even if at the beginning it does so only on rare
> occasions, ever so cautiously. But then the real You
> will see that you really do not have to fear, you do not
> have to be ashamed. The fear comes mostly as a conse-
> quence of the shame of exposure. By this process you
> will remove the phantom world you have created out
> of the false impressions of your childhood. You have
> no idea what a tremendous relief it is to remove this
> phantom world and live in reality. You will live in
> freedom, you will find it is no longer necessary to
> betray the best in you or in another. (*PGL 66*)

What the Higher Self is Not

The higher self is the expression of God within, whether experienced on the personality level as an openness to love and truth, on the transpersonal level as the inner teacher, spirit guides, or the immortal Soul, or on the unitive level as cosmic consciousness. The higher self is by nature moral as well as pleasurable. However, the higher self is never moralistic or perfectionistic. Those are qualities of the mask or superimposed conscience—the idealized self—not the natural or innate higher self. We need to learn the difference between our true higher self and the false impostor.

Martha asked for a dream of guidance from her higher self, and received the following: "I am driving a car with three people in the back seat. One is a happy, sexy man who is reaching out to a beautiful woman sitting beside him. The third person is an old woman who looks disapprovingly toward the other two." Martha could recognize the sensual couple as spirit guides encouraging her to enjoy life and sexuality more fully, but she could not identify the third person.

In a subsequent Pathwork session on whether or not to take on a major new responsibility in her already crowded life, her helper asked her to sit on a pillow representing her higher self and see what guidance it had for her. She immediately spoke, "Of course you should take on this job. It would be a good thing to do and you should do it. The only reason you won't do it is because you are lazy and irresponsible."

I stopped her. "Martha, that is not your higher self. The higher self never says 'should.' It always gives you options and respects your free will. It also always loves you and doesn't put you down like that voice did. Who is the voice that you are confusing with your higher self?"

"I think it must be my grandmother," Martha responded. "My grandmother was the one who sent me to Sunday school and was always reading the Bible to me and telling me what I should and should not do. She preached at me all the time."

Only later did Martha realize that the third figure in the car in her dream was her grandmother. She was symbolic of Martha's distortion of her higher self: a judgmental, moralistic, bitter old woman. By confronting this image falsely posing as her higher self, she came closer to her inner truth.

The higher self may sometimes offer confrontive guidance to us, saying "no" to something the little ego greatly desires, or directing us to undertake difficult and challenging tasks. But it always does so with respect and love for the total self. The higher self always offers us choices while helping us to grasp the consequences of our negative choices. The higher self may lead us into the strictest of self-disciplines, but never does it deprive us of positive pleasure in life.

We must learn to distinguish the voice of the superimposed conscience from the voice of the true conscience, to let go of the mask of good appearances while affirming the true desire to serve others, to release all the outer "shoulds" and "musts" of the perfectionistic mask and instead to find the truth within.

The Emanations of the Three Selves

The three realms that we embody—the mask self, the lower self, and the higher self—each send forth different emanations. These emanations are in the form of colors, smells, and feeling tones on the vibratory level. They are not normally visible, except to those who have a psychic sensitivity. But we all instinctively respond to these emanations, and we can learn to tune in to the qualities of the different selves.

> It is important for all of you to try to train your inner
> eye to see yourselves and others from the spiritual point
> of view. You will feel when you come in contact with
> the higher self a very distinct difference from the mask
> self, once your intuition has awakened, even if the
> outer experience may sometimes be similar. (*PGL 14*)

The vibrations of the higher self are always pleasurable, reassuring, and real. In their presence we feel a quickening of life energies; we feel invigorated and renewed. The quality of higher-self energy is of relaxed activity, harmonious movement, a trusting and loving attitude, ease and self-assurance. The colors of higher self emanations are pure and clean, whether bright or subdued in hue.

By contrast, the emanations of active lower-self energy are jagged and sharp, usually lacerating and painful. Or, if the lower self is expressed through passivity or dependency, its emanations have a gluey, life-denying, stagnant quality. The colors are usually dark and sinister. However painful, the vibrations of the lower self often feel like a relief in contrast to those of the mask which are consistently unpleasant.

> The mask self presents a very ugly color, often sickly
> sweetish, and its odor is also sickly and nauseating.

192 THE UNDEFENDED SELF

> We in the spirit world even prefer the emanations and
> effects of the lower self, unpleasant as these may be,
> but at least the lower self is honest. (*PGL 14*)

The mask self obscures the light in a way that is more indirect and harder to detect than the lower self. The mask often utters half-truths, or apparent truths, where the content of the words sounds good but we sense there is something wrong. This is a crucial sensitivity to develop, because evil cannot thrive in the political or personal world unless we blind ourselves to the real energy behind the "sugar-coated" words and promises. The double-talk of those attempting to justify racism, sexism, child abuse, or even genocide may be sprinkled with references to "Christ," a "higher good," or "the will of God." Thus is truth perverted and love distorted to obfuscate evil intentions. To recognize evil for what it is, in ourselves and in others, we must expose the falsity of the mask. To do this we must develop a trustworthy perception of the intentions and emanations behind verbal expressions.

Children usually respond immediately to the underlying vibrations, because their innate sensitivity has not been dulled by the over-development of the rational verbal mind. A child will instinctively shy away from a relative who approaches with sweet words but with a perverse or hostile intent.

Talk coming from the mask often confuses us. We vaguely sense when others are not "practicing what they preach," especially when exhortations about a higher purpose seem intent on making us feel bad or inadequate, or promoting some cause or cult or person as superior to us. The uncertainty we feel in such cases needs to be trusted, for the higher self will never promote doubt about our innate goodness. Even though God is beyond rational understanding, an experience of the higher self does not leave us feeling confused. It makes us feel good and empowered to be in the presence of the benign reality of our divine nature.

As we learn more about the way these three selves express themselves in us, we will also develop a sensitivity to the real intent behind the words of others. As we learn to recognize the half-truths and rationalizations of our mask, we will not be led astray by others. As we learn to sense our own buried lower-self motives behind our stated intentions, we will become much more attuned to the truth or falsity of others' intentions. As we develop our own integrity, being willing to stand firmly in our own truth, we will be more sensitive to whether or not others speak the truth.

What Is God?

In the last chapter, on the lower self, we asked "What is evil? What is the essence of the negativity that manifests in each human being as the personal lower self?" So now we need to ask "What is God? What is the core of that divine energy that reveals itself in the personal higher self?" While we recognize that any answer is only partial, we deepen our understanding by exploring the question.

God is the essential life-force, the creative movement of energy, the spirit that moves through all things. God exists as the finest vibratory movement of the universe, an energy or force field finer than can be measured. This force is constantly moving, changing, proliferating, even evolving, becoming more and more known to itself, more and more conscious.

God is also the space through which energy moves, the background and ground of all being, beyond movement. We can approach God when we become as still, alert, and relaxed as possible, in both mind and body, and listen to the play of energy/consciousness within which animates us.

God is bliss, intensity, now-ness, infinity, totality, reality. We come closest to God-experience when we are nakedly, vulnerably real, openly accepting, fully present.

God is love, moving in patterns of greater and greater inclusion and awakening, moving in ways that assure the reunion of everything that has ever split its awareness off from knowing its oneness with the source. In human life divine love shows itself in the laws of karma, the operation of cause and effect, through which we learn what in us causes pain and what leads to love. We come closest to God when we surrender to spiritual law, that profound love which directs our lives back to the source.

At our core we humans are one with this limitless essence of all life. The life force at our core never dies; it just constantly changes form in an infinitely creative movement. It breathes, moves, vibrates through us, as us.

> Every individual consciousness is universal consciousness. It would not be correct to state that it is a part of

> it, for a part implies it is only a little of it, a fragment of a whole. But wherever consciousness exists at all, it is all of original consciousness. This original consciousness, the creative Life Principle, individualizes itself in varied forms. When individualization passes a certain point and progresses beyond the state when it knows its connection with its origin, a disconnection comes into existence. Thus consciousness continues to exist and to contain the possibilities of Universal Consciousness, but it is oblivious of its own nature, its laws, and its potentials. This is, in short, the state of human consciousness as a whole.
>
> When you begin to become aware of the Life Principle's ever-present nature, you discover that it has always been there but that you have not noticed it because you were under the illusion of your separate existence. . . . You may begin to notice its ever-present power as autonomous consciousness or as energy. The separated ego-personality possesses both; but the ego intelligence is by far inferior to the Universal Intelligence you potentially are, whether or not you realize and utilize it. (*PGL 152*)

God embraces all dualities, including good and evil, male and female, light and dark, life and death, and all the realms of experience and archetypal figures which represent those dualities. Evil is merely a distortion of the life force, not a force with equal power of its own. Similarly, death is not the opposite of life, since death is only a temporary, transitional stage for the one life force which goes on beyond the cessation of any single life form. Since our human consciousness is so steeped in duality, it is hard for us to conceive of a reality beyond duality—a life that does not die, a goodness that cannot be vanquished by evil. But such is the unitive reality underlying all appearances. Such is God.

The Higher Self as Cosmic Consciousness

To experience the higher self in its totality is to know God. When we fully identify with the place in which we are flowing with divine energy, we can experience total love and total bliss, even if only momentarily. We start by contacting this feeling in those areas where we are already open, and we gradually build the capacity to sustain the good feelings.

We all believe we are most afraid of pain, but actually pain is much easier to sustain than bliss. Bliss, the All-Consciousness, is more threatening to our idea of who we think we are. It shatters our isolated sense of self; it is a shock to our usual expectations. It breaks through all our negative and limiting beliefs about ourselves and others. So we must slowly open ourselves to more and more of the good within and around us, in order to learn to build and sustain our capacity for bliss.

Eventually we may experience what the Guide calls "the cosmic feeling" or others have called "cosmic consciousness."[1] This is the experience of the unitive level of God, where all dualities are resolved.

> The cosmic feeling is an experience that no longer splits off feeling from thinking. The experience of oneness is total. It is an experience of bliss, the comprehension of life and its mysteries, all-encompassing love, a knowledge that **all is well and there is nothing to fear**. The total absence of fear is something that is very hard to visualize for the average human person because you are partly unaware of the existing fears and partly so used to life with them that it does not occur to you that life could be otherwise. . . .
>
> In the state of the cosmic feeling you experience the immediacy of the presence of God within. The immediacy of this incredibly powerful presence is at first shocking. The good feeling is shocking. It is as if literally an electric shock went through your entire system. Therefore the ego-personality has to grow sufficiently strong and healthy so that it can acclimatize itself to the high vibrations of the inner presence of God manifesting in the outer person. This manifestation is then experienced as your eternal reality and state, as your true identity. The moment you find yourself in this state you will know in a most profound way that you have always known what you now rediscover, that you have always been what you now experience yourself to be—that none of this is really new; you had only temporarily cut yourself off

---

1 For personal descriptions of the state of cosmic consciousness, the reader is referred to Richard Bucke's book, *Cosmic Consciousness*.

> from this state of feeling and knowing, of experienc-
> ing and perceiving life as it really is. (*PGL 200*)

While the direct experience of God—cosmic consciousness—is a desired result of our spiritual work, it is a gift of grace that cannot be forced. As we keep seeking God, we will gradually remove the obstructions to our vision of ultimate reality.

The Higher Self and the God Image

When we first try to make contact with God within, we will instead be confronted with our limitations and misconceptions, our images of God. Since we have all been taught that God is the supreme authority, our images of God are distorted in whatever direction our early childhood experiences with authority were distorted. If we experienced authority as punitive, we will expect a harsh, judgmental God. Hence we may resist finding our own Godselves for fear that we will meet self-judgment and guilt. If we experienced authority as indulgent, we will expect our God-self to serve our own ego desires, and will be disappointed and impatient, perhaps even lose faith, when we must instead learn the lessons of taming the ego to serve the Greater Self.

In every culture, God-images are further reinforced by the characteristic misunderstandings within institutional religion. Religions originate with the direct God experience, the realization of cosmic consciousness, of their founders. However as the teachings or practices of the founder(s) become rigidified over time, distortions set in which reinforce separateness and special-ness of the adherents of this particular religion or sect, thus creating dualistic attitudes which promote one way of understanding God or practicing the path to God *versus* another way. These cultural mass images are further reinforced by the particular ethnic identity and social history of the adherents, e.g., a history of persecution, which create further distortions in the idea and perception of Ultimate Reality, or God. Judaism and Christianity, like all the world's major religions, each have their particular distortions.

The mass images of institutionalized religion and the God images resulting from the cultural history of these religions become further mixed with our personal responses to authority in such a way as to confuse us about the nature of God and discourage us from pursuing the experience of God. Often, then, we can begin to find our way back to a genuine search for God only through some avenue other than the institutionalized religions in which we were raised. Here are stories about negative childhood experiences with religion, mixed with negative experiences of authority, which resulted in distorted God images. These stories derive from Jewish, Catholic, and Protestant backgrounds:

1) A Jewish experience:
Eli felt he could not open to God; to do so would be foolish and even dangerous. He had been a child in Poland when the Nazis invaded. He and his father had escaped, but his entire extended family had been killed in concentration camps.

Eli remembered being seven years old and standing with his father, watching the Nazi soldiers parade into their town. His father had spoken Eli's worst fear, "They'll never be stopped, never." Eli, who feared his father's cruelty, had felt so horrified and betrayed by this dark certainty that he had fled into the crowd and hidden for the rest of that day. Just a month later, however, when Eli listened through a closed door to his distinguished and beloved grandfather reassuring the town's Jews that surely they had nothing to worry about, Eli found himself echoing his father's certainty that before long, "We will all be dead. They will not be stopped." Many times since then he'd wished that as a boy he had been strong enough and brave enough to scream his own dark truth at his grandfather, to insist that the old man leave with them rather than passively await the awful death which came a few short months later.

Eli's deep pessimism had become mixed up in his mind with the saving of his life. Had he and his father been benignly optimistic about the Germans, the way his grandfather had been, none of the family would have survived. A large part of him still lived in the terrifying reality of that Poland of his childhood where the impulses of his beloved grandfather were not trustworthy.

He was quite certain that humankind's propensity for evil outweighed the potential for good, and he painfully but certainly expected the human race to come to the same end via nuclear holocaust that the Jews of Poland had come to via Hitler's genocidal holocaust. "None of us will survive" echoed frequently in his thoughts. As a noted speaker to audiences about the threat posed to humanity by nuclear weapons, he found himself echoing the grim beliefs of his own forlorn, bitter child, pounding on the door of humankind's deafness and denial about the danger he felt so palpably.

If there were a God, Eli was furious at Him. He could not forgive Him for allowing the horror of Hitler's evil. This evil he had met, face to face. This was real. If this was also God, then God swaggered with the brutal march of the Nazis and spoke in the terrifying voice of Eli's cruel father. Such a God was only a ruthless and irrational punitive force; it would be humiliating to speak with, much less pray to, such a God.

After years of feeling his pain and rage at what he felt was God's betrayal, not only of him personally but of Jews and of all humankind, Eli began to awaken his longing to hear a different voice within him.

In the course of a Pathwork intensive retreat in which Eli had sought to reverse his pattern of self-destructiveness, Eli released a lot of anger toward his father who had been brutal with him, often beating him as a child and constantly criticizing him as an adult. Eli had come to understand that his own deeply ingrained self-hatred was not a voice of truth but was instead the voice of his lower self, speaking as his internalized father. He began to see this as an inner Devil, intent on destroying him, just as the Nazis had been intent on destroying the Jews. In his self-destructiveness, he was perpetuating the lethal anti-Semitism he abhorred. He began to realize that his deep negativity could not be overcome with just his limited human goodness; he needed something more. He needed God.

In his intensive journal, Eli wrote: "Faced by the Devil, I acknowledged my powerlessness over him. I agreed that I (my ego-self) couldn't match him, stop him. I had seen his work. My helper invited me to ask God to help me, to pray to him. I couldn't. I admitted I was lost. I didn't know how to pray. I couldn't say the word 'God.' I said I couldn't forgive Him, and then sobbed and sobbed, saying it over and over. After a while my heart was still and peaceful (in 'neutral'). My helper asked me if I yearned to open my heart yet more to God, and I did, but I couldn't go any further. I couldn't open it yet, but at least I had let go of my opposition to opening, let go of my tenacious unforgiveness."

After this session, Eli went back to his room and found himself unexpectedly preoccupied with mathematics. Later he wrote: "Became aware of why I had been doing algebra equations all afternoon: I had put my beliefs, my life, into the conviction of the triumph of evil, and was not even aware that there had to be something to balance the equation."

Eli opened to the idea that evil must be balanced by good, that his lower self must be balanced by his higher self. And further, that the design in the universe that created the balanced algebra equations might also be the same larger reality which created and allowed both good and evil. Thus he began to open to the idea of

God as that which encompasses the whole, all dualities, including good and evil, and is larger than both.

Eli's experience as a Jew had created in him a God image of a capricious or even hostile authority, and of people as more capable of evil than good. He began to find his way back to a more benign view of the universe through exploring and releasing his childhood feelings of rejection by his father and oppression by the Nazis. Further, his natural mathematical talent helped him to understand that he was out of balance in his over-emphasis on the dark side of life.

2) A Catholic experience:

James, whose story introduced Chapter Three, was sent to parochial schools throughout his childhood, and had taken Catholicism very seriously. By age seven he was already convinced that he had committed a mortal sin by missing Mass one Sunday. He was terrified of suffering eternally in Hell.

At parochial schools James had been taught that "God is everywhere. God knows all things." [2] Thus he knew God would know when he disobeyed the Commandments. And since the Commandments taught in the Catechism included proscriptions against ever getting angry or disobeying his parents or the Church or school authorities, as well as rules about always being honest and pure in thoughts and words, he was sure he had failed God many times.

As a boy James tried very hard to be good, and by normal standards he was a quiet, obedient child. Still, by the Catechism standards he felt like a constant failure. His self-worth was further undermined by his total belief in the Catechism's words which he felt were spoken directly to him, "We are born without God's grace. We are not holy and pleasing to God. We do not have the right to Heaven." [3] Even though he had been given the sacraments of baptism and later communion which would help him get to Heaven, he was convinced that he could never do enough to please God.

By the time he was an adolescent, James began to rebel against the strictures of his Catholic upbringing. When his sexuality appeared in full force, he knew he could no longer meet the demands of his Church. He felt he had only two choices: to sink under the weight of this terrible judgment and try to suppress his sexuality and his "bad thoughts," or just accept that he was irrevocably bad and go ahead and be bad/sexual,

---

[2] Taken from *My First Communion Catechism*, published by the Confraternity of Christian Doctrine, Washington, D.C., 1942.
[3] *Ibid.*

hoping against hope that the Catholic final judgment was wrong. It felt like a risky choice; he might still spend eternity in Hell. But his sexuality was so overwhelming that he simply could no longer deny its claims on him.

When he went to college, James began to read widely, including modern psychology, and his rejection of Catholicism now took on a more intellectual base. He read deeply books from Eastern mysticism and began to open to another view of God. Zen Buddhist meditation practice became for him a way of re-connecting with his childhood seriousness about God, but with none of the trappings of religion which had been so oppressive to him.

James's Catholic experience had led him to an image of God as demanding, rejecting, anti-sexual and punitive, whom he—a mere mortal with normal sexual desires and inevitable human flaws—could never please. He felt he had to reject either God or himself—an intolerable choice. Yet his concern with ultimate questions, wanting to know the deeper meaning of life and of death, continued to preoccupy him, and eventually led him back to God, through a path that led to a direct, non-moralistic experience of Ultimate Reality.

3) A Protestant experience:

Martha had grown up in a small rural town attending the local Lutheran church. She remembered Sunday school as pleasant but boring and she recalled her family at church always putting on a show of respectability and normality, acting like everything was just fine. But at home her father was drunk a lot, violent with her mother and the children, and barely able to provide for his family. Church was phony; home life was harsh, scary, and real. Her mother was oppressed and overwhelmed, unable to be a source of comfort to Martha. The real patriarch was not God or Jesus, but her alcoholic father, who dominated the household. God and religion, she came to believe, were mostly just for show, a mask you put on to please other people. Religion had nothing to do with reality.

As a child Martha would often escape from her oppressive house and spend hours alone in the countryside and at the creeks nearby, becoming intimate with the plants and the creatures of this place. Here she was close to the benign pulse of life, finding comfort and reassurance in the cycles of the days, the rhythm of the seasons. Nature, not religion, became her salvation.

When she grew up, Martha's spiritual hunger was first assuaged by being introduced to Native American spirituality which had as its center a love of the earth seen as both the teacher and comforter for humans. Mother Earth was a Being she could love and who clearly was central to her well-being. She started to read everything she could about earth-centered religions, where the Goddesses were as important as the Gods, the Grandmothers as wise as the Grandfathers.

Through her Protestant experience Martha had an image of God as both ineffectual and pretentious. In order to find her way back to her spiritual nature, she had to go through her connection with nature. This also allowed her access to her own feminine Godself which had been denied by the patriarchal religion and the patriarchal household in which she had grown up.

The hunger for spiritual experience will find a way to reach through to even the most cynical soul. This longing may come as a desire for love or for knowledge of the universe. For James it came as a hunger for answers to ultimate questions; for Martha it was a longing to connect more deeply with the earth; for Eli his yearning was to release his dark pessimism and find a balanced universe. All such longings to know more deeply, love more deeply, connect more deeply are ultimately a desire to experience a more unified state of awareness than that afforded by the normal disconnected ego. This longing will lead us to seek God within and will result in contact with our higher self. As we seek this connection, we must recognize and gradually discard all the cultural and psychological distortions of the God image.

> Every smallest inner deviation and obstruction are hindrances to understanding the inexplicable, limitless greatness of God, who cannot be limited into words. We have to be concerned with the elimination of hindrances, step by step, stone by stone, for only then will you glimpse the light and sense the infinite bliss.
>
> One hindrance is that, despite the teachings you have received from various sources, you still unconsciously think about God as a person who acts, chooses, decides, disposes arbitrarily and at will. On top of this you superimpose the idea that God is also just. But these ideas are false. For **God Is**. The justice comes from the working out of spiritual laws that also just **are**. God is,

among so many other things, life and life force, the
great creative power at your disposal. You, made in
His likeness, are free to choose how you make use of
this power. You learn over time that deviation from
spiritual law, from the way of love and truth, brings
unhappiness. And acting in accordance with spiritual
law brings happiness. You are completely free to
choose as you wish. You are not forced to live in
bliss and light. You can if you wish. All this means
the love of God. (*PGL 52*)

Surrender and Resistance to the Higher Self

The experience of the transpersonal and unitive levels of the
higher self comes only when the outer self, the adult ego, can
learn to surrender itself to the larger reality within the self. This
becomes possible only after we have faced and released oppressive and limited images of God carried over from childhood and
past lifetimes.

"The ego must know that it is only a servant to the greater
being within. Its main function is to deliberately seek contact
with the greater self within." (*PGL 158*) The ego's job includes
the work of facing our obstructions, so that we can hear and
heed the messages of the higher self.

In surrender of the ego we become as open and tender-
hearted as we were as children. "Unless you become as little children, you cannot enter the Kingdom of Heaven." We fear this
surrender because in our openness we become vulnerable to the
images of authority—parental authority and God or religious
authority—which we encountered when we were very young
and undefended. Thus we must meet again the instances in
which our trust in authority was betrayed, and our faith shaken.

*Carol longed to know God, to experience her higher self. She read all
the spiritual literature she could, from the basic texts of different world
religions to New Age writings. Intellectually she believed in spiritual
reality, yet she was unable to experience it firsthand. She knocked, but the
door remained closed to her.*

*In the course of working on her earliest childhood memories, Carol
spontaneously re-entered the reality of her infant self. Born prematurely,
she had been left in a hospital incubator for several months, and her
mother had been too ill to care for or even visit her.*

Lying on a couch in her Pathwork session, Carol began to speak in a strangled, tense voice, "Where are you, where are you?" Her feeling tone alternated between desperation and impotent rage. Encouraged to kick and scream, Carol allowed the full expression of her infant's anxiety. After this strong wave of feeling had subsided, she spoke in a tiny, sad voice, "I feel so abandoned, so betrayed. This isn't the way it's supposed to be. Where is she, where is she?" Now grief replaced rage, and she gave over to heaving sobs. When the crying had completed itself, she became quiet, and briefly entered an empty, open space in which she thought she heard the music of angels.

*Later, Carol reviewed her infantile regression thoughtfully, "This is just the way I have felt about God. Abandoned, betrayed, left alone to cope by myself, without help. But I see now that this was my choice. As soon as I was old enough to fend for myself, I inwardly vowed to never again be as vulnerable and needy as I had been as an infant. I made a strong identification with my ego, and I haven't wanted to let go because I knew I'd have to fall back to this terrible raw vulnerability again. I have all this time unconsciously identified God, or my own higher self, with my mother who was not there. Now for the first time I have some hope that I can contact something—a guardian angel, my own soul, my higher self—that **was** there for me, **is** there for me, even when my mother was not. I know that to hear God's voice I will need to come to God from my raw need rather than my adult intellect."*

On the path to the higher self we fall into various painful and fearful states of consciousness. Negotiating these states, the ego learns to become "transparent," thinned out, so that other, deeper realities can come to the surface. Since the higher self is a streaming of involuntary energies, we must learn to flow with our own involuntary processes which moved strongly through us as children, before we developed an ego. As we let go of control, and allow the involuntary, we will gradually sort out which impulses come from the higher self, and are therefore trustworthy, and which come from the lower self, and therefore need to be confronted or contained. We will certainly need to open up the childhood fears and vulnerability which underlie our ego controls. As we learn to tolerate all our involuntary feelings, we open ourselves more fully to the flow of spirit within.

> The not letting go always reflects the inner, spiritual struggle about what to trust: the little ego or God

within. In order to trust God within, the interim
states of consciousness must be "traveled through,"
as it were. And only too often, the self wishes to avoid
pain or confusion, emptiness or fear. Whatever the
state, it must be temporarily embraced, so that it can
be explored, understood, and dissolved.

This is why the resistance to letting go is so strong.
You prefer the status quo in which you avoid falling
into those other states of consciousness that must be
traversed in order to let go and create and expand your
life. You prefer the status quo even though the state
of letting loose, of letting God, feels wonderful, rich,
light, joyful, and safe. As you make the choice to let
go into these other states, the resistance to letting go
diminishes gradually. It can never be done in one
single decision. It is a decision and commitment that
must be repeated many times. (*PGL 213*)

Appropriate letting go into involuntary processes must
include the discipline of self-confrontation of the negative
impulses which emerge from the lower self. Until the ego has
developed this innate discipline, then surrender to the involuntary seems dangerous. Over time, we learn to trust the
unfoldment of our inner material, and to work with our negativity in safe and appropriate contexts. We learn to trust the
self-regulating nature of the creative evolutionary life process
itself as it moves through us. "Recognition of this must help
you to come again a step nearer to the **real life that leads itself**
from within you." (*PGL 153*)

Exercises for Chapter 8:

1. Write out fully an experience you have had of the higher self. Also include in what ways, if any, you feel changed from the experience.

2. Write a list of your own best qualities, the places where you feel the higher self "shines through" your present personality. When you have completed this list, explore what relationship, if any, this list has to aspects of your mask self. Explore apparent similarities and real differences.

3. Look within to discover if you have any shame about claiming your higher self qualities. If so, explore how this betrayal of yourself relates to ways you may have betrayed love coming from one or both of your parents. Did you take the more loving parent for granted and pursue the less loving one?

4. Look at your life for how open or "spiritually well" you feel in different areas: e.g., being alone with yourself, being with people of the same sex, being with the opposite sex, giving your best to your work, being in nature, being with children. Ask yourself how (relatively) relaxed, open, trusting, real you are in these different areas. In a prayer or ritual, invite your higher self to lead you into greater openness in those areas where you currently feel blocked or closed.

5. Visualize your higher self as an inner teacher/healer/companion. Write out a description of this higher-self being who lives inside you. Then create a dialogue between the ego part of you and this being (that is also you). Label each voice and write out this dialogue. It can be on some subject in your life that is currently troubling you, or you can simply listen in for whatever guidance wants to come now.

Releasing Lower Self Attachments

"When you ferret out your negative intentionality,
you can no longer deceive yourself that negativity
'happens' to you. You must come to terms with the
fact that your life is the result of your choices.
And choice implies the freedom to adopt another attitude."

—Pathwork Guide Lecture 195, *"Identification and Intentionality:
Identification with the Spiritual Self to Overcome Negative Intentionality"*

Michael's Devil:
Exploring the Roots of Forbidden Fruit

Michael came to the Pathwork specifically to deal with his attachment to negative sexual fantasies. He was newly married and deeply loved his wife. Sensing the possibility of a more loving and ecstatic sexual union with her, Michael wanted to remove what was, for him, the major obstacle to a more loving sexuality.

His most frequent fantasies were about sexual encounters with prostitutes, especially with "queens." Queens live in the nether world of sexual ambiguity, born as men but identifying themselves as women. They exhibit feminine secondary sexual characteristics while retaining masculine genitals. Michael had experienced numerous one-night stands with queens and still felt turned on by fantasies about them.

This dream had prompted Michael to begin work on his sexual issue: "I am in an urban environment, in a porno district, where there are some queens working as prostitutes. People are cheering a helicopter above them, which is doing some very fancy flying down several city streets, around a triangular building. All the buildings are very tall and the streets are narrow.

"The helicopter is enormous, like the Queen Mary, and also very flexible with a long tail that bends like an accordion. The helicopter is doing complicated and very dangerous tricks, 'hot-dogging,' trying to go around the triangular building very fast. As it makes a sharp turn around one building, the tail swings wide, out of control, and crashes into another building with a terrible crunch. I had felt the danger coming, and was now nauseated by the sight of the destruction."

The sexual imagery was obvious to Michael. He associated the triangular building with the female "pubic triangle" and feared that his own sexual energy, tied up as it was in doing "tricks" with queens, was terribly self-destructive. In his work on this dream, Michael identified with the helicopter pilot:

"I'm in charge here. I'm in the cockpit. I've got this enormous power at my command, and I get a big charge out of doing these tricks, impressing everyone below. I enjoy the excitement and the danger. I'm aware that the helicopter does a kind of 'crack-the-whip' around the buildings, but I feel invulnerable. Suddenly I'm aware that the tail is totally out of control, that disaster looms, and then. . . sudden death."

Michael said the feeling of impending disaster was familiar, as if he could almost remember having died suddenly in a sexually charged situation in another life. The feeling was also reminiscent of his encounters with prostitute queens, toward whom he felt alternately paternalistic and frightened. Imminent danger was part of the sexual turn-on. Sex and danger, power and the dark side, excitement and destruction—somehow they all ran together, and he knew he needed to separate them in order to let go of the negativity bound up in his masculine sexuality.

He reviewed his early sexual history. As far back as he could remember, Michael felt aligned with his mother against his father. His parents had fought, usually about his father's excessive drinking. An only child, Michael knew that his mother favored him and scorned his father. His mother confided in Michael, sharing her complaints about her husband, including her sexual dissatisfactions. His mother was also flirtatious with him. Parading around the house nude, or semi-nude, Michael's mother often asked her son to massage her neck, or wash her back when she was in the tub, or tell her how she looked in her clothes. As an adolescent Michael had been obsessed with sexual fantasies about his mother.

To little Michael, his mother was the "queen" of the house, his father the impotent king, and Michael the crown prince. The incestuous energy between mother and son, even if not acted out, was intense and clearly dangerous: What if it got out of control and they broke the ultimate taboo? What if his father found out? In reviewing his earliest associations of sex with danger, and how he was later involved with the "forbidden fruit" of queens, Michael began to understand his contempt for "boringly normal" married heterosexuality. He also sensed that the growing intimacy with his wife threatened to reawaken the taboo sensations associated with his mother.

Then he dreamed: "I am in a dark place, probably a subway in New York City, trying to avoid a devil-character who is seeking an alliance with me. He wants to give me powers, including the ability to fly, in exchange for 'selling my soul.' He is a spirit, and can change his form in any way.

"He says to me, 'Guess where I am going next?'

"I feel a tingle in my head, and then realize he is in my brain. He gives me an invitation to have sex with him, and reminds me that he can change form. Then he becomes a very seductive, beautiful queen. He is there with another queen. They both have weird genitals, where the skin is barely attached to their bodies, like an appendage that isn't theirs. Both want to have sex with me, which we know has been arranged by the devil spirit. The queens start to argue, however, and then their genitals fall off."

In his next session, Michael acknowledged that the dream underlined his childhood fear of castration as an aspect of his incestuous involvement with his mother. But, beyond the psychological level, Michael sensed that he had made a pact with the devil, one which he now wanted to illumi-

nate and change. In the session Michael spoke both sides in this dialogue with the devil:

Devil: "You need me. Let me be in charge of your sexuality. I will make you powerful."

Michael: "No, get out. I don't need you. I don't want you. I want to choose love, not what you offer me. I want to believe that love is more powerful than you."

Devil: "Remember, I couldn't come if you didn't want me."

I intervened, suggesting that Michael explore his attachment to the devil-force.

Michael: "I feel the power my negative sexuality gives me; it's the excitement which drives the machine. The sexual power inside me wakes up everything and makes life worth living."

I then asked, "Who would you be without it?"

Michael: "Without it I would be my father—a depressed, impotent conformist. He is a hollow mask, someone who settled for too little, who got rigid and proper, and then drank to unwind and got silly and stupid and childish. He's already dead; he has rigor mortis of the mind."

Devil: "See, I give you your life. The kind of sex I can offer you is your life. You don't need any other feelings."

Michael: "You give me power with a terrible price tag: pain, guilt, and separation from the woman I love. Also you constrict my feeling life. I don't want to have just sexual feelings. I want to be able to expand my intimacy with my wife, to be sad and angry, to know joy and fear, to feel all of life. I hate your narrow preoccupation with sexuality."

Devil: "I give you power through sex. That's all there is."

Michael: "Who are you and what do you want?"

Devil: "I want power and separation. It's all I know about."

In later sessions Michael reflected on his question about the identity of the devil. He began to recognize the devil as a destructive and willful child wanting constant attention, instant gratification, and power over others. Underneath this lower-self child, he found a needy child, who believed he needed power as compensation for feeling unloved. Michael knew that what he really wanted was mutual love, incompatible with total childish selfishness, and yet he knew he was still attracted to the power and danger of forbidden sexuality. So Michael asked again of this devil-child, "Who are you and what do you want?"

In another dialogue in which Michael played both parts, his lower-self devil began to sound more and more like an emotionally distressed child, reminding Michael of a tough adolescent boy he had once counseled while working in a home for disturbed teenagers. Michael remembered a time, after the boy's tired and preoccupied mother had visited along with three of her eleven children, when the boy went out back of the home and started pulling up saplings from a young forest. Michael raced up to him, grabbed him by the shoulders, and yelled at him, "What are you doing?" The boy, eyes shining with hate, glared and said nothing. Michael softened, and then, calmly but insistently, asked the boy repeatedly, "What do you want? What do you really want?" Silent for a long time, the boy finally answered quietly, tears filling his eyes, "I want my mother."

Michael choked up on recounting this story and, for the first time, realized how little real mothering he himself had received. To his mother, he had been husband and lover, father and comforter, but rarely a child receiving maternal care and reassurance. Michael's subsequent work focused on grieving for the mother he did not have, for the nurturance he did not receive. His emotional life began to expand to include more frequent bouts with grief and anger.

At the same time, Michael started to feel more compassion for his own disturbed and willful inner child; he began to have patience with him, to want to help him grow up and realize that he was loved and did not need to act out negatively. Michael was awakening the "good parent" within who could nurture his inner child.

He began meditating more regularly and making more contact with his higher self, the spiritual essence he had always known was his true identity. This self, he knew, loved and accepted every part of Michael, including the devil/lower-self child. Past use of psychedelic drugs had given him a real taste of his expanded self, though he had also used the drug experience as a substitute for emotional growth.

For a while Michael found his sexual feelings with his wife diminishing as he started focusing more on his love for her. And then once, when his lovemaking was flowing out of his love, and he was feeling flooded with a new kind of strength—the powerful union of sex with love—he developed a sudden, sharp pain in his left hip and had to stop to attend to it. Temporarily identifying with the energy that had "attacked" him, Michael again spoke with the devil's voice: "No, I won't let you bring the two energies of love and sex together. Don't you know that it will kill you! You'll be overwhelmed! Never will I let you get it together. Return to me; it's so much safer."

Michael knew that what would be overwhelmed through his surrender to the unified flow of loving sexuality was only his ego control, not his real self. So, remembering that the devil was a defense of his confused child, he confronted the devil again, saying, "I know that the flood of unified feelings is scary to you. I know it brings back fear of incest and feel-

ings of being overwhelmed. I know you think you are protecting me by splitting off my sexuality from my heart."

Michael was then able to feel and share with his mate his childhood fears, his confusion and isolation. As soon as he shared these feelings, he knew he also needed to confront the devil directly. "I no longer need the defense of split-off sexuality that you keep tempting me with. I want to bring it all together. I say 'no' to your negative will, and I consciously align with my higher-self intention to love and to express my love sexually." The pain in his hip gradually receded. ·

Michael began to make a daily practice of visualizing uniting his sexuality with his heart feelings, and letting go of the sexual fantasies which he knew split the sexual life force. Through his meditations and visualizations he strengthened his contact with his higher self.

(Michael's story continues in the Prologue of Chapter 10.)

Releasing Lower Self Attachments

As Michael learned in his dreams and dialogues, the lower self, which he called his inner devil, has a life of its own, an agenda of its own, a spiritual form of its own. It will fight to stay alive and accomplish its aim of separation. It thrives in hidden-ness, festering in the unconscious where it is easiest to thwart our conscious good intentions. It prefers an emotional climate of denial, self-justification, confusion, and dishonesty. When we keep ourselves ignorant of our own lower self, it will command us to fulfill a destructive pattern in our lives despite our conscious wish to let it go. Until Michael brought the dreams of his unconscious into the light of awareness, he was trapped in his pattern of compulsive negative sexuality.

The lower self is also out to convince us that it is our best pro-tection, that we can be safe, or powerful, or have pleasure only if we follow the path of egocentricity and negativity. Michael's devil was constantly arguing against his surrender to love and vulnerability. Until we unmask the true intentions of the lower self we will remain caught in our negative life patterns.

We experience the unconscious grip of the lower self whenever we cannot change what we consciously wish to change. Even when we stop blaming our parents, our culture, or God—even when we have discharged many of the childhood hurts behind our images—we may still feel that we cannot help being the way we are; that this is simply our "human nature." This apparent helplessness in the face of the lower self results from a deep and largely unconscious **attachment** we all have to negativity. This attachment derives from both our **intent** to stay negative and our **pleasure** in being negative.

Negative Intent, Negative Will

We can discover our negative intentions by examining areas of unfulfillment in our lives. We may consciously wish for all the right things—love, happiness, a fulfilling work situation, creative self-expression. Yet we may simultaneously fear or defy the fulfillment of our conscious wishes for any number of unconscious reasons. We may be unconsciously punishing ourselves or others, or perversely refusing to embrace happiness or trust in the universe simply because it threatens our ego control.

We need to find the level of the lower self in which we choose, of our own free will, to defy our divine connectedness with all life in favor of our egocentric limitations. This level may appear in the form of a demon or a devil, an archetypal negative voice of the collective negative unconscious which we share with all humans who exist in duality. Only when we make conscious this deeper negative choice to resist life do we have the opportunity to change it.

Discovering the negative intention to stay split-off from our divine core, to stand in opposition to the love, truth and pleasure in and around us, is at first a shocking discovery. It is hard to believe we actually say "no" to the very things we most want in life. And yet the discovery that the "no" is within us, not outside us, leads to knowing freedom and realizing maturity. Sometimes a negative intent toward some aspect of life only becomes clear when we are already beginning to make other choices, as in the following case:

Sophie was a young woman recently divorced from an older man with whom she had never enjoyed sex. She was now in love with a gentle young man whom she really loved and who had helped her to relax sexually to the point that, for the first time in her life, she had experienced orgasm. But she was having many doubts about the relationship and was tempted to leave her new lover. Soon thereafter she dreamed that she went home to her ex-husband, who became murderously violent when she told him she was now orgasmic.

In her Pathwork session, I asked Sophie to talk as the dream character of her ex-husband. Speaking as him, Sophie realized that she harbored within her a voice that was repelled by her new-found loving sexuality. The voice said, "Now see what you've done. You have given away your only power advantage, the power of withholding, which you have used all these years to control men. What a lousy choice you've made! Now you will just be a wimp with men; you will go slavering after them, and any man will be able to have you. If you are going to keep any self-respect at all, you'd better choose to withhold again and leave this young man."

Sophie identified this voice as that of her negative intentionality. A part of her was terrified of and enraged at the vulnerability that her more open sexuality represented, and wanted her to close down again by leaving. Making this negative intent conscious helped Sophie stay in the relationship and continue to open to a more fulfilling sexual love.

> It takes considerable time and growth to accept that, where there is unfulfillment, the inner intention is different from the outer conscious desires, wants, and intentions. You must eventually discover this truth of life: that there must be something at work within you that thwarts the wished-for fulfillment. But even when this, at first purely conceptual, acceptance develops, it still seems impossible to conceive that an actual inner 'No' exists in regard to the conscious 'Yes.' Hardly anyone can believe to begin with, that what he so ardently strives for is denied by himself for his own inner 'reasons.' The disconnectedness from this inner voice is the primary problem. Any work concerned with genuine self-search and development must go in the direction to unearth this inner negation, this inner No-saying voice. (*PGL 186*)

It is a great step forward when we can face and experience our unconscious intent to persist in destructive attitudes and patterns, to say "no" to what we say we want. Once we see that we choose unfulfillment, negativity, and suffering, we no longer blame the world and others. We assume responsibility for the creation of our lives and redirect the creative energy.

> The mere word **intention** connotes that the self is in charge; makes a deliberate choice, **intends** to do, act, be. Even when you own up to the worst destructive,

cruel, brutal attitudes in you, there is always an implica-
tion that you cannot help being the way you are. When
you ferret out your negative intentionality, you can no
longer deceive yourself that negativity "happens" to you.
You must sooner or later come to terms with the fact
that your life is the result of your choices. And choice
implies the freedom to adopt another attitude. . . .
That the self deliberately chooses a course of denial,
spite, and hate, even at the price of suffering, is
tremendously difficult to admit. But once this is done,
the door opens to freedom, even before one is actually
ready to step through this door. (*PGL 195*)

An understanding of negative intentionality—the inner
choice of a part of the soul to stay negative toward life—usually
comes only after much personal work. We must first develop
and learn to identify with our compassionate, objective
observer self (as presented in Chapter Three) and then learn
about our particular misconceptions about reality, our
"images," and how these recreate negative repetitive patterns,
or vicious circles, in our present life (as discussed in Chapter
Five). We must learn to remove the mask (as explored in
Chapter Six), to accept the existence of the lower self (as examined in Chapter Seven), and finally to ground ourselves in our
higher self (as discussed in Chapter Eight). Usually all these
steps are necessary preconditions for our having the spiritual
strength and maturity to face our deepest distrust of life and
self represented by our negative intentionality.

*Sophie had done considerable work on her hostility toward men as
it related to having been sexually abused by her alcoholic father. She
had seen her images of distrust and how she justified her hostility, and
had many times discharged her rage, her grief, and her deep pain. She
had seen how she had re-created the untrustworthy relationship with
her ex-husband. And even though her new relationship was going well,
she kept finding that her distrust was a barrier to surrendering more
deeply to love.*

*In one Pathwork group Sophie spontaneously discovered "memories"
of other lifetimes with her father. She felt they had been doing this dance
of power and control, abuse and betrayal, in countless replays, with each
of them alternating the roles of victim and perpetrator. She wanted to
understand why she had chosen her father this lifetime, and tried talking
imaginatively to him from her new awareness of lower self intentionality:*

"I chose you. I knew you would abuse me, and be crude, and I chose you. Now I have all the excuse I will ever need to hate men. You gave me that excuse, you bastard, and I'm glad, because now I can choose to separate from you and all men, forever. I will never trust, never give in, never love. I will stay separate and aggrieved forever. Ha!"

Here was a clear statement of her underlying negative intention, the choice to justify hate, withholding, and spite. With this awareness of the part of her committed to her negative view of men and relationships, Sophie could soften the hold it had on her life. She prayed to change her fundamental alignment from a negative, distrusting one to a positive, trusting view of men. Only now that she had unearthed her deep negative will and had chosen to relinquish it did her prayers have a deep impact on her unconscious and allow her to create a fulfilling love relationship.

Making Negative Intentions Conscious

Whenever our negative patterns—areas of disharmony and unfulfillment in our lives—feel deeply entrenched, we need to look for hidden negative intentions and to put them clearly into words. We can listen within for the voice that might be saying:

"I intend to withhold from life. I don't trust that freely giving myself will be appreciated or returned. I will hold out against other people, and punish them by not giving what they want from me. That's how I'll be powerful."

"I want to cheat life—to get more than I give. I've been deprived by my parents and now it's up to life to make it up to me. I don't want to engage in a give-and-take."

"I like blaming and being the victimized child—it's easier than growing up and being a self-responsible adult."

"I intend to stay deprived and unhappy in my life—that will surely hurt my parents and others who love me. I won't be happy out of spite; I'll use my misery as a weapon to punish others."

"Being cold and cruel makes me feel powerful. The more unattainable I am, the more others will have to come after me. I don't care if it's also lonely; I just won't feel."

"I am hopelessly bad and do not deserve any pleasure or goodness in life. I will see life as a punishment and never have joy."

We hold on to these negative intentions because they are familiar. We made these negative vows long ago; they are an expression of our main images about life as hostile, painful, or threatening. Our defenses against pain eventually solidify into a pervasive negative or distrustful attitude. To open up to a positive view of life and self is initially unfamiliar, and threatens the "safety" of our defenses.

The fundamental agenda of the lower self is to convince us that we and life are bad, untrustworthy, and hopeless, so that we will maintain our defensive separateness and not surrender to the life force or God within and around us. Our negative intentions are an expression of our deepest fears that the lower self is our ultimate reality. That is why it is especially important to keep a clear identification with the compassionate, objective observer-self and other aspects of the higher self as we do this work of uncovering our most deeply held "no" to life.

Some of our negative intentions arise from a mass or cultural image that life is a battle or struggle, and that therefore the route to happiness is to be more powerful than others and to get our own way. This mass image says that egocentrism is "smart," whereas a life based on love and compassion is "dumb" and will make us weak. To challenge our own negative will often means challenging negative mass images about life. We must learn that egocentricity will never make us happy. The way to fulfillment is through trust of life, a willingness to engage with others, to enter the human and planetary life cycles of giving and receiving.

Why We Choose Negativity

As long as we identify with the little ego, we behave toward our own higher self much the way a child behaves toward his parents. We see God as an outer authority who will invade or crush us if we say "yes." Our God-images, as discussed in Chapter Eight, define our unconscious picture of our higher self and stand in the way of our personal surrender to life.

We believe our "no" is a guarantee of autonomy. "The child equates giving up the resistance with capitulation of his individuality." (*PGL 195*) He resists; therefore he is. The struggle for autonomy and freedom from outside authorities is appropriate for the child and young person, but easily becomes distorted for adults into resistance to life and to God.

We also hold onto negativity both as a denial of and defense against the real, and often painful, feelings of childhood and as a means to punish our imperfect parents.

> The holding on to negative will directions is due to
> a refusal to assume responsibility in life, to deal with
> 'un-ideal' circumstances. It is an inner insistence to
> 'force' the 'bad parents' to become 'good parents,' as
> if one's own misery were a weapon. This misery then
> becomes a means to punish life (the 'bad parents').
> (*PGL 195*)

When our resistance and our spite are carried on inside our own psyche, we identify with only a fragment of our consciousness—either the unconscious child self or the separated little ego. Then we resist or punish the greater consciousness or higher self in us which we identify as the feared authority. Resisting the higher self wastes a great deal of energy, and precludes the development of a more expansive self-concept and experience of life. We say "no" to the very life force that could sustain us.

As we recognize the limitations of the child-self and little ego, tasting the greater self that we could be, then we can relax our fearsome autonomy and self-destructive spite, and surrender to our vaster potential.

Relinquishing Negative Intentions; Affirming Positive Intentions

Once we are fully aware of the negative intent, and especially its basis in false images about ourselves and the world, we have to take the plunge into the unknown region of a new choice. This is the choice for positive intention and energy, and for the greater reality beyond the limitations inherent in negativity. The Guide calls this **relinquishing** or going into the "abyss of illusion." We leap into the mysterious larger reality and away from the image-based, known but limited reality, overcoming our fears of annihilation precisely by leaping into them.

> To give in or let go of your negative will seems tanta-
> mount to falling headlong into the abyss. Yet the abyss
> can only disappear if you let yourself sink into it.
> Then, and only then, will you learn that you do not
> crash and perish, but that you float beautifully. You
> will then see that what made you tense with fear and
> anxiety was as illusory as this abyss. *(PGL 60)*

To know who we really are, we must make the choice to support and trust life and to release our petty egocentrism and the negative intent toward life based on our fears and resentments. The choice for love, hope, and goodness requires surrender of our tightly held identification with the little ego-self. If sincerely felt, our prayers of positive intent to seek and follow God's will in our lives will have a profound impact on our soul substance.

We benefit most from positive affirmations when the distorted ideas and negative intentions have first been unearthed. Sophie's commitment to surrender to her new love relationship became much more powerful after she uncovered and chose to release her negative intentions toward men. When we release attachment to our negative will, we create an empty space. The commitment to positive energy then "fills in" the space. In this way truth replaces untruth, connectedness replaces separateness, self-esteem replaces self-denigration.

As we release a negative intent to withhold from or to cheat life, the following affirmation is especially powerful:

"I intend to give all of who I am to life. I will trust that my freely giving myself will be appreciated and returned. I want to be a full participant in the give-and-take of life."

As we relinquish our attachment to blaming, deprivation, or victimization, the following is especially helpful:

"I choose to grow up and take my place as an adult among other adults. I take responsibility for myself and for creating my own happiness in life."

As we let go of our intentions toward power in the form of hostility and cruelty, we can affirm the following:

"I relinquish my coldness and my cruelty. I choose love rather than power. I want to have all my feelings, so I open to my vulnerability."

As we release our negative commitment to unworthiness and despair, we assert:

"I give my best to life and I deserve the best from life. I am a divine manifestation of God, no less and no more than every other human and natural expression of the Life Force on this planet."

Good will—the choice to align with love and truth—is our gift to God. Neither insight into the childhood origins nor active discharge of our negative feelings are sufficient to transform negative patterns. We must also change the alignment of our **will** away from the preservation of the fearful child or destructive ego toward the acceptance and manifestation of God's will in our lives. Through the work of relinquishing and realigning, we slowly gain faith that being "in God" will serve our personal and planetary fulfillment infinitely more than egocentric resistance to God. As we name and relinquish our most deeply held negative beliefs, we leap into an expansion of our spiritual self.

> The lower self should be identified; the spiritual self identified with. The ego as objective observer makes the identification, but gives itself up voluntarily so that it is integrated into the spiritual self. (*PGL 195*)

Understanding the Deeper Levels of Our Negativity

Perhaps the single most important contribution of the Pathwork Guide is the teaching about how negativity becomes so firmly entrenched in the soul substance of human beings—why we keep making negative choices even after we know certain behaviors are wrong or destructive for ourselves and others. Why can't we just "wake up" and start making positive choices? Why are human beings so perverse?

The Guide's answer to the puzzle of human perversity begins with an understanding that we experience life according to our images which create vicious circles, in such a way that our negative world view and negative choices constantly reinforce each other. Our everyday perceptions of the world are not reality but are a product of our illusions, but we have gotten so used to seeing life according to our negative expectations that we rarely question our assumptions about reality. This keeps us trapped in a negative and limited world-view.

Understanding the innate lower self of every human being gives us another part of the puzzle. Originating in the ancient choice of divine substance to separate itself from the whole and identify with its separateness, the lower self is deeply antagonistic to the natural flow of life, because to surrender would mean death for its separate ego-based existence. The lower self is a perverse part of us that fiercely resists the call of life toward integration and union, supporting its separateness through the defenses of self-will, pride, and fear. The choice to stay separate has become deeply settled in our soul substance, through many lifetimes of repeating negative choices. The negative will directions of the soul need to be brought to consciousness and then released in order to further our alignment with God on our journey home to wholeness. We need to make the leap from the limitations of the known—our limited and negative ideas about life—into the vastness of the unknown mystery of Spirit.

Negative Pleasure

Yet another part of the puzzle of human perversity lies in an understanding of how negativity gets mixed up with the Life Force, or pleasure principle, so that we fear that surrender of our negativity will entail loss of the excitement and pleasure it affords us. The "lower-self land" that fills our newspapers, T.V. shows, and secret dreams and sexual fantasies is still a place of pleasure, or at least irresistible excitement, for many of us, however ashamed we may be of the charge we get from this negativity. In a sense, the lower self holds part of our natural capacity for pleasure hostage; otherwise, we would surrender our negativity much more easily.

Michael, whose story introduced this chapter, consciously wanted to realign his sexuality with his love for his wife. He knew that his happiness lay in relating to her sexually from his present love, not from his fantasies of past loveless experiences. Yet, even with the strongest good will, he still had to meet the places in him which were "hooked" on negative sexuality, where his excitement lay in the forbidden, where the "devil" held sway.

When, like Michael, we become willing to meet the demons feasting on our destructiveness, we perform a kind of personal exorcism worthy of our greatest respect. Here we exhibit the heroism of meeting the dragon head-on, feeling the threat of its hot breath upon us, slaying it, and eating its flesh, thus reincorporating its power within us. We walk a heroic path when we choose consciously to meet the secret pleasure in our many dark temptations.

> When you find yourself stymied in your attempt to overcome negativity, it is extremely important to sense deep within yourself the pleasurable aspect involved in this negativity, regardless of how much pain exists in your surface consciousness. The difficulty of ridding yourself of destructiveness is, of course, due also to other reasons which you have already verified—the desire to punish life or to force life to meet your expectations. . . . But these reasons are not the deepest difficulty in shedding negativity. It is necessary to first sense intuitively, and then to feel very specifically, that pleasure is attached to your negativity. *(PGL 148)*

Negative attitudes and negative choices stay locked into the psyche because they become "mixed up" with the excitement and pleasure of the Life Force. "When it is understood that the painful aspect of negativity can be abandoned, while the pleasurable aspect will increase with positive attitudes, only then can negativity transform itself." *(PGL 148)*

What Is Pleasure?

Pleasure is the sensation of the life force flowing through the body. The essence of pleasure is not different from the cosmic state of bliss, a giving over of the ego to the unobstructed flow of life energy.

What we are calling "negative pleasure" is the sensation of a particle, a split-off piece, of the life force, which has temporarily gotten attached to a negative life situation. Just as the ego is a split-off piece of universal consciousness, so negative pleasure is a fragment of universal bliss.

> Negative pleasure is always, in some way, more geared to gratifying ego goals than fulfilling the real and legitimate needs of the entity for bathing in the light of pleasure supreme. . . .

> As long as you identify with the tight ego-structure,
> real, total pleasure becomes impossible, because it
> depends on the ability of the ego to let go of itself and
> to let itself be carried and lived through by a greater
> power within the body and soul. (*PGL 177*)

As long as we hold onto the little ego and to destructive attitudes, we impair our integrity and create agitation in the body-mind. In this state we cannot create the condition of relaxed inner receptivity necessary for the experience of pleasure supreme. Pleasure flows unobstructed only when our inner being is at peace and thus able to attune finely to the cosmic rhythm as it moves, pulsates, breathes through us, as us.

> Pleasure is made possible when the state of mind and
> emotions is quietly confident, calmly expectant and
> receptive, patient and unanxious, unhurried and
> unworried. (*PGL 177*)

This state of relaxed openness to the cosmic flow of life is rare, as our usual condition is a contracted ego state of fear and refusal to surrender our pride and self-will. So we all live in various stages of numbness, unavailable to the full pulsation of our life force.

And yet, since human beings cannot live without pleasure, we find our pleasure in what is familiar, in states of agitated overactivity or will-less passivity. And because we are defended against the tender and vulnerable flow of our inner sensations and feelings, we become addicted to an intense level of external sensory stimulation. The more numb we are to the vulnerable flow of inner experience, the more we will intensify the external assault on our senses in order to feel **something**. Or we collapse from our hurried, action-packed lives, and expect to find pleasure in being completely passive and taken care of by others. These false or partial pleasures are never deeply satisfying, but until we learn how to relax into our deeper selves, we stay hooked on the pattern of alternating high intensity with passive collapse.

Attachment of the Life Force to Negative Situations

When the pleasure principle, or Life Force, attaches to situations of passivity and/or stagnation we call it masochism. When the pleasure principle attaches to situations of over-exertion of power, control, or forcing, we call it sadism.

The persistence of sadistic cruelty in our collective psyches stems from the pleasure we derive from fantasies of conquest, exploitation, and revenge. This is the nucleus of humankind's attachment to war and other mass cruelties, as well as to all the family wars and emotional atrocities we commit in our intimate lives. We even speak of "sweet revenge" and "delicious cruelty." The tenacity of masochistic self-destruction, on the other hand, also depends on the pleasure we imagine from being passive, "done to," not having to be responsible for ourselves or our lives. If there were not excitement and sexual pleasure attached to sadistic and masochistic acts and fantasies, they would not endure so powerfully in the human psyche.

> If the positive life principle were not involved and
> inadvertently used, then evil, or destructiveness, would
> be of very short duration. (*PGL 135*)

When the pleasure principle is strongly attached to negativity, then evil gains in intensity and tenacity. Whenever negativity is powerfully acted out, painful guilt feelings may come flooding into the psyche. In order to ward off this pain, the person numbs himself further, cutting off the warm feelings of human connectedness, thus making it more possible to perpetuate future violence. Thus in the extreme case of the serial killer, there is a constant escalation of the stimulus of negative excitement in order to obliterate the pain of guilt and the grief over disconnection, until finally all normal human empathy is destroyed.

A convicted killer and rapist of young boys declares, "If I do escape, I promise you I will kill and rape again, and I will enjoy every minute of it." His "enjoyment" of his sadism is shocking, and yet his perversity stimulates our nervous system. How do we otherwise explain the incredible prevalence of violent and perverse material in our popular culture? Somehow the acts of sadistic sociopaths stimulate and attract a part of us, even as we are morally repelled.

Even "normal" people can be drawn into extreme acts of murder, rape, and torture if a sufficiently perverse mass culture stimulates their appetite for violence and numbs their innate conscience, destroying their humane feelings, as in the participation of "good Germans" under Hitler or, more recently, "good Serbs" in what was Yugoslavia, in the collectively insane process of genocide. Acts of torture and rape are not just carried out under orders; those who participate take pleasure in their actions. It is this attachment of pleasure to violence and evil that we must investigate if we are to understand its tenacity in our souls.

Origin of Negative Pleasure

How does the life-force or pleasure get attached to negative situations? We will explore first the origin of negative pleasure within the psyche of the child, and then extend this to the level of our collective psyches.

In the universe of the child, all experience is united; it is one continuous flow of life. The child does not separate herself from her life experience. She has not yet developed a separate, discriminating ego able to make clear discernments, especially where her parents are concerned. The child experiences an intense flow of energy and pleasure in simply being alive. She is less defended against life than adults who have learned to separate from their environment.

The small child is not yet able to discriminate between positive and negative life circumstances. She loves her parents and needs their presence to feel secure. Thus she takes pleasure in being with them, whether or not they deserve this love. When treated with cruelty or humiliation, rejection or withdrawal, the child "attaches" the pleasure and love she feels for her parents to the negativity she experiences at their hands.

She will then re-create in adult life the ways she was related to as a child, not only because this pattern is familiar but also because she actually now experiences pleasure—including tasting the openness she had as a child—in re-experiencing the negative patterns from childhood. Childhood victimization "matures" into adult masochism and self-destructiveness.

Nancy was working on her problems with her job as a nurse. She knew she had chosen her profession largely to please her powerful father, who was a doctor, rather than listen to her own longing to pursue her interest in spirituality. Now she was dissatisfied with her job.

When I asked her what kept her attached to pleasing Daddy, Nancy reported a strong tingling sensation in her thighs, moving toward her genitals. She knew it had something to do with staying "one down" with Daddy, letting him be "on top." I had Nancy lie on the floor with a pillow over her pelvis representing her father on top of her. Nancy wriggled with pleasure considering being pinned down by him, and realized that she actively enjoyed being held under him, being his little girl, passive and unable to move, totally controlled by him.

After a while she decided to struggle out from under the pillow to claim her own life and independent world view. However, as soon as she was free, she pulled the pillow back on top of herself. Her pleasure was still attached to not being herself, to being Daddy's girl.

She had taken an important step in understanding her attachment to her unwillingness to become who she was as an independent person. She still found pleasure in her masochistic surrender to Daddy. Until Nancy's recognition of this negative attachment, her self-betrayal had been a mystery; now her self-responsibility deepened immeasurably.

Pleasure is often attached to masochism—self-denial—as a way to perpetuate the victimization we experienced as children. If our independence was suppressed in childhood, pleasure can get attached to enmeshment and dependency which feels cozier than the lonely assertion of a separate self.

Pleasure can also get attached to sadism as a way to compensate for childhood hurts. For example, if we were mistreated as children, and felt entirely helpless, we may now take pleasure in feeling powerful over others. Albert, whose story introduced Chapter Five, was caught in such a cycle of attaching pleasure to revenge for his mother's sexual abuse of him in childhood.

Whether a child grows up to identify with victim or perpetrator depends on many factors, but either identification will be sustained by the pleasure mixed in with early mistreatment. The child's feelings of pleasure and denial of pain originally "softened the blow" of parental inadequacies, helping him not to be devastated by his situation.

Karl's mother used to play a bizarre game with her little boy. In the middle of some nursery game together, she would suddenly lie flat on the floor and pretend to be dead. Karl would attempt to arouse her, screaming,

"Mommy, Mommy, wake up! Mommy, what's wrong!"

She would continue her pretense until the little boy became frantic, running around in circles, terrified. Only then would she "wake up" laughing and say, "Fooled you that time! Fooled you again. Here's Mommy, I'm o.k."

He would, of course, fall into her arms crying with relief.

No matter how many times his mother repeated the game, which she did from the time Karl was three until he was eight years old, the boy was always devastated.

As an adult Karl was especially considerate with women; he prided himself on being a "nice guy." However, he acknowledged to himself and to me another, darker side, which only surfaced in occasional sexual fantasies. In them he would be with a strong, sexy woman who was coming on to him with great bravado. He would take her up on her offer and begin sex play, but just before intercourse, the woman would become scared, vulnerable, child-like, wanting to stop. But he would push through, forcing himself on her sexually, keenly enjoying the fear behind her initial bravado.

Fear had been the emotion Karl's mother elicited from her little boy in order to prove not only her power over him, but also his love for her. She manipulated his emotions to satisfy herself that she was loved and needed. In this way fear became equated with intimacy, control with pleasure. Now part of Karl's sexuality was attached to enjoying the fear he evoked in the controlling woman—a perfect mirror image of what was done to him as a child, and a precise compensatory punishment toward the woman (Mother).

If we are thoroughly honest with ourselves, we can all find places where we experience pleasure in controlling or hurting ourselves or others. Our sadism and/or masochism may be deeply buried or denied. If that is the case, we may need to wait patiently for these attitudes to be revealed. Often, however, our negative pleasure can be detected rather quickly through looking at our sexual fantasies or behavior.

Distortions in Sexuality

Lower-self attitudes that may be denied or repressed in other areas of our lives are often clearly laid out in the sexual arena. Unfortunately, this area is also so overlaid with false guilt and shame that the real inner situation is obscured. This guilt, as with all false guilt, results from the powerful perfectionism of the mask, reinforced by parental and societal injunction, which makes us believe that we ought to be more loving, decent, or sane than we really are.

The task, therefore, is to release the false guilt induced by the idealized standards of the mask, and face **whatever is** in us. Then we can learn to fully acknowledge and experience our negative pleasure, including sadistic or masochistic sexual fantasies. "When you find the parallel between the outer problem and the pleasure current in your sexuality, you will be able to make the frozen energy fluid again." (*PGL 148*) Eventually, the free-flowing life-force of our sexuality can be extricated from the negativity to which it has become attached.

We now know that most child abusers were abused themselves as children. And it is not just that this is the way they have come to expect children to be treated. Their sexual pleasure is also attached to this negative situation.

In the abusive situation, the powerful focused excitement of adult sexuality overwhelms the child's innocent unfocused sexuality. Just as the child does not have a focused ego, his sexuality is not yet concentrated exclusively in his genitals. For the child, sexuality is not separate from the whole of his body which is open to the undiluted streamings of pleasure and love. Forced to focus only on the sexual and genital dimension of pleasure, the child is robbed of the sweetness of full-body pleasure, physical safety and innocent play which are his birthright as a child. If the abuser is also a loved one, the loss includes the splitting of his sexuality from his heart or love, because the experience of being sexually used and over-stimulated and loving the abuser all at the same time is too painful and confusing to bear. When the child's natural openness is violated to gratify an adult's sexual obsession, his innocence and trust in life are abruptly lost. The child who has been abused usually grows to either hate sex or become obsessed with it.

As an adult, the abused child will be powerfully attracted to re-creating his negative history. Pleasure has become attached to "feeding off" childhood innocence, so he may find mutual adult sexual interaction much too threatening. He may therefore seek partners toward whom he feels inferior (like a child) or toward whom he feels superior (treating the other as though she were the child). Pleasure may be attached to submission or to control, in compensation for the helplessness experienced when he was a child. Or the sexual act may even become an act of displaced revenge against the person who first abused him.

Whether or not we were actively abused as children, everyone has an inner situation which is similar. We are turned on now as adults by whatever was painful to us as children. The unhealed child within us is always seeking to replay early abuse in just the same way that we compulsively and unconsciously re-create other childhood hurts from parents. We have become hooked on the pleasure of unfulfillment, if not of active abuse.

Working with Our Negative Pleasure

Acknowledging negative pleasure, letting ourselves know what turns us on, even if we may be ashamed of it, brings the energy of this distorted pleasure "out of the closet" where it can be accepted and transformed. This is not easy. We fear bringing our sexual and pleasure distortions out into the open because we unconsciously fear that if we expose our negative pleasure we will have to give up all pleasure and all sexuality in order not to be "bad."

> The attachment of, or connection between, pleasure
> and destructiveness has been instrumental in the wide-
> spread guilt feeling mankind has about all experiences
> of pleasure. This, in turn, is responsible for numbing all
> feelings. For how can the pleasure be liberated from the
> destructiveness if both are considered equally wrong?
> And yet man cannot live without pleasure, for life and
> pleasure are one and the same. When pleasure is linked
> to destructiveness, destructiveness cannot be given up.
> It feels as if life has to be given up. (PGL 148)

But this is not so. Instead we can reclaim the undiluted plea-sure behind our distortions which is so much more powerful than the small bits that squeeze through the narrow keyholes of our negative fantasies and distortions.

Everyone has distortions of sexuality. Everyone has elements of sadism or masochism in their sexual expression or fantasies. Masochism says: "Stagnation and self-punishment are sweet. Pleasure is in not doing anything, in being 'done to' without any responsibility for myself. Or the pleasure is in being 'punished' for being sexual and being 'forced' to have sexual feelings I do not have to be responsible for." Sadism says: "Power is sweet. Pleasure is in having power over others, and especially in 'paying back' all those who were so much more powerful than I was as a child." When we courageously face our sexual distortions, we release powerful energy for transformation.

After two years of marriage, Patricia's husband Jack became intensely attracted to a younger woman, Laurie, who was also Patricia's friend. Being in the Pathwork together, the three friends committed to staying open and honest with one another even as they entered the painful terri-tory of this love triangle. Patricia's unhappiness at Jack's feelings for Lau-rie quickly escalated into an agony of victimization for her; she was often tempted to threaten divorce and frequently indulged her passionately held moral superiority. And yet, since she also felt loyal to preserving their mar-riage, she elected to keep going through her pain. Patricia regularly ranted and railed at both Jack and Laurie, alternately feeling herself to be their judge and their victim; she sobbed her grief at not being Jack's "one and only" eternal romantic love.

After months of self-imposed agony, Patricia finally decided that there must be more to learn from this situation. Since, short of threatening divorce, Patricia was unable to control Jack's love feelings and his desires, she decided instead to surrender to whatever she could learn for herself, regardless of what happened to the marriage.

On a day spent in meditation, Patricia found herself repeating over and over her commitment to knowing the truth in this painful love triangle. "I just want the truth," she kept repeating to herself, "however painful or unflattering." Then she became very receptive, willing to listen to whatever came up. After a moment or so of deep inner silence, in which her whole body-mind seemed unusually still and focused, Patricia started to have sex-ual feelings in her genitals. As she tuned in to the feelings she realized, with a terrible shock, that she was actually turned on by Jack's love and sexual desire for another woman. Spontaneously she found herself visualizing her husband and Laurie making love, and then she had a fantasy of all three of them making love together and realized that the images turned her on. She was shocked. She almost shut off her feelings completely, but was coura-geous enough to acknowledge the truth to herself. Somehow Jack and Lau-rie's attraction for each other also held pleasure for her. She was actually turned on by the negative situation which also distressed her.

This awareness led to a great deal of further work. For the first time in her life Patricia allowed herself to have sexual fantasies of being with a woman and being with a couple. As she worked with these fantasies, she realized that they stemmed at least partly from the physical deprivation she had felt in the absence of deep bonding with her mother. Not having had the physical affection she needed as a child had led to a buried desire to "unite" physically with a woman.

Further exploration led to her understanding that she had felt stimulated sexually in the "triangle" with her mother and father. Neither of her parents was physically demonstrative, with each other or with the children. Patricia had craved more affectionate contact with both of them. As a child she had active fantasies of spending the night between the twin beds of her parents. She had imagined that she might get the affection and physical closeness she longed for by coming between them, being in the middle, feeding off whatever unknown urges must have sometimes drawn them together in the night. Patricia became aware that her present situation re-created the intensity of being "in the middle" between her parents. Again she acknowledged how her sexual energy was unconsciously tied to the love triangle she consciously abhorred.

Positive healthy sexuality can be re-claimed only if we first claim it in its distorted form, and then gradually learn to separate the pleasure from the negative situation. We can learn to extricate our sexuality from our sadism and masochism without losing our sexual enjoyment, and we can learn to separate our pleasure from our revenge and exploitation of others without lessening our capacity for real pleasure.

The Transformation of Negative Pleasure

The first step in the transformation of any aspect of the lower self is to allow ourselves to become conscious of its operation within us. We need to feel and to know our attachment to negative pleasure.

> It is not sufficient to know this generally. It must be brought back to your specific circumstances. What is the outer manifestation at this moment that causes you continuous anguish? In order truly to resolve these conditions, the blocked and paralyzed energy must be made fluid again. And this can only happen when you begin, as the first step in this particular phase of your development, to ascertain the pleasurable aspect in your destructiveness (including self-destructiveness).
> (PGL 148)

Actually, this is the gift of exploring our entrenched negativity. Locked in every destructive pattern is essential life energy, bound and hidden in pockets of cruelty and sloughs of stagnation in our souls. As we meet and release this distorted energy trapped in us, we will build our capacity for true pleasure and reduce our fear of destructive pleasure. In this way we will gradually expand our potential for bliss.

The possibility of increased pleasure and capacity for bliss is one of the principal motivations for transformation. And the understanding that the pleasure current is one great undivided force, only temporarily manifesting in attachment to negativity but much more powerful when not so ensnared, gives us a powerful incentive for transformation.

Exercises for Chapter 9:

1. In some area of disharmony or unfulfillment in your life, find and then state clearly your own negativity—your resentments, bitterness, rage, and blame.

a. Then find and put on paper your own negative intentions toward this situation—the attachment you have to the negativity and to the unfulfillment, the part of you that wants it this way. Does it, for example, feed your negative conclusions about life, or does your misery punish those who you believe hurt you? Are you exacting vengeance on someone?

b. Then see if you can find the negative pleasure in this situation—the part of you that enjoys this negative situation, that "gets off" on the pain or unfulfillment, that enjoys the victimization or the control.

c. Trace back into childhood to see if you can find the prototype or origin of this connection between unfulfillment and pleasure. How and when did your life force become attached to this kind of event?

2. After you have uncovered your negative intentionality and explored the pleasure current attached to it, consider if you are willing to be transformed in this area. Write out clearly the positive attitude you would like to embrace—the positive will and positive pleasure you would like to substitute for the current negative attitude. In your meditations, send this new positive affirmation deep into your soul substance.

Transforming the Lower Self

"Through the gateway of feeling your pain
lies your pleasure and joy."

—Pathwork Guide Lecture 190, *"The Importance of Feeling All Feelings"*

Michael's Devil: Transforming Lust into Love

Michael, whose story introduced Chapter Nine, was working to transform his sexual obsessions into a whole, healthy passion. After the exploratory work with his sexual "devil" described in the first part of his story, Michael had the following dream:

"I am visiting a friend who lives on a mountain. Talking in the kitchen, we look out the window and see that a storm is headed our way. Dark clouds fill the sky, coming down directly over our heads; there is a feeling of great danger. Through the kitchen screen door I notice a foot of water has already accumulated. I go up to the balcony outside, and I see more flooding in the distance. Suddenly the balcony collapses under me, and I fall on a power line.

"The line stretches from where I am all the way down to the valley. I slide down with the power line between my legs; it feels like a sexual 'live wire' between my legs, powerful but benign. It connects the dangerous 'high' place with a safer place in the valley, ending at a high school football field covered with only about two feet of water. As I slide off the line, I discover I am unhurt and that the water is much less dangerous down here."

The "water" of Michael's emotions had been attached to the "high," dangerous places of his drug use and distorted sexuality. This place was giving way, and he could no longer stand there. Michael's feeling about the power line he rode to safety was that it was an expression of his essential spiritual energy, the life force that was at once sexual, loving, benign and powerful. The dream expressed his growing capacity to "ground" his sexuality in the larger current of his spiritual power.

During this phase of Michael's Pathwork I did many sessions of core energetic work[1] with him so that he could build his capacity to sustain and ground a strong energetic charge. To experience the combined sexual and spiritual force which he longed for, Michael needed a strong container, a body with the capacity for ecstasy. He was strengthening his ability to feel passion and pleasure directly in his body, without having to generate unwanted sexual fantasies in his head to sustain a charge.

*I felt confirmed that we were opening up his capacity to ride his inner "power line" when Michael had a series of dreams about snakes. The snake is the archetypal image of the **kundalini**, or essential Life Force energy, that moves, snake-like, up the spine. The snake is also symbolic of sexual energy, and has been demonized in Western religion.*

---

[1] Core Energetics is a therapeutic modality for working directly with physical and emotional energies and energy blocks. Dr. John Pierrakos, psychiatrist and Eva Pierrakos's husband, created Core Energetics out of his formative work in Bio-Energetics and his grounding in the Pathwork Guide Lecture concepts.

Michael was terrified of snakes; he recalled with horror the memory of being chased by a pack of older boys running after him with a dead snake on a stick. He reported a dream:

"A group of boys is chasing me and I run into my basement. Then I see a snake coming after me, sniffing my feet. It's undulating, and I feel very scared. Then the snake begins to grow fur and to look a little like my cat Pansy, so I am not quite so frightened." Michael knew clearly that he had to meet his snake-like sexual energy, but he also knew that it would be less frightening than it had been in the past.

Working on the dream, Michael first spoke as the furry snake: "I am primitive, collective, primordial energy—squiggly, vibrating, unintelligent. I live in your basement. I like to see you [ego, intelligent Michael] squirm." Michael was then able to affirm, as Michael, "I accept you as mine—my pure raw sexual/primitive energy." Michael realized that his fear of the pack of boys chasing him reflected the distortions of his masculine sexual energy that originated in his childhood. As a child his sexuality had been tied up with attraction to his mother, but to have felt that fully would have been tantamount to incest, so he had shut down his energy and only later acted it out in "forbidden" sexual encounters.

Michael then had another snake dream: "I am in a room with another person who looks a lot like me, though older and wiser. Suddenly I see a two-foot banded snake coming off the radiator, and I am frightened. The other person says quietly, 'You haven't noticed yet, but there are snakes all over you.' I look up and am horrified to discover that there are indeed tiny snakes, thin as vermicelli, all over my body. I start pulling at them frantically, and discover that some break apart, like glass snakes. The other person speaks to me gently, 'Notice that the snakes are not hurting you. Just let them be, and you will discover they are harmless.'

"As I calm down, I realize the snakes are not poisonous, and I become curious about them, noticing they are of many varieties. One is a kind of suction snake which has attached itself to my leg. I discover it has a child-like quality to it, as though it were needy and had attached itself to me as a way of getting nourishment. I begin to feel I am seeing the snakes for the pure energy that they are, including the child-like neediness that is part of my sexuality. I am seeing the 'child behind every snake.'"

Michael's work on this dream included seeing the snakes as his animal sexual nature, which he had associated with the "devil." But now, with the help of the older, wiser man, representing his higher self teacher, he saw that the ominous part of the devil was gone. The snakes were benign, an expression of his kundalini or Life Force, which includes sexuality without the evil and guilt attached.

What had been frightening actually was seen to be child-like, even needy. He realized the suction snake was himself as a little boy, wanting to suck, full of unfulfilled oral needs. Michael had not been breast-fed, but as a child often had fantasies of sucking his mother's breasts, and as an adult he had a strong oral component to his sexuality. He committed to bringing his oral neediness more into the open, in his relationship with his wife, and also with himself, so that he could learn better how to nurture himself. He knew his inner little boy needed for him to also become a better parent to himself.

Shortly thereafter, Michael had two dreams which confirmed what had been happening in his waking life. Michael had been having fewer sexual fantasies about queens and was more fully present in lovemaking with his wife.

"I am in a spy movie, pursuing an attractive woman who is actually a queen. I think she may have been sent to entrap me. I keep trying to be alone with her, but we are constantly interrupted. When we are finally alone and she is naked, I move toward her genitals and I'm shocked to see that there is nothing there, only scar tissue."

Michael began to realize that, in reality, "there is nothing there." The queens were no longer exciting to him. And he could sense that behind the negative excitement was old pain, now faced and left behind. All that remained was the scar tissue, the reminder of the pain.

*He had a second dream which confirmed his inner change: "I visit my wife in a basement apartment she has taken in town. I meet some queens and transsexuals. I do not find them attractive, only sad. Suddenly I am aware of two men looking in the picture window of the apartment—angry men, gesticulating for me to come out. They remind me of the depraved characters in the movie **Deliverance**, men who violently forced others into humiliating, terrifying sexual acts. But somehow I am not afraid as I go outside to meet these two. I tell them confidently that they must be looking for someone else, not me. 'It is a case of mistaken identity,' I say to them calmly."*

Michael was no longer identified with the negative sexuality that had been the expression of his inner demon, his lower self. Now he could confidently face that side and say, "No, I am not the one I was. You can no longer claim me for one of yours." After this dream especially, he noticed that his infrequent sexual fantasies involving queens often ended up picturing his wife instead, with whom his sexual self-expression felt increasingly rich and full. The "basement apartment" where his fantasies once dwelt was now her apartment; it no longer belonged to the queens.

Around this time Michael also started feeling a great deal more powerful in his work and in athletics. He found himself more focused, assertive, and self-directed, and less prone to distraction. His love for his wife deepened, as he saw her more clearly for herself, rather than feeling vaguely threatened by her as a feminine presence unconsciously merged with his mother.

The many emotions which had been fused in Michael's early sexual energy around his mother were now being sorted out, and hence his emotional life was much richer. His need for nurturing and some appropriate re-mothering was being met by me as his Pathwork helper, without any conflicting sexual energy. His need for sexual and romantic love was being met by his wife, who was also a source of nurturing for him. And his need to care for others was being met by giving to his own inner unloved child and by caring for his cat Pansy.

Transforming the Lower Self

The transformation of the lower self is the heroic journey for our times. The hero's path for our day is to go inward, not outward; to travel deep into the basements of our inner darkness, where we will meet and transform our devils and demons.

More than any of us realizes, our personal power has been restricted by unconscious negativity. As Michael discovered on meeting his own sexual distortions, we can safely release the energy of negative pleasure trapped in the unconscious and thereby greatly enhance our real pleasure and vitality. When we lift the mask, we will be impressed by the raw creative power of the lower self, for it is indeed more authentic and passionate than what has concealed and suppressed it. But eventually we realize that indulgence of lower-self power never leads to sustained happiness, and we come to long for the deeper power which is aligned with love. So we meet our own unloving attitudes and passions in order to release them into their original nature, thus reconnecting our personal energy with the power of God.

The ripple effects of taking the hero's journey of personal transformation empower everyone we meet. Surrendering bitterness and blame, we know that our unhappiness exists in direct proportion to our own unredeemed lower self. Because we take responsibility for our unhappiness, those around us are released from guilt and coercion and are enabled to relate to us more openly. Furthermore, each step we take through our own inner darkness inspires courage in those who observe us. Ultimately, the transformation of the lower self benefits the whole of creation: each defense dismantled, each demon de-energized, and each distortion resolved releases that much more energy into the collective pool of positive life energy.

Yet it remains true that it is a rare person who will consciously undertake this journey, and fewer still will choose it as a way of life. It is neither easy nor painless to see our own lower self clearly, without denial and without self-denigration. It is difficult to stop blaming others and to take full responsibility for our own happiness. To see ourselves with clarity and compassion takes a strong, resilient self-esteem which will become deeper and more grounded the more we do this work.

For those who make the choice, nothing is more exhilarating than transforming inner distortions, coming home to our essence as truth and love. This odyssey includes consciously choosing to meet the negativity and limitations in us which, if left to operate unconsciously, would result in negative life circumstances. Painful life experience eventually teaches us to look within for our own negativity. In consciously undertaking this journey, we speed up this process as we align with the inner teacher in this great school of life, moving with the evolutionary processes which will bring us home.

Because our own lower self is what we most fear, confronting it bravely increases our capacity for fearlessness. We are doing nothing less than engaging and exorcising Satan, the distorted energy of God. This distorted energy has existed in all of us since the earliest of times, since the invention of the ego, since we left the "Garden of Eden," the state of unified and connected God consciousness.

The journey of self-realization takes many lifetimes. Each stage of the journey requires great patience with ourselves, based on the understanding that whatever feeling or insight temporarily threatens to overwhelm our self-esteem is only a small part of an immense undertaking.

> Do not ever forget that you are not your ugly traits.
> But at the same time do not negate or deny them. . . .
> It is necessary to acknowledge the ugly aspects as part
> of you and take responsibility for them before you
> can truly understand that you are not these aspects.

> It is possible to be responsible for them without
> believing that they are your only reality. Only when
> you first take responsibility for them can you come
> to the wonderful realization that you are not them,
> but that you carry them with you for a certain
> purpose. Only then can you come to the next
> step of integration. (*PGL 189*)

Activating Higher Self Energies

We cannot reach the heart of the lower self without also having a strong connection with the higher self. As we reach deeply into and transform our worst selves, we must simultaneously be learning to identify with our higher selves and reaching for all the spiritual help available to us. We need to align our energy with the positive intention to embody the best that we are, to know our true spiritual identity, even as we meet the worst in ourselves.

The most important ingredient in the transformation process is our good will; **we must be willing to be transformed**. Good will can be encouraged and developed in this work, as we learn to deepen our alignment with the higher self, but it must already exist in the individual to some extent before transformation can begin. It creates the spiritual underpinning, the safety net, the stage on which the inner characters are invited out from the shadows to be seen for who they are.

When we accept the task of transformation as the purpose of life, we find joy and meaning in acknowledging and releasing distorted energy and consciousness back into their original divine essence.

> To the extent that life is led in such a way, to that
> degree consciousness—as a whole, as it permeates all—
> is less split off into its particles and more unified.
> (*PGL 189*)

Letting Go of the Lower Self

Letting go of a piece of the lower self can be a simple matter of apologizing for negative acts we know we have committed. To say "I'm sorry" genuinely can go a long way toward clearing the air. Or we may need to be more specific: "I see now that my competitiveness made me undermine you when you needed my support. I can see that I hurt you, and I'm sorry. I'm committed to releasing my competitiveness so I can be there for you in the future." When the truth is said, the pain of real guilt felt, and the commitment to act differently in future is made, we can apologize and, likely, be forgiven; the karma is finished. Sometimes it is that easy.

Activating Lower-Self Energies

Often, however, the lower self needs not only to be brought into awareness and confessed to another, but also to be released energetically through physical self-expression. Our bodies have "solidified" certain negative or repressive attitudes through muscular tensions and structural distortions. By releasing these tensions we reclaim the energy behind our negative attitudes, thereby gaining much greater freedom of movement and a new integral vitality. Release of these tensions can sometimes be helped by others, through deep tissue massage, core energetics, or other forms of bodywork, or through healings. As we take responsibility for the tensions and distortions in our own bodies, we will find ways to discharge the negative energy safely and appropriately.

Finding the proper expression is not easy. We tend to have an either/or attitude toward expression of the lower self. Either we repress it in order not to be bad—which can leave us feeling stifled, numb, phony, depressed, and resentful—or we express it carelessly and hurtfully, and end up feeling guilty and self-rejecting.

There is another way. We can create safe environments where the work of discharging bottled-up hostilities can go on with support and guidance. Even the energy of latent murderers and rapists, power-driven leaders or masochistic followers can be released and transformed safely in the context of supportive groups and individual sessions with trained helpers, counselors, and therapists.

There are many recognized ways for expressing negative feelings on inanimate objects. We can use a rubber hose to beat up and destroy phone books.[2] This is especially useful for someone who was never allowed to make messes as a child, or who needs to experience his destructiveness. We may use a tennis racket or a padded rubber bat to beat on a couch, bed, or pillow repre-

---

2 This technique was originated by Dr. Elisabeth Kubler-Ross for her "Life, Death, and Transition" workshops.

senting someone (or a negative aspect of someone) toward whom we are angry. We can throw a "temper tantrum," flailing hands and feet while lying on a bed; we can "choke" a towel or a padded rubber bat, and so on.[3] We can talk to or beat up on pillows representing parents or others with whom we have "unfinished business." These active energetic expressions of the lower self allow people to work through the feelings involved without hurting anyone. However, the presence of a trained group leader or helper is necessary to ensure the proper and safe use of these techniques.

For some people substituting inanimate objects for real people at first seems artificial. But that awkwardness can be overcome, and learning to work with symbolic representations is far better than either the repression of negative energy or its destructive expression with others. Symbolism helps us to realize that the energy in need of expression is our own, with only a marginal relationship to whomever we think deserves our anger, bitterness, or blame. This leads us to reclaim the original pure energy behind our negativity.

> The groping toward finding the lower self seems
> confusing, until you find the method and the manner
> in which it becomes possible to accept destructive
> impulses and desires in you without condoning them,
> to understand them without hanging onto them,
> to evaluate them realistically without acting them
> out. You need to avoid the traps of projection, self-
> justification, self-righteous exoneration, blaming
> of others, and making excuses for the self, or the traps
> of self-indulgence, denial, repression, and evasion. It
> requires continuous inspiration from the higher forces
> within and a deliberate articulation in requesting their
> help, in order to awaken and maintain awareness of
> the destructive aspects and the proper method of
> handling them. (PGL 184)

Our task is to look directly into the heart of our own distortions—to awaken the negative feelings behind our numbness and denial, so we can discharge them and let them return to their innate identity as pure energy.

---

[3]These techniques are used by Bio-Energetics and Core Energetics therapists, and were originated by Drs. Alexander Lowen and John Pierrakos.

Feeling Our Feelings

To come out of denial and numbness, we need to feel the passionate energy of the lower self behind our cool disguises.

A woman who had been working on herself for many years first met in a dream the intense cruelty behind her "coolness." Her personal work had recently focused on her fear of being home alone at night, when her husband was away at work. She relates her dream:

"I am home alone. I wake up and someone is pounding on the door in a very demanding manner. I get out of bed wearing a flimsy pink nightgown. I start looking for a robe but cannot find it. The pounding continues and gets insistent. I open the door expecting to see my husband. Instead, standing in front of me is an attractive but ominous man, a David Bowie type—androgynous, slim, slicked-back hair, a dapper dresser in pleated pants, a leather pilot jacket with fur collar, a white scarf. His ice-cold blue eyes complete his menacing appearance. He strides into the room as if he owns it.

"The dream changes. I turn into a frenzied killer. The man is on the floor. I have something in my hand, a bunch of knives, a metal device, or perhaps just long, dangerous fingernails. I am shredding the man below me, mutilating him, attacking him like a mad dog. Part of me is distant—my objective observer is watching this scene, being amazed at my killer energy—even while the other part of me is busily shredding him.

"The dream changes again. I 'wake up' from the previous dream. It is as though I am coming out of the psychotic break I entered when I became the frenzied killer. I look down and see that what I had thought was the man I was mutilating was in fact my cat and I am mashing her under the arch of my foot. As I look down I see my cat looking up at me meowing piteously and saying, in effect, 'What are you doing to me?'

"Then I really wake up, shocked at myself. My cat comes up to me and jumps into bed with me. I find all I can do is sit there, numbly stroking her. Much later, when I was able to work on the dream, I realized that it is the answer I have been praying for: to understand why I experience nighttime terrors, and to understand and meet the lower self. I did not know until this dream that my real nighttime terror is of myself, my own killer. In the past my lower self expressed itself more like the cold androgynous man, numbed to feelings, cold and cruel. In this dream at last I see my passionate cruelty, my killer energy. When I 'wake up' within the dream and see what I am doing to my cat, I realize how destructive this energy is.

"Since working extensively on this dream, I have much reduced the fear of nighttime and being alone. I now have access to the energy and source of my fears and hence no longer have anything to fear. I have met the enemy and it is, indeed, myself."

The dreamer met her personal killer, the destroyer of her own soft, feminine, trusting, kittenish energy. Such an encounter leaves her more able to take responsibility for her nighttime terrors, no longer so vulnerable to her negative fantasies. The androgynous man is an archetype of the cool, dapper sophisticated devil. Such a character denies his human passion and only calculates his power advantage. The dreamer takes the mask off this cool character and exposes the passionate killer underneath.

The lower self is at its most dangerous when we numb both the passionate cruelty and the soft vulnerability behind the negative attitudes we harbor. When we are cut off from our own feelings, we can easily deny the vulnerable humanity of others and thus rationalize our cruelty toward them. Our cruelty, and our unconscious excitement in being cruel, then become a substitute for the real flow of life that feelings represent.

The more numb we stay, the more we may have to escalate our negativity in order to feel anything. By contrast,

> The more you acknowledge your hate, the less you
> hate. The more you accept your ugliness, the more
> beautiful you become. The more you accept your
> weakness, the stronger you are. The more you admit
> your hurt, the more dignity you will have. These are
> inexorable laws. This is the path we tread. (*PGL 197*)

Seeing Evil as a Defense Against Pain

We are greatly helped in our work to face and transform the evil in ourselves when we understand that all our distortions are ultimately a defense against pain. In any particular lifetime, the childhood pains—of loss and rejection, invasion and abandonment—are the pool of feelings which get covered over by our defenses of hostility or withdrawal, sadism or masochism. In the soul's journey there are also hurts from past lives—separation from loved ones, betrayal and self-betrayal—which resulted in a predisposition toward certain character faults and distortions in this life.

At the cosmic level the evil in us is our defense against the pain of our choice to separate from God. The greatest pain in the soul results from our false belief that we are only our separated limited selves, unable and unworthy of connecting to the whole of self and of life.

When we choose to stop numbing ourselves and stop denying our pain, then we can reclaim the innocent self we were before we created the defenses that make up the crux of the lower self. The pain of all our hurts may be quite intense, but it also softens us and completes itself in the process of being felt. Our personal pain leads us quickly to the most basic pain in us all, that of feeling separate from God, and the false belief that we are not worthy to reconnect with the wholeness of life.

When we defend against pain, we rigidify, become defensive, and lash back in characteristic modes. Feeling the pain and discovering that we can tolerate it begins the process of releasing our defenses. We learn to bend like the willow instead of staying upright but brittle. We are no longer ashamed to weep, to mourn, and to forgive. Our souls return to us as we reclaim all our feelings—our anger, grief, and fear can turn into joy and exhilaration if we let all our emotions flow.

We especially need to feel the grief of the hurt child behind our defenses.

Julie was working on her criticalness toward others, whom she often dismissed as unredeemable. As a result she had few intimate relationships and was beginning to feel the pain of her isolation. She had the following dream:

"I am a child again on the red-haired horse I got when I was fifteen years old. I am beating my horse, Big Red, with a whip, harder than I ought to, and telling the horse how bad it is not to be behaving the way I think he ought to behave. The dream is very real; this is a scene I remember vividly from adolescence, when I did abuse my large, patient, trusting horse."

Following a suggestion from me, Julie became the child beating up on her horse represented by a large reddish brown pillow. When I asked why she beat up on her horse, she responded, "Because I am angry. I'm angry because I am always alone and I don't feel like anyone loves me. My parents keep telling me everything I do is wrong and nothing I do is right. I just want to hurt something, so I don't have to feel how hurt I am inside. I'm going to stay tough instead."

Now that she had seen her lower self in the form of the adolescent who abused Big Red, she thought it should change and she turned her critical impatience toward herself. In a later session, Julie expressed her judgmentalness toward her lower-self adolescent represented by another pillow. Julie began to beat the pillow and to yell at it, "Why are you so stubborn? I want to beat some sense into you. Who are you and why don't you wake up? Wake up!"

As Julie brought her fists down to the pillow yet again, she saw the face of the mean, defiant adolescent she had been, only this time the face began to change. With her arms still stretched up to hit the pillow, she looked down and saw a new face. Looking back at her with soft, pleading eyes was the face of a frightened, cowering baby fawn. Julie crumbled and wept, holding the pillow representing the frightened fawn/child underneath her toughness. At last she knew the vulnerability hiding beneath her defense.

> "Through the gateway of feeling your weakness
>   lies your strength.
> Through the gateway of feeling your pain lies your
>   pleasure and joy.
> Through the gateway of feeling your fear lies your security
>   and safety.
> Through the gateway of feeling your loneliness lies your
>   capacity to have fulfillment, love, and companionship.
> Through the gateway of feeling your hopelessness lies true
>   and justified hope.
> Through the gateway of accepting the lacks of your
>   childhood lies your fulfillment now." (*PGL 190*)

Feeling the Pain of Real Guilt

In addition to feeling the real pain of our lacks in childhood and our losses in adulthood, transformation of the lower self also requires that we be willing to feel the pain of our real guilt for abandoning or rejecting others. In our negativity we have transgressed spiritual law, creating pain for others by our negative choices and personal flaws. This kind of pain is often more difficult to feel than the pain of having been hurt by others.

> In the days of pre-psychology, religion had indoctrinated humanity with a distorted, debilitating guilt feeling. False guilts; fear of a punishing god; guilt that did not make it possible for people to raise their heads in dignity and in the knowledge of who they ultimately

> are. In order to straighten out such distortions, the
> pendulum must always swing temporarily into an
> opposite extreme, until the right balance, the truth,
> is found. Thus, the entire psychological movement
> has turned away from feeling the pain of guilt.
>
> But the real guilt for your own distortions must be fully
> seen, faced, felt, understood as to all their ramifications
> and chain reactions. Otherwise you can never be in the
> clear with yourself. Unless you do so, you cannot be
> whole; you cannot look at yourself with love and
> respect. You cannot be who you really are. (PGL 201)

Feeling the pain of real guilt means taking responsibility for having created a condition causing pain to others. This is hard to do and initially feels like a blow to one's self-esteem. And yet there is no pain that is more fully releasing and transforming. The pain of real guilt is soft, and completes itself in the process of being felt. Through allowing this pain fully, we can know we are forgiven by God. We have paid the price and are released from our guilt.

The pain of real guilt and the pain of our own real suffering are different from the "hard" pain of blame, which is a means of trying to punish those who hurt us. The message of this hard pain is always, "See how miserable I am. It is all your fault." Our misery then becomes the weapon to punish parents or others who have hurt us, and there is no intent of extending forgiveness.

The pain of real guilt, true remorse, is also different from the pain of false guilt, which results from not living up to expectations—our own or those of others. The excessive *mea culpa* of false guilt reinforces the mask, giving the message, "See how good I am because I feel so bad," or "I am so bad that you must not expect very much of me, and you should feel sorry for me." Clearing away these distortions allows the simple, softer pain of real guilt to be felt, while maintaining our personal dignity and awareness of our divinity.

Acknowledging our real guilts and feeling their pain is a marvelous cleansing process and is the true meaning of the age-old ritual of confession. This process may be followed by an act of restitution—either a simple "I'm sorry" or more extensive acts of righting our wrongs. When we ask within ourselves for the right kind of restitution in each case—neither denying nor exaggerating the wrong we have done—the answers will come. Above all we need to know that we are already forgiven, already loved in our entirety. For there is nothing we can do, feel, or intend that surpasses the power of God to forgive.

Patience in Healing the Lower Self

In addition to good will, the most important element in the healing process is patience. We must remember that the lower self is rooted in the very origins of human consciousness which is dualistic. It began with the first separation of part of God from all of God. It began with free will, which gave us the capacity to choose separateness, and has been reinforced by wrong choices made by human beings down through the millennia. To think we can repair the damage entirely in a single lifetime may be the utmost in arrogance. In any case, it is bound to lead to frustration and despair, so we must be patient.

Julie was an outdoorswoman, born in the American Southwest. She loved to camp and felt entirely peaceful in the desert. With people it was different; with them she often felt distrustful and separate.

When Julie began work on her lower self, she visualized it as a tough, paranoid, greedy, power-hungry, street-wise adolescent boy—an extreme version of the adolescent she had been who had abused her beloved horse. In her visualizations she would take this street kid out to the desert and she saw him sitting silently with her for long periods of time. He was too proud to ask for help or even to interact with her. When he would eventually need something and would deign to ask Julie, he did so with a snarl of contempt. Julie would answer, just the minimum, and wait.

She carried on this visualization for months, and each time she tuned in she found that the street kid was softening just a little, beginning to realize that someone (Julie's own higher self) was there for him. For the first time he had a reason to trust. But still Julie was willing to wait, in faith, for the coming together of her lower and higher selves.

Julie felt that this healing visualization was also a picture of her incarnational choices. She knew that her ability to be trusting with other humans was deeply flawed. When she started the Pathwork she felt nearly incapacitated in that respect, and she suspected that it reflected lifetimes of difficulty and mistakes. Her soul's choice to be born and raised in the desert this time was just what she had needed to solidify a connection with nature and with her higher self. This would afford her the strength to finally take on her lower self, after lifetimes of acting it out unconsciously.

We can only take one step at a time. Often we are afraid to wake up to our lower self because we fear the realization of how much disarray or destruction it may have wrought. Anxious that we might then have to change everything at once, we shrink from a task that threatens to overwhelm us.

Diane had been in denial about her alcoholism for years. As she began to wake up to the reality that she was alcoholic and to recognize the devastation her illness had caused for herself and her children, she felt horrified. Everything was such a mess; how could she ever straighten it all out?

Then she had this dream: "I am washing my hair in a sink and I discover to my horror that I have my head stuck under the faucet and I don't know how to get it out. At first I panic and try to jerk my head out, while the water is still running. I hurt my neck and get an unwanted gulp of water; I feel like I am drowning. Then I hear a quiet voice inside me which says, 'Slow down and take it one step at a time.' Somehow I am then able to think clearly. So first I turn off the water faucet. Then I carefully turn my head to the side and I find that, little by little, I can indeed extricate myself, step by step, until I am free."

Residing quietly beyond the lower self is always the light and wisdom of the higher self, guiding us every step of the way. The lower self is a dark shadow that attempts to dampen the light, to distract us from the soft, steady glow that is constantly present to guide us.

Meditation to Re-Educate the Lower Self

Once we have found the lower self and felt the pain behind its manifestation, we can re-educate it with the help of the higher self. In the Pathwork we work actively with both the lower and higher selves in our meditations. We do this work in meditation only after we have established the capacity to calm the outer mind, through concentrating on the breath or through some other centering practice. Then we can engage the conscious ego in the work of contacting, understanding, and re-educating the lower self. Thus meditation becomes an active dialogue among three parts of ourselves: the positive ego, the lower-self child, and the higher self.

> The conscious ego must reach down and say, "Whatever is in me, whatever is hidden that I ought to know about myself, whatever negativity and destructiveness it is, should be out in the open. I want to see it. I commit myself to seeing it, regardless of the hurt vanity that may result from it. Wherever I am stuck, I want to be aware of how I deliberately refuse to see my own lower self and therefore concentrate on the wrongs of others." This is one direction of meditation.

> The other direction must go toward the universal, higher self, which has powers that surpass the limitations of the conscious self. These higher powers should be called upon for the same purpose of exposing the destructive little self so that resistance can be overcome. The ego-will alone may be incapable of accomplishing this. But the ego can meditate to request the higher powers to help.

> . . . .

> When the lower self begins to express itself more freely because the ego allows it, receives it as an interested, open listener, you must collect this material for further study. What reveals itself should be explored as to its origins, its results. What underlying misconceptions (images) are responsible for the overt self-destruction, the hate, the spite, the malice that come out?

> . . . .

> The next step in meditation is to re-educate the self-destructive child (and the adult lower self) that is now no longer entirely unconscious. The child with its false beliefs, stubborn resistance, spitefulness and murderous rage, must be reoriented. (*PGL 182*)

As a little girl, Judith had been terrorized by her mother whom she had seen as a wicked witch.[4] Now Judith was aware that her own lower self was a re-creation of her mother's witch—a defense Judith used to

---

[4] The witch as a symbol for destructive female energy is ingrained in children's unconscious mind through frequent exposure to European fairy tales. These tales themselves derived from the archetypal, and also historical, struggle of the patriarchal, Christian, or rational world-view to suppress the matriarchal, pre-Christian, or intuitive world-view. The true witch was a healer or priestess of the pre-Christian, Goddess religion who became demonized by Christianity.

distance herself from intimate contact. Created as a defense against child-hood pain, Judith's lower self no longer served her, but had nonetheless taken on a life of its own. Now it kept her shut down even when she was consciously ready to open up.

In meditation, Judith began a three-way dialogue in which her adult ego invited both her lower-self witch and her higher-self angel to speak. Immediately she saw her witch come toward her in a menacing way, trying to keep her down and stop the dialogue altogether.

Judith persisted: "I want to have my feelings back."

The wicked witch replied: "Don't you realize that is impossible? Your feelings will kill you. That's why you created me. I kept you from going crazy as a child, so you better thank me and let me keep control of things."

Adult Judith: "I do thank you for saving me from feeling too much vulnerability when I was a child. But I don't need your protection anymore. Now I want to be able to feel vulnerable, because I am around people who are safer than my mother was. Now I want to love and be loved; please release my feelings."

The witch: "No, I want to hold on and feel my power to scare you and other people. I want power more than anything else."

Judith then invoked the greater power of the higher self. For a while she saw and heard nothing. Then slowly she saw a woman robed in white light emerge from behind a curtain.

This angelic figure spoke to the witch: "You say you want power. But what do you really want?"

The witch suddenly turned into a little girl and spoke with a child's voice: "Love is what I want. But I don't believe I deserve it. I have to be good to get love. If I had been good, my mother wouldn't have been so mean to me. So I must be bad. Since I'm bad anyway I'll act bad and scare people, so at least I'll feel powerful."

The witch now dissolved fully into the little girl Judy, who began to cry quietly. Judith saw her child-self peeking out from behind a curtain. She also saw the angel opening her arms to the child. The little girl came across the room and onto the lap of the angel, cuddling for a moment but then becoming scared again.

Little Judy: "There are lots of witches here, you know. Not just me."

In her meditation Judith now saw a whole line of girls and women behind little Judy—an entire female lineage emerged, including her mother, two grandmothers, and yet more female relatives. "They all need love too," said the child Judy. "They have witches' voices because they are scared and lonely too. There was no one to love them either."

Judith now witnessed little Judy coming toward her, leading the whole row of women/witches. She saw the angel as a goddess robed in white taking the hand of the child and all the other women and forming a circle with them, urging them to find their voices and their strength as women of true power without the distortions. Judith began to hear the words and music of "Song of the Soul" in her mind; a chorus of girl children and women sang together.

It takes practice to open up a connection with both the lower and higher selves in meditation, but doing this kind of meditation speeds up the work.

Seeing Divine Qualities Behind Faults

Under every fault needing transformation is a divine quality. This divine quality already exists even before the fault is transformed.

For example, under laziness is a positive ability to relax and take life as it comes, without rushing to control it. Under hyperactivity, on the other hand, is a positive ability to act and move out into life. Under judgmentalness is the ability to make positive and precise discernments. Under sloppiness, on the other hand, is an ability to let go of ego control and allow life to flow without interference.

Usually we find that our finest qualities are right next door to our worst faults. As the faults are gradually transformed, the corresponding good qualities are not lost—as we sometimes mistakenly fear—but are instead strengthened and balanced.

Even the worst aspects of human nature, when faced, discharged and transformed, yield a divine kernel. Murderous rage can turn into passionate assertion. Cruelty can become positive, creative aggression.

> No matter how actually ugly some of these
> manifestations may be—such as cruelty, spite,
> arrogance, contempt, selfishness, indifference, greed,
> cheating, and many more—you can bring yourself
> to realize that every one of these traits is an energy
> current that is originally good and beautiful and
> life-affirming. By searching in that direction, you
> will come to understand and experience how this is
> true specifically; how this or that hostile impulse is
> originally a good force. When you understand it, you

have made a substantial inroad toward transforming
the hostility and freeing the energy that is either
channeled in a truly undesirable, destructive way, or
is frozen and stagnating.

You have to learn to fully acknowledge that **the way
the power manifests is undesirable, but the energy
current that produces this manifestation is desirable in itself.** For it is made of the life stuff itself. It
contains consciousness and creative energy. It contains
every possibility to manifest and express life, to create
new life manifestations. It contains the best of life.
(*PGL 184*)

The deeper we go into our faults, the higher we can go into
our essence. And the opposite is also true. The more connected
we are to our essence as divinity, the more courage we have to
face all the distorted, unhealed aspects still remaining in the
psyche. Truly this journey brings out the best in us, allowing us
all to be heroes and heroines of the inner path.

Taking Full Self-Responsibility

When we take full responsibility for the lower self, we
expand beyond our limitations into an expanded identity.

Taking full responsibility for your distorted, demonic
traits will, paradoxical as this may seem, liberate you
from being identified with those aspects. You will
know fully that you are you and that these aspects are
but appendices or attachments, which you can draw
into yourself as you dissolve them. That is, their basic
energy and undistorted nature can become part of
consciousness that you manifest. (*PGL 189*)

*Patricia and her husband Jack had created a love triangle with Lau-
rie, as described in Chapter Nine. All three of them conscientiously
explored the compelling impulses which kept them in this mutually punishing relationship. Patricia's work on this issue included facing her
temptation to separateness and self-righteousness, which were so much
easier for her than keeping her heart open in the face of pain. She had
glimpses of an inner persona as a nun—morally superior and sexually
uptight—whom she began to call "Mother Superior." Jack saw how his
fear of commitment made it easier for him to split his desire for intimacy*

into attraction for two women, rather than "put all his eggs in one basket." Laurie explored her dependency on a strong older man to make her feel safe.

Eventually they were able to let go of the triangle. Jack chose to risk giving his full commitment to Patricia. Laurie chose to move away from them, so she could start a new life and create a relationship of her own. And Patricia chose to relax her moralism and give her full sexual love to Jack. Their marriage was immeasurably deepened by the truthful consciousness they had brought to this painful experience.

Several weeks after Laurie moved away, Patricia was walking alone in the woods when suddenly a full-blown past-life scenario presented itself. The setting was the Middle Ages, perhaps in the south of what is now France. She saw Jack as the lord of a small manor, a powerful yet self-centered man who, among other things, would occasionally exercise his right (the "droit de seigneur") to initiate sexually any virgin living on his land. She saw herself as his uptight, moralistic wife who was constantly putting him down and judging him. She saw Laurie as the beautiful daughter of one of Jack's guards. In that life Patricia had eventually left her husband and had entered a convent, forswearing men and sexuality, and living out her life in solitary bitterness, except for one very predatory affair with a younger nun. "Jack" eventually married "Laurie," but continued his decline into egotistic self-indulgence which "Laurie" was not strong enough to confront. "Laurie" had lived out her life in painful dependency.

After this startling past-life revelation, Patricia saw that this time they had all done the necessary inner work so they would not have to re-create the errors of the "past." In a way that she could not explain, Patricia felt that the work they did in this life also helped the people they once had been. She had a sense that the lives of past and present interpenetrated and that by doing the inner work and making the right choices now, three souls were being healed. With this reincarnational revelation also came a sense of great dignity and respect for herself and the two others involved. They had indeed helped one another to meet deep unresolved soul issues and had together journeyed toward wholeness.

Letting Go to God

As we identify and experience the lower self, including the negative intent and negative pleasure, and as we release our defenses and feel our underlying pain and real guilt, we also continuously affirm our essence as beings of light, angels of

God. We hold in the light each aspect of ourselves in need of transformation.

Then, when we have done our very best in facing some area of negativity in us, we let go and release the whole process to God. As much as we can accomplish with the best intentions in the world, we—the little ego—cannot accomplish transformation alone. We must invoke the spontaneous energies of our higher self, and the guidance and grace of God and God's spirit world, to effect the transformation.

Prayer and meditation, positive affirmation, and invoking the energies of the higher self, are important tools at every stage of the transformation process. We could not possibly face the depths of the lower self without the constant reassurance, support, forgiveness, and guidance from the higher self.

Transformation does not proceed in a linear fashion. Stages constantly overlap and intertwine. For a while we may be working on the mask, and then on aspects of the lower self, and then all that has to be postponed until awareness of the higher self has been strengthened enough to allow consciousness of those aspects that still stand in need of transformation. This is the ever-deepening spiral of growth.

Exercises for Chapter 10:

1. Write honestly about some event in your life in which you feel you behaved badly. On paper, confess clearly what you feel were your flaws in this situation and where you erred. If other people were involved, write a simple letter of apology to each of them (which you do not need to send).

2. Once you have located a negative attitude in yourself, state it clearly, and then list the ways this harms you in your life, the consequences or "price you pay" for holding onto this or that negative attitude.

3. In meditation, allow a dialogue between the ego, lower self and the higher self. After centering yourself, select an issue or disharmony in your life. Invite the lower self to speak about its part in the issue, and allow the ego-mind to relax and just listen. Then invite the higher self to speak to the issue, and let the ego just listen to it. Then allow a dialogue among the three selves about the issue. The higher self may appear as a benign angel or other archetypal figure; the lower self may appear as a child, or a demon, or anything else. Allow the higher self to talk directly to the lower self. Your ego is the moderator. Write out or draw this exchange to capture the energy of your inner characters as they are revealed.

4. List five of what you feel are your faults. Find five corresponding positive qualities which are "right next door" to these distortions in your psyche.

5. Take one of your character faults and invite in the spirit of forgiveness to surround and bathe this flaw. How do you see your fault differently when you look at it in the light of its being already forgiven?

Creating Our Lives
from the Higher Self

"The innate potential of all human beings to create
is astoundingly underestimated. It is infinitely greater
than you could possibly realize now. . . . Most people
do not know of their dormant capacity to create
and re-create their lives consciously."

—Pathwork Guide Lecture 208, *"The Innate Capacity to Create"*

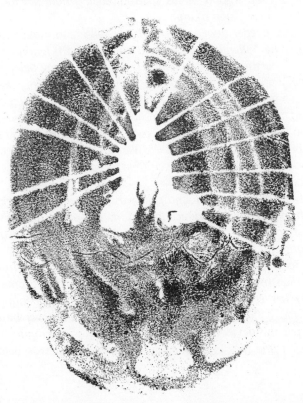

Susan's Retreat: Journeying Toward the Feminine

At forty years old, I began to experience a powerful visceral yearning to become a mother. Earlier in my marriage I had occasionally had such twinges, but I had convinced myself that such longing was either a displacement of my desire for more intimacy in my marriage or was a metaphor for my "mothering" of Sevenoaks, the spiritual center which Donovan and I had created and which had, indeed, become our "baby." I had effectively dismissed my earlier urgings as those of a biological will which did not, in my estimation, equate with God's will for me or for us.

But what moved through me now was not to be dismissed; its urgency was consuming. Yet in opening up a vision of myself as a mother—quieter, more feminine, more inward, more on the land—I also released the deeper layers of my inner "no," which I had not known about until this challenge was brought.

Old images, fears, and dualities were revealed: motherhood meant confinement, dependency, powerlessness, being out of control, loss of personhood. On the other hand, the intense giving demanded by my spiritual work with others offered creativity and effectiveness, but felt barren. The split of motherhood versus spiritual calling haunted me, even as I groped for a new vision of unity.

An even deeper duality emerged: my self-identity as a "daughter of the patriarchy," identified with mind and will, both fearing and longing to plunge into the more feminine, receptive side of my being from which I felt deeply separate. Choosing to go toward my feminine, sexual, fertile, unseen self felt like going into a Void—unknown and unsupported.

I had a dream in which my mother, sister, and I were riding in a limousine to Dad's office. The bureaucracy hadn't caught up to the fact that he had been dead for nine years! We were still caught in the world of masculine values; we had not yet been able to be women together and were still riding in the man's car.

Perhaps the most profound split was between my faith in my guidance which affirmed this direction and my self-doubt and despair which continued to surface, especially each monthly time I discovered that I was not pregnant.

My feelings flip-flopped. As Donovan and I rode back from a movie several months after we had decided we wanted to become parents, I suddenly felt enveloped in darkness and bleakness, hearing cackling, hostile voices, "Who do you think you are? You'll never be able to do this." I felt the devils telling me I was wrong and arrogant to want so much from one life. Instead of an annunciation, I was being given a denunciation. My lower-self despair and self-doubt were what allowed this demonic assault on my faith; yet I emerged from the encounter feeling my determination strengthened.

About a week after this "attack" of darkness, I experienced an ecstatic moment, an opening into clear vision, sweet sexuality, and blissful readiness. In an intensive period of working with couples on their sexuality, I felt fully in my body, healthier than I had ever felt in my life, and I started running down the hill on the path to the pond, shouting with delight to the universe, "I'm ready! I'm ready!" I dove into the pond, feeling energized, exquisitely sensitive, happy, and full. And praising God, "Thank you God. I'm ready. Thank you."

But then, the next month, when my period came, I experienced the most intense disappointment I could ever remember feeling. I felt barren, bereft, needy, crazy. It was as though I had just lost the most precious thing in the world to me. I wailed and wailed. I lost faith in my ability to become a mother. I saw how deep was my despair about feminine spiritual fulfillment. The areas where I still longed for more fullness were precisely those areas in which I could not exercise my ego-will— in sexuality, spirituality, and in motherhood. I could only open to receive the grace of God through me.

The difficulty and vulnerability of this did not strike me as long as I was more defended against my longing. But I could no longer deny my longing. My wanting to surrender more fully was physical; I could taste it. And I could not will it. I could do nothing. I could only let go. I committed to giving up the displaced struggle of the will. I prayed to let go and let God. This unleashed a powerful need for Donovan. I felt often like a needy child, a baby possum wanting to cling to its mommy's belly; Donovan responded well to my aching, archaic need.

After months of not getting pregnant, we looked into the possibility of adoption. At this same time, we visited Donovan's new granddaughter Pamela who was beginning life in difficult and precarious circumstances. I already loved this sweet girl child, which intensified my grief about my own barrenness.

I sought further guidance. This came: "The child that you are to have can come only as a result of further purification. Therefore continue your purification process and nourish your faith in this process preceding motherhood. Purify the emotions: see your anger, jealousy (which I felt whenever I saw a mother and child), competitiveness with other women, and distrust. Purify the will: see the forcing current, and the despair at having to give up the outer will. Release the overactivity of the will, the straining to control. Purify the mind/thoughts: Be aware of the limits of the mind, and do not strain for more. Stop the negative process of making judgments and jumping to conclusions. Allow for more not-knowing. Settle into unknowing as the precondition for a deeper knowing which can only emerge from the receptive side of your being. Release the busyness of the little mind, and allow space for a different kind of knowing to emerge. Also, purify the body. Gently, patiently clean up your diet, add more exercise, enjoy the water in your house.

"Welcome the purification process. Attend to it. And let go of the conception process. What is needed will happen of itself when the time is right. There is nothing you can or should do about this. Truly give this over into the hands of God. The goal is not conception, but purification; the birth of your own true feminine Godself, not the birth of an outer soul. As long as you attend to the inner process, you will not displace expectations, needs, or value onto the outer event. You are enough as you are. Your principal task on earth is self-purification and self-trans-formation—not mothering or helping people or any outer task. Do not let yourself be distracted by the outer focus."

I went into a slump after this guidance, incorrectly equating letting go of my ego demand for fulfillment on my terms with having to let go of fulfillment itself. But slowly my faith returned as I kept affirming my longing while knowing that only God completes the creation.

My work on the anti-feminine in me continued. I was shown my strong images of the "woman of God" as the nun—ascetic, invulnera-ble, not needing anyone. Connection to spirit is all that matters, with contempt for human life and needs and bodies (especially female ones). Deep distrust and hostility toward the instinctual life of the body. I dreamed of a corpulent primitive Goddess in a verdant forest. In a later scene in this same dream, I saw people digging steps in an icy mountain and helping me up the steps. The Goddess is unthink-ing obedience to the primal urges of sexuality and procreation, fertility and the body, before reason or morality. Was I, then, the ice maiden, being carefully led up the steps to Heaven, while beneath are the passionate chaotic urgings of an open-hearted, sexual, primitive being? Is she also me? In my conscious self, the claims of order have won out over the claims of instinct. I long to reconnect with earth and passion, coupling and chaos. I need to begin again, from the ground up, as it were, to claim the feminine.

As the awareness came more fully that I must find my feminine full-ness in myself, to know I am enough as I am, I found an inner voice that said, "Never. If I must become my own mother and nurture only my own inner child, then I refuse. I'd rather die."

For several weeks thereafter, I descended into sickness and a kind of inner death. Severe headache, less severe but constant nausea. Inhabiting an utterly gray-black bleakness, only occasionally highlighted by bursts of red anger. I felt like I was dying. I was angry at God, at death, at all who have died, including my father, and all who will die, including my mother and Donovan. And nothing mattered. I lived in existential aloneness, facing death and fearing nothingness. I sensed that beyond that black curtain lay a new life. But not for me, not then.

My journal tells of this time, in June of 1981, "I lay face down on the hard tile floor, joyless, burdened by the day's heavy, slow heat, while the whining fan above my head turned mercilessly and without meaning. Flashes of medieval Christian and Buddhist monasteries—places where death is understood. Knowing I will die. Donovan will die. My mother will die. And a child to whom I give birth might die. Death is. This isn't the deepest spiritual truth I've touched, but it's a step along the way, and one I've skipped. Death is. And giving birth will not save me from death. And God will not save me from death. And my anger about it will not stop it from being true."

For days, my head continued to throb. I felt more removed from my longing to have a baby, as I saw that one of the unexamined reasons for wanting to give birth was to deny death. Sitting in meditation, my body became a skeleton, covered with a shroud. I became the wind gently swirling dust around and through the skeleton. Great empty spaces, no self, only the Void. The wind, not even the skeleton.

I had a fragment of a dream: "An announcement is made, in ominous tones: 'The dead will eat at large metal kitchen tables and will dig in the garden.'" But I was too sick to either eat or work in the garden.

And then, in the middle of this bout with death and despair, a vision was revealed to me. One evening shortly before bed I started sliding down a negative spiral, until I slipped into an entirely dead space where my life had no meaning, and where I might just as well be dead. Ordinary human life felt gray and worthless. My mind was blank, and I fell into a vast bleakness. Just before I thought I might absolutely slip off the edge into death, I felt a ringing certainty. Conception will happen in July and I must prepare myself for it by having a five-day retreat alone, fasting some and meditating a lot, preparing myself inwardly. The flash of certainty came and then it left. I doubted at first, but still essentially believed it was to be, and had always been meant to be so. I heard a light spirit laughter with the announcement. I assented, "Thy Will, not mine, be done."

I began my retreat. My journal tells the story:

"7/2/81: I am enjoying my simple, quiet retreat. Low energy and fasting. Gentle, rainy day. My mind has slowed down some. I am waiting, enjoying the present simplicity of just being.

"I have only a glimpse of what I am doing here, something to do with Becoming Woman, preparing my body and my soul for conception, whether physical conception or spiritual conception, I am uncertain. I am preparing the sacred vessel. I want to open to life, to nurture and open myself and await filling, however this is meant to happen. What is it I seek—a rebirth? an initiation? I want to go into the dark and the unknown to discover what? A new self? An old self? A woman self? A God self? This retreat does feel like an archetypal initiatory process of withdrawal from the outer for renewal from within. I await in faith whatever will come."

*"7/3/81: This morning I am bitter and angry. My basal temperature has shot up which probably means that ovulation has passed again without my becoming pregnant. And this was supposed to be the magic month, when **it** would happen.*

"I feel hostile to God. What good does it do to want? What's the point of retreat, of trying to get closer to God?

"I begin to see my bitterness as a state of soul that exists beneath my attempt to make life give me what I want. Are my visions and dreams just more subtle versions of my demands on life to deliver what I want—when, where, and how I want it? I feel now that sharp bitter taste, that barren blackness, that lack of faith that gnaws at my soul. I feel you and acknowledge you as mine.

"Today while weeding the strawberries in the garden, I began to glimpse that the state of no thought, just being, is my practice now, the necessary antidote to my grabbing impatience toward life."

"7/3/81, later: After a nap I woke up with stiff neck and stiff upper back, the protest of my pride and my will. This is exactly where in my body I need to let go, to melt with trust of the Divine Will, to stop trying to direct my life from my little ego will. But I can do no more than observe and accept my stubbornness and my fears. I cannot force myself to let go.

"In zazen I felt my simple beingness. Behind aching, behind death, I AM. Behind willfulness, behind efforts to let go of willfulness, I AM. I felt aligned with trees and birds, both abundantly present near this wonderful little retreat cabin. I felt immensely sad at first. What makes their lives meaningful? They live and they die. Why do birds sing? What do they have to sing about? Just being. Is that really enough? For them it is."

"7/3/81, still later: I feel a deep cynicism such as I have rarely known. A deep distrust of self and life. What makes me think I have a connection to Christ? Is spirituality just superstition and wishful thinking? I feel waves of bitterness and doubt, which I start to see as scary faces zooming in and out of consciousness. Cackling witches mocking me and my serious goodness. Devils pointing at me with mockery and humiliation. Old crones and tough, mean young men pointing at my barren belly and laughing. These faces travel with me. I accept them."

"7/4/81: On awakening, still fasting, I had an extraordinary few minutes of no-self, aware only of streamings of energy, but no form. A voice in my head asking, 'What is it? What is it?' Letting down to a deeper level of not-knowing, sitting in this vast yet fully energized spaciousness. And then another voice, 'This is it. This is it.' This sparkling sea of energetic formlessness. Aware of breathing, but not who breathes. Then slowly form returns. For a long time feeling essential femaleness—roundedness, breasts, belly, vagina—mammalian, but not yet human. And only slowly do I know myself as human woman, evolutionary sister to all who have gone before. Reborn. Female.

"For hours I walked around in the summer woods outside my cabin in a state of blissful connection, feeling intimately related to every growing, living thing in the woods around me.

"Later I fell again into my bitterness and despair, focusing on my confusion about my time here. What am I doing here? I may never know. What makes me think I know what I am doing? I don't know. And, furthermore, I don't need to know. All I can do is follow the deepest instincts, the deepest sense of guidance I have about what I am meant to do in this part of my life. And that is all I can do."

"7/5/81: I fell asleep early last evening and dreamed: 'I am at a picnic to which many people formerly in my life are invited. We are eating baked potatoes in a ritual manner. The eating of the potatoes comes right after I have walked through many rooms of a museum of old crafts—by and for women only—with my mother. My mother is looking at the eighteenth century 'period' furniture; I am engaged with the folk handicrafts. The headmistress of the museum is a great big African woman. I notice that one sewing project—of stuffed animals—is incomplete.

"I woke up from the dream, in the middle of the night, craving a baked potato. Such a basic food, directly from the belly of the earth, a round woman-food, pregnant with new life. After my three days of fasting, I was starving for a potato!

"I felt an urge to make a midnight raid on the garden to dig potatoes. My mind argued that it didn't make sense to do this and I should just go back to sleep. But the primordial yearnings took over.

"And so, into the soft rain of the pitch-black night, I took my flashlight and walked to the garden, feeling happy and adventuresome. I knelt in the earth, and, offering prayers of thanks to Mother Earth, pulled some potatoes. I carried them back to the kitchen cradled in my arms like tender babies, and offered them to the cooking pot. I developed the powerful idea that this was to be a ritual meal uniting me with all women, with the archetypal Feminine in all life. I walked alone around the kitchen with a chant of union with the Goddess, and prayers to let down into the deep rhythms of woman in my body and soul, and to know my specific individual task of female creation.

"Then I sat down to my ritual meal, at the kitchen table decorated with dried wheat fronds—my offering to the Goddesses of abundance and fertility. After eating my potatoes, I walked around a while, praying a few more prayers to goddesses. And then I drank some milk slowly, savoring my linkage to cows and mothers of all species. Only after my meal was complete did I realize that I had gone through a death and rebirth and had, as my earlier dream had predicted, sat at the large metal kitchen table and dug in the garden.

"I walked slowly back to my cabin pondering this night's dream image of a museum of the Feminine, presided over by an archetypal female figure. However far my mother and I may seem from our primitive nature in our current interests, we are both held in the power and energy of the African caretaker, Eve, our primal mother. And a stuffed animal (for a baby?) remains yet to be sewn.

"All evening I heard a background noise that sounded like drum beats. Either rain dripping from the roof or Fourth of July Independence Day fireworks or the bass rhythms from records being played in the distance. Sounded like African drums. Primordial rhythm. Today I celebrate my interdependence with all that is feminine."

"7/6/81: What I have learned from this retreat: that my nature, and hence my inner God, is deeply feminine—quiet, slow, of the earth, reflective. That I can release knowing and even form, and come back to essence. I also learned again how deep goes my self-distrust and feelings of worthlessness as a woman, and how much I have substituted mind and masculine will to cover over these aching pits of feminine emptiness. And now I have chosen to go into the wound of my self-rejection, to fall to the very bottom and see its untruth, so I may again come to the surface, only *this time with the soul dents 'filled in' with my true femininity. My path to healing is through the wound itself."*

"7/7/81: Last day of my retreat. I awoke slowly, resting for a long time in the half-sleep. Breathing to my belly and feeling small shivers of pleasure that started in my vagina and wriggled upward. I am waking up to becoming an open space for the creation of new life. I have a sense that the inner job is done, the vessel has been prepared. All I need do now is wait in faith."

I went home from my retreat and prepared a room for the baby, still not knowing how a child would come to us but confident she would. Exactly nine months later, Donovan and I became the adoptive parents of his eleven-month-old granddaughter Pamela, after her natural parents had given her up for adoption. My soul had been carefully prepared to become the mother to this beautiful baby girl, the true daughter of my heart.

Creating Our Lives from the Higher Self

Human beings are incredibly creative. We are like children at the sandpile—creating, destroying, and re-creating the infinite forms and expressions of the human spirit. Whether or not we ever create a painting or a poem, we each are the creators of our lives. Our lives are our art, the outer manifestation of our inner spirit.

> The sum total of all your conscious, semi-conscious, unconscious, explicit and implicit thoughts, beliefs, assumptions, intentions, emotions, feelings, and will directions—conflicting as they may be—create a definitive result. The result is your present experience and the way your life is unfolding for you. Your present life expresses exactly, like a faultless mathematical equation, what your inner state is. It can thus very well be used as a map into your inner regions. (*PGL 208*)

In the story that introduces this chapter, I related how awakening my longing for a child became the beginning of a journey of transformation.

As I worked through my rejection of the Feminine, slowly dismantling the masculine ego fortress with which I had been secretly identified, I entered a space where that identity could die and a new woman-self be born. By aligning with becoming a receptive vessel, I helped create the inner soul condition through which outer motherhood could manifest.

As we gradually understand that our lives are our creations, we can turn our focus and caring more directly into conscious creation of our lives from our higher selves.

> There is an enormous difference between those who
> unwittingly create, never knowing that their unwise,
> erroneous thoughts, their destructive feelings, and
> their unchecked negative wishes bring about a result
> as surely as if they were to commit a conscious act;
> and those who attempt to check, to test, and challenge
> their concepts, who seek the truth and adjust their
> ideas, thought processes, and aims, and who purify
> their feelings by going through them with courage
> and honesty. This latter attitude toward life can then
> result in **deliberate creation** of one's life. (*PGL 194*)

The creative process is a constant dynamic between probing the unconscious inner causes of our unhappiness and reaching out into new, more productive life directions. We seek to open to the full and focused flow of life through us, at the same time that we try to understand and remove our inner hindrances.

Positive creation comes from aligning ourselves with the higher self within us. The positive life stream is always available; we have only to remove the obstructions to experience and know it as our true self. Within us is everything we need to create fulfilling, serene lives.

> All the answers, all the knowledge, all the power to
> create, to feel, to enjoy, to experience—all worlds exist
> within. For the true universe is inside, while the exte-
> rior world is but a reflection, like a mirror image. Every-
> thing you ever need to know about yourself and your
> life exists within and this knowledge can be actualized
> if you learn to focus. . . . Creation and re-creation are
> primarily a focusing. If you want to create from your
> inner being, it must be a **relaxed focusing**. If you try
> to create from the ego level alone, it will be a tense,
> anxiety-producing focus. The outer ego will, the
> willpower, is needed. But by itself it creates with a
> willfulness that lacks wisdom and understanding,
> vision, and depth. (*PGL 208*)

Each of us can find within us what we need for our fulfillment. In order to open to this unlimited Source, we must
actively find and unravel our distortions, and then we must cease
activity and allow the deeper self to speak and act through us.

Scientists and artists have shared the experience that their
most creative achievements, or most profound insights into
the nature of the universe, came after letting go of mental
hard work and allowing some deeper wisdom or vision to
come through them. Having touched into a deeper reality
where a mathematical truth, a beautiful painting, or an
exquisite piece of music already exists, the job is then to craft
it into a form that will make it understandable, audible or
visible in our world.

All creation is a matter of "channeling" the inner reality to
the outer, bringing into manifestation the wisdom, love, and
beauty inherent in the universe. Our lives are vehicles for channeling the divine into earth reality.

The process of positive life creation may be likened to that of
the gardener. We must use our conscious ego self to plant the
seeds of our longing and water the plants through our affirmation. But we alone can never grow the plant. For that we must
allow the life force to work through the soil we have prepared.
Along the way we need to learn from the feedback we receive
from the garden—where to enrich the soil, how to control the
bugs, when to eliminate the weeds. Just so, in positive creation
of our lives, we first focus and then we let go. We accept our
limitations and then we open to larger energies. We listen
carefully for the feedback life gives us and work to remove
obstructions. We affirm new directions and await their manifestation. In this way we human beings co-create with God.

Self-Creation and Self-Responsibility

We can create our lives in positive directions only when we
are willing to be self-responsible for our lives as they are now.
The greatest enslavement of the mind is to succumb to the victim mentality where we believe that who we are is entirely a
result of others' actions upon us. When we are trapped in this
belief, we remain helpless, humiliated, and unable to change or
exercise whatever choices are open to us. We demand that
others change first in order to make us feel free or powerful, or

whatever. We expend all our energy trying to change others or circumstances. In that way we stay unfree.

It is true that we may, at any particular moment, need to blame others or rail against society or parents or fate, in order to release our feelings, and to acknowledge where we are still caught in our helplessness and hopelessness. But when we continue to hold onto beliefs of victimization, we betray the deepest truth of our being, which is that we are free, creative agents of divinity, however temporarily limited and distorted, and however constrained by karmic circumstance.

When we experience ourselves as being **in** this limited, dualistic world, but not necessarily **of** this world, we will know ourselves to be one with the Creator. Our task is to bring into manifestation as much of our inherent divinity as we can by learning to be positive co-creators of our world. The first step is to take responsibility for our own life creation as it presently manifests.

We are responsible for our own lives simply because there is no one else who possibly could be. We are constantly subjected to many outside influences and conditioning, past and present, and yet it is only we who direct our life experience moment by moment. However chaotic our lives may feel temporarily, we are the ones making the choices in the present.

This truth must not be used to put ourselves down when our lives are going badly nor to aggrandize ourselves when our lives are going well. It is easy to distort the idea of self-responsibility into blaming ourselves for the "bad" things in our lives, or taking credit for the "good" things. The creation of our lives is not a matter of ego blame or ego credit, as the creative forces that shape our lives include complex unconscious, collective, and circumstantial forces that are way beyond the control of the little ego. However, it is also true that we, at both our conscious and unconscious levels, are solely and ultimately in charge of our own personal life choices.

We each manifest a unique set of realities, organized as a separate self. We are each a complex expression of what is possible for human beings to express and experience. We are much more than our separate skin-encapsulated selves. And yet we are also each a distinct self, embodied separately. This particular life in which we stand needs to be embraced as the manifestation of our unique centers of creative consciousness—both our lower and our higher selves, at the levels of ego-personality, inner child, and transpersonal soul.

As we learn to recognize the creative center within, we can learn to create our lives much more harmoniously. We learn to create consciously from our higher self rather than to create unconsciously from our lower self. But in order to learn to create positively, we first accept responsibility, without blame, for our negative life creations.

Martin was a talented and successful journalist who occasionally also wrote short stories and screenplays. But his personal life was miserable. Martin had spent many years in trying to make a heterosexual relationship work for him. Occasionally, however, he would sneak out at night and have a loveless homosexual encounter. Gradually it became clear that, even though he liked women and had established some good friendships, he could no longer deny his basic homosexual orientation.

As he openly acknowledged his homosexuality in his Pathwork sessions with me, Martin continued to indulge in short-term heartless "backroom" sexual encounters that left him feeling emotionally and spiritually unclean. He was caught in a vicious circle of needing validation for his sexuality, yet hating that part of himself and therefore seeking out degrading and self-punitive encounters, thereby reinforcing his self-hate and leaving him even more desperate for validation.

He longed for a committed love relationship that would satisfy both his companionship and his sexual needs. Yet he seemed unable to establish a lasting relationship with a man, and this created tremendous inner unrest. Why couldn't he find the right mate? Why was life so rotten?

Having been raised a secular Jew, Martin acknowledged his distrust and lack of faith in God. He raged against life's unfairness, shaking his fists at God and feeling like Job. In the midst of one of his complaints, Martin was suddenly flooded with memories of his stepmother physically abusing and emotionally humiliating him, with his father remaining distant and unprotective. This triggered more rage. He remembered how totally helpless and victimized he had felt as a child with her, and cried out his fury mixed with grief, in heart-wrenching sobs. His deprivation in adult love seemed a terribly unjust re-creation of his childhood agony.

While he was doing his inner work, Martin was also opening up his social life. He had started to attend services at a gay synagogue where he met intelligent, open men, who were interested in more than sex. He even started a relationship, but it broke up after only a few months.

This reawakened Martin's despair. I asked Martin to imagine that, contrary to his feelings, the breakup of this love affair was exactly the motivation he needed to go still deeper in his process to discover the causes of his deprivation within himself. Now he raged at me as well as at God. But even as he did so, a part of him was simply witnessing the rage and his belief in life's unfairness, without being quite so attached to the negative beliefs that underlay the rage.

Martin came into his next session deeply thoughtful.

"I really want to understand why I stay unfulfilled in my life. Is it really my creation or is it just somehow my lot in life to be unhappy? What's going on?"

"Imagine," I suggested, "that the unfulfillment in your love life is the subject of a short story or screenplay you are writing. Imagine that you are the author of this story. How does this change how you relate to the unhappiness in your life?"

Martin then shared, "In my writing, I always create stories of unhappiness and lost hopes. Just the way much of my life turns out. I believe that happiness is not for me. For others maybe, but somehow I am specially cursed and my stories always have bittersweet, sad endings. An embittered Tennessee Williams life, filled with short, unhappy relationships."

"Can you imagine a different story?" I asked. "How do you feel about happy endings? How attached are you to bitterness and despair?"

This was a useful metaphor for Martin and he began to explore how much he disliked happy endings, regarding them as phony. The stories he liked best always had a bitter quality—great possibilities that never quite materialize, disappointed hopes and defeated dreams. These, and only these, seemed real to him.

"Consider again that you are the author of your life," I repeated, "How might you create a different kind of story, not just one that repeats the disappointments and disillusionments of your childhood?"

"You mean I could rewrite this sad script of Martin's life! What a far-out idea! Well, for one thing, I'd like to see my current lost love as not the ending of the story, but in fact an opportunity to precipitate a new beginning."

"How would you do that?" I asked. Martin didn't know, but felt deeply committed to the idea that, as author of his life, he could indeed write the script he would like, not the one he had previously felt helplessly doomed to re-create from childhood. He knew now that he would stand by his longing for a committed relationship.

Martin added to his regular spiritual practice a prayer to align with happiness and a visualization of fulfillment. He began to feel that happiness was not just for other people or for phonies. It could be real and it could be his. Several months later Martin met a man who also wanted more than a casual encounter, and they began what turned out to be a complete and enduring relationship, which appears to be a life-long commitment for them both.

When Martin shifted his identification away from being the victim of some tragic script written by a hostile God, and toward being the author of his own life, he came into his enormous creative potential. He was now identified with his higher self rather than believing himself to be the helpless child.

In a similar way, in my story introducing this chapter, I first took responsibility for having created my own unfulfillment, assuming that my own attitudes had kept me from my heart's longing. As I descended to meet my inner barriers, I was mostly able to keep looking at my self-doubts and despair as only aspects of myself, which I was large enough to embrace, rather than being defined by my limitations. My identity gradually expanded from one who had rejected her femininity to one who could embrace herself as an aspect of the universal Goddess. As this higher-self identity became more firmly who I was, my motherhood could manifest.

Identification with the Higher Self

In our transformation work, we learn first to identify with the positive ego in its functioning as objective, compassionate observer. As our identification with detached and loving self-observation deepens, we become the bowl of awareness itself, rather than the contents of that bowl.

To expand on the metaphors first introduced in Chapter Three on the observer self, we switch our identity from being an observer in the audience (the observer self) to being the one who wrote the play which contains our diverse inner characters (the creative soul). We shift from being the observer of the house where our different parts live, to knowing we are the builder of our soul's house. We accept that our life manifestation is the result of the creative potential of both our lower and higher selves. We change our self-identity from being the listener to the different radio stations—the different "channels" within our psyche—to being the one who turns the dial, and is thus responsible for what we manifest. This understanding of responsibility for ourselves and our lives is a very deep, creative level of the soul in both its higher-self and lower-self aspects.

Our self-identity gradually deepens even beyond the level of self-responsibility for our life's creation. Eventually, we drop to the deepest level of the higher self, in which we can identify with the totality of life. We drop into a state of unitive consciousness. At this level we can know ourselves as an expression of the one life force, an aspect of the whole. We learn to let life live through us rather than imagining that we, in our ego identity or even as our unique creative soul, are in charge.

To follow the earlier metaphors, we see that it is God who writes the play, and we assent to our role in it; it is God's house that is being built and we assent to the creation of this particular building; the radio which contains our many inner channels is actually the instrument of God. Ultimately, the job of the ego is to assent to the positive, creative movement of the divine life force moving through us, as through all things, wherever it leads.

> The ego must know that it is only a servant to the
> greater being within. Its main function is to deliber-
> ately seek contact with the greater self within.
> (PGL 158)

As we come to know and identify with our higher self, at deeper and deeper levels, we can express the gifts of our unique personality in an egoless way. We experience resolution of the dualities that normally plague us. We can feel both alert and relaxed, intensely sexual and deeply spiritual, compassionate and confrontational, totally present and wisely detached, happy yet peaceful.

> It is the kind of happiness that is, at one and the
> same time, dynamic, stimulating, exciting, vibrantly
> alive, and yet peaceful. There is no longer any split
> that comes from separating these concepts and making
> them mutually exclusive, which is what the dualistic
> ego does. (PGL 158)

The experience of the higher self is the greatest experience of pleasure available to human beings, an experience of being open to cosmic streamings as they come through physical form. At the beginning of our work on ourselves, this experience of our higher self may be fleeting and come only in rare moments. Later we may forget or even deny its reality. But gradually we come to be anchored in this new experience of self. We shift our identification away from the peripheral layers of self and into this center as our true identity. We come to know that this is who we always are, underneath the fog of our everyday forgetfulness.

Meditation for Positive Creation

In our meditation we can work with uncovering the inner causes of our outer unfulfillment, and we can bring into existence the conditions for positive life creation. Like any act of creation, meditation for positive manifestation involves both the active principle and the receptive principle, both doing and not-doing, affirming and allowing.

> The conscious mind assumes the active part by speaking the word, by concisely formulating the intent. . . . The soul substance is the receptive principle. The more one-pointed and unconflicted is the statement, uncontaminated by secret doubts, due to unrecognized negativities, the deeper and clearer the soul substance will be imprinted. (*PGL 194*)

The basic steps for positive creation are: 1. align with the longing by forming a clear concept of what is desired, making sure this desired state is in harmony with truth and with love for the self and for others, 2. impress this concept on the soul substance, 3. create a visualization of the new state as an inner reality, 4. affirm and allow the fulfillment, 5. wait in faith.

At any point in the process of manifestation, when we encounter obstacles, we go back to uncovering the lower self causes of our unfulfillment. We stay open to the feedback of our lives as to where further work is needed to remove the obstacles.

Summary of Self-Work Required for Positive Life Creation

In our Pathwork, we learn first to observe and then to take responsibility for the lower self, manifesting as unfulfillment and disharmony. Only then can the higher self manifest as harmony and fulfillment. The following steps, summarizing the Pathwork as outlined in this book, must be followed to create the grounding for positive creation.

Steps on the Path of the Undefended Self

Chapters 1 and 2:
a.) Align with the intent to unify the self, to bring all aspects into awareness. Practice honesty with self and others.

b.) Identify faults and disharmonies along with good qualities and harmonies. Accept pain and discomfort along with good feelings. Release perfectionism and demands on life to be other than it is.

Chap. 3:
c.) Develop and learn to identify with the objective, compassionate observer-self, through the practices of daily review and meditation.

Chap. 4:
d.) Learn about and begin to accept the many different aspects of self, including the three selves of mask, lower self, and higher self, and the developmental stages of inner child, adult ego, transpersonal soul, and union with God.

Chap. 5:
e.) Uncover patterns in daily life which reveal images—misconceptions about reality. See how childhood hurts are re-created in the present. Articulate images clearly.

f.) Allow childhood hurts to be fully felt, released, and forgiven. Open to the spontaneous energies of the undefended child.

g.) Impress soul with the true concept to replace misconception. Meditate in dialogue with inner child, calling in divine help to promote healing.

Chap. 6:
h.) Understand and then release identification with the idealized self-image, the mask self. Explore ego distortions (overly passive or overly controlling) and learn to be both flexible and firm.

Chap. 7:   i.) Face and accept the existence of the lower self. Identify where pride, self-will, and fear manifest.

Chap. 8:   j.) Claim and learn to identify with the higher self. Allow the streamings of spiritual energy through the body-mind.

Chap. 9:   k.) Where negative patterns persist, uncover attachments of the lower self to negative intentionality—ill will toward self and others—and negative pleasure—sadism and masochism.

Chap. 10:   l.) Release these attachments through fully understanding and feeling what they are doing to the soul. Take full responsibility for the lower self.

m.) Allow the pain of real guilt and accept forgiveness. Affirm positive intention and allow positive pleasure in self and life.

Chap. 11:   n.) Create life from the higher self. Surrender to deeper and deeper levels of God within.

The Creative Dance of Spiritual Evolution

Our evolution toward more personal fulfillment is assured. In the course of our soul's journey toward reunion with God we will gain more faith, more centeredness, more truth, and more love in our lives. We will become better able to face and release our buried negativity that manifests as negative life experience. We will be able to transform our inner "no" into a deeper and deeper "yes" to life.

The process may at times seem unbearably slow; at other times dizzyingly rapid. For a while we will expand toward greater fulfillment; and then we will temporarily contract. Our personal spiritual evolution moves in a spiral form. We circle around the same inner issues and difficulties, but each time at a deeper level, as our ability to learn from our life experiences increases. Eventually we come to the nub or psychic nuclear point of some negative pattern. We then replace this with a truthful and loving attitude, and our lives spiral out again, this time with more positive life creation.

The process of our spiritual evolution, like all other creative activity, includes some periods of active work and other periods of relaxed receptivity. For a while we may work at creating a new inner reality in order to manifest differently. And then for a while we may need to let go of change and come to full acceptance of whatever limitations we experience now. We work to change what we can in ourselves and to let go of what is not yet ready for change. We await our own unfoldment with patience, even as we also work on those areas in ourselves that are ripe for transformation.

We learn to find a balance between the role of directing consciousness and the role of receptive surrender to the flow of life. We need to allow for both focused activity and trusting receptivity. We are capable of choice, direction, and follow-through in the active creation of our lives. **And**, as long as we live in duality, our knowing is partial and our life creation is constrained by karma, so we also need to surrender to the greater intelligence beyond our limited human mind. We are each capable of enormous creativity and also we are each merely a speck in the larger creative design of cosmic life pulsating within us.

The movement of our spiritual path is one of gradually expanding our identity into greater unity. As soon as we consolidate one identity, our path will move us toward disintegration of this known self, this now "false unity." Old forms and beliefs must be broken up to allow new energy, expanded consciousness, a more profound unity. For a while we know what we know, and then we let go of the known and allow the vastness of the unknown to overwhelm us. Going into the inner depths, with the sure guide of our higher self, we come to a yet deeper integration of self, a fuller identity, where more of who we are is held in the light of love. We must be willing to let our knowing dissolve, even into despair, so we can pass through the "dark nights" of our soul, meeting previously unmet inner material, coming into a new and expanded self. Each time we go through this process of death and rebirth of the self, we hold our knowing a little more lightly and our faith gets a little more grounded.

Spiritual growth is a process of steadily expanding our boundaries, eventually to include the entire spectrum of human possibilities. Then we know, not just theoretically, but from our deepest experience, that there is no separation between us and any other human being. Ultimately we expand even beyond our human boundaries, to be one with all of nature, with the rest of the universe, in which we learn to humbly take our place.

In expanding our identity we learn to embrace our dualities—our lower self and our higher self, the conscious and the unconscious within us, our separate ego and the flow of universal life force pulsating through us. In allowing our creativity we incorporate our polarities—our masculine and our feminine aspects, our focused work and our letting go into chaos, our fullness and our emptiness.

Through this path of acceptance of all that we are, we become whole.

Creating Heaven on Earth

The possibility calls out to us to re-inhabit ourselves and our planet in an entirely new way. We are called not only to know ourselves as children of God, but to know God within ourselves. We can re-enter the Garden of Eden, this innately gorgeous planet we call home, not as dependent or rebellious children, not as conquerors or victims, but as co-creators of love, beauty, and harmony.

When we begin to awaken to our true nature as divine beings, we will treat ourselves, other humans, and the non-human world with infinite respect and caring. We will know that love is our true home, not fear or hatred; that creation is our destiny and cooperation is our natural mode. We will find our unique place in the web of creation and let go of our egoistic defenses of pride, self-will, fear, and separateness.

However, in order to awaken to this deeper faith in ourselves, we also need to wake up to the temporary reality of our lower self which fears and denies our essential divinity. Though we fundamentally want to love others and to enjoy our connection with all life, we have gotten side-tracked into believing that instant gratification of our self-will and our pride will bring us happiness. We have forgotten our deservingness and lost our connection with the whole. Once we acknowledge the lower self, we can wake up to it as an illusion. It can be transformed. We can reclaim its creative vitality and let go of its limitations.

We can remember who we are and what all human beings know in their hearts:

> That we are each enough as we are.
> That we are each ultimately good and deeply connected to all life.
> That we have within us all that we need to make us happy.
> That we are lovable and capable of loving others.

> That the most pleasurable way to live on the planet is in a community of nourishing, supportive relationships.
> That we are capable of deep intimacy with a primary other.
> That we can find friends who will support us on our path of spiritual and emotional growth.
> That we can find our true work in the world—what we are uniquely called to give—which will also meet our real needs.
> That we can find our right place to live, our grounding on this planet.

> That this is ultimately a benign universe.
> That there is order and meaning to our lives which we can gradually uncover from within.
> That the process of facing and accepting all of our inner selves will bring peace, love, harmony, happiness, and fulfillment in our lives.

As we drop our defenses and embrace all of who we are, we come to know our true identity as God-inspired beings. We embrace our free will and choose harmony, love, and respect over divisiveness, fear, and destruction. We choose both connection and individuation, rather than separation or self-denial.

We hear the call to fulfill a vision of harmony on earth. We know the longing. We attune ourselves to create from love and trust, even as we stay awake to the limitations intrinsic to the human condition in its present state of evolution. We open to and affirm the best in ourselves and our fellow humans. We acknowledge and work to transform the worst in ourselves and our fellow humans. And we keep alive the vision of creating heaven on earth, of entering the new Eden of awakened consciousness.

Exercises for Chapter 11:

1. How would you like to contribute to creating "heaven on earth?" What is the deepest dream of your soul for yourself and for this planet? Don't be shy. Be willing to claim, on paper, your grandest longings. Notice, as you write, any feelings of shame, fear, distrust, or cynicism as you contemplate giving birth to your dream. Then dialogue from your higher self with each of your negative responses, seeing if you can reassure the fear and stand by the truth of your longing.

2. What obstructions or distortions within you stand in the way of fulfilling the dreams you revealed in Exercise 1? What is your plan to work on transforming these obstructions?

3. Look back on your spiritual path. See where you have success-fully taken responsibility for a negative pattern in your life. Name the underlying specific negative attitudes you unearthed. How have you replaced those with positive attitudes and how has that changed the creation of your life? Can you see the spiral form of your work on this issue—how you may have circled around your specific distortion at deeper levels until you came to resolution?

4. Explore the question of your own faith. How anchored would you say that you are in identification with and trust in your higher self? in a Higher Power in the universe? How trusting are you that your life and path are ultimately directed by this Higher Power and your own higher self? How attached are you to "blind faith"—a need to believe in a benign order so as not to have to let go and open to the unknown? How willing are you to open up and question everything in your life, to adventure into new territory?

Chart of "Steps on the Spiritual Path"

A Map of the Human Psyche
and the Inner Work of Transformation

Chart of "Steps on the Spiritual Path"
A Map of the Human Psyche and the Inner Work of Transformation

The work of transformation is vast—from strengthening the positive ego to releasing the ego, from uncovering the wounded inner child to finding a spiritual identity that was never wounded, no matter how horrific our childhood. In addition to maps of the psyche which attempt to show the many kinds of consciousness we are, we also need maps to help us identify the different kinds of work appropriate to the different levels of our identity. The work at one level, and the stance of the helper—whether working as counselor, therapist, spiritual friend, healer or spiritual teacher—is quite different, sometimes even contradictory, to the work at another level.

For example, in doing inner child work, the helper needs to keep exquisitely clear boundaries and to allow for the transference of childhood feelings onto the helper. But at the level of making a soul connection, the helper needs to be able to thin his boundaries and make deep transpersonal contact with the person whom he is helping (the person we in the Pathwork call the "worker"). Furthermore, in the work of co-creating spiritual community, *all those* on a particular path—including helpers and leaders, who are also workers on their own paths—need, at some time and in the right place, to be willing to expose and share their human flaws and failings as well as to stand by their inner Godself.

The level of creating authentic and intimate human relationships assumes and requires practicing a fundamental equality among all humans. We must eventually learn to see everyone, even our spiritual teachers, as our brother or our sister, and transcend the illusion that we can find someone who will be our perfect Mommy or Daddy and who will tell us how to lead our lives. A central paradox about the spiritual path is that we need to find human spiritual teachers to whom we can surrender our misplaced autonomy, even as we also need to learn that our ultimate surrender is only to God and to our own spirit guides which can be found by every seeker who looks deeply enough within. We humans are all children, and expressions, of the one God—no matter how shallow or profound, unified or diverse, are our understanding and manifestation of our true nature and origin.

In the Pathwork where helpers aid in the psychological work of helping others to transform the defenses formed in childhood, and where helpers and workers also co-create spiritual community, it is imperative for the helper to be as clear as possible at every point about what level s/he is working on with her/his workers. Otherwise, the transference that is an inevitable byproduct of inner child work will become confusing and unconsciously cloud both the work of creating community and the work of making soul connection. The only antidote to this confusion is our growing consciousness and clarity about what is appropriate to the helper-worker interaction at every step of the way. The chart on the following pages was created out of my need to gain further clarity about this complex subject.

I began with the map outlined in Chapter Four, "Embracing the Child, Adult, Ego, and Transpersonal Selves." This map of the human psyche shows how the four developmental stages—child, adult ego, soul or transpersonal level, and the unitive level—intersect with the three selves—mask self, lower self, and higher self. The same map is reproduced on the left side of the following chart of "Steps on the Spiritual Path" with, however, the addition of a level of human relationships which I had not included in Chapter Four. This level is a necessary step in creating spiritual community.

On the right side of this chart is a description of the work of transformation to be done at each of the developmental levels. "The Inner Work" includes the spiritual practices to be done on one's own, and the more active and inter-active work to be done with a helper. These two columns are written as instructions to the spiritual seeker. The far right-hand column on "Stance of the Helper..." is written to those who work as helpers in the field of personal transformation—whether as counselor, therapist, spiritual friend, healer, or spiritual teacher. The instructions to the helper illustrate what is the appropriate and needed stance toward the worker at that level of the work.

I have produced a more expanded version of this chart as a four-color rainbow-hued poster for hanging on walls which is available from the bookstore at Sevenoaks Pathwork Center.

Developmental Stage and Task:	THE THREE SELVES		
	The Mask Self	The Lower Self	The Higher Self
Child Self *Re-educate inner child to become autonomous adult*	Phony child behaving in reaction to expectations of others, trying to avoid vulnerability of being real. Submissive or rebellious child, in reaction to parental authority projected onto others.	Selfish, willful child who wants only his/her own way. Negative, wounded child defended against feeling pain and disappointment. Superstitious and not autonomous.	Spontaneous, loving, creative child, in touch with spirit. Open, undefended child, able to feel and be vulnerable. Open to spiritual reality, without preconceptions.
Adult Ego *Strengthen Positive Ego Mind;* *Align with* *Spiritual Self*	Idealized self-image of ourselves, which we present to the world and want to believe is who we are. Perfectionistic demands on self and others. Character defenses of the Mask: a distortion of a divine quality: submission (Love), aggression (Power), or withdrawal (Serenity)	Personality faults. Egotistical, selfish ego which wants to be master of all it surveys. Alternately, a weak dependent ego which will not take responsibility or lay claim to what it deserves. Pride, self-will, and fear (aspects of lower self on all levels)	Good qualities of the personality. Positive ego will, serving the Spiritual Self. Makes positive choices. Observes and accepts all aspects of the self. Pursues spiritual discipline and follows through on guidance received. Personal strength: Love, Power, or Serenity.
Human Relationships *Integrate Self with Others*	Patterns of dependency and/or separateness. Blaming and Projecting own issues onto others.	Manipulative and dishonest relationships based on specialness and self-importance (me vs. the other).	Relationships that are both autonomous and mutually loving (me and the other).
Soul/Transpersonal Level *Heal Personal and Collective Soul;* *Surrender to God*	No more mask.	Personal soul: Negative soul directions, with intent to perpetuate duality. Personal soul dents, karmic distortions. Collective soul: Negative archetypes and demonic impulses. Attachment to negative power and separation (evil).	Personal soul: Positive soul directions, with intent to unify. Personal soul gifts and desire to serve. Collective soul: Positive archetypes and angelic essences. Surrender to inner guides and to God.
Unitive Level BE IN GOD	No more mask.	No more separating impulses; no more lower self.	Creative Presence; Love and Truth. BEING HERE NOW

	THE INNER WORK		Stance of the Helper in the Helping Relationship
	Spiritual Practices	**Work with a Helper**	
PRAYER ... MEDITATION	Question all fixed ideas/images/attitudes; allow open attention and curiosity about the self. Meditate and pray in dialogue with the inner child. Call in positive adult ego and Divine Mother/ Divine Father to re-parent the inner child.	Open to emotional reality of inner child. Discover how childhood images create and distort present reality. Externalize unfelt feelings from childhood including anger, grief, fear, and joy. Allow loss of childhood illusions.	Work with transference: Actively analyze how childhood reality is re-created in the helping relationship. Allow positive and negative transference: projections of "perfect" parent and "disappointing" or "monstrous" parent
WORK WITH BREATH, RHYTHM ...	Use a journal and practice Daily Review to discover personality patterns. Meditate to develop and strengthen capacity for objective and compassionate self-observation. Use prayer and affirmations to align with Love and Truth.	Look honestly at life patterns and what they reveal about the self. Accept opposites within the self; "bad" faults as well as "good" qualities; pain as well as pleasure. Differentiate self from others; create resilient, effective ego. Recognize and allow present-day feelings as they arise. Make connections with past if relevant; release the past to function in the present.	Negotiate clear and reliable contract, clear boundaries. Promote ego differentiation from helper. Do not engage transference: Work with adult issues, not re-creation of child relationship. Be appropriately self-revealing. Allow feelings rather than strongly encouraging them.
DAILY REVIEW ...	Meditate and pray to open the heart, practicing forgiveness of self and others. Engage in compassionate service.	Make interactions conscious: negotiate relationship. Practice realness/vulnerability/confession/forgiveness. Experience brother/sisterhood.	Engage with whole self: share more, support connection, confront separateness. Shift from transference to intimacy; allow peership.
PRAYER ... MEDITATION ... JOURNAL,	Pray, align, and affirm positive intention. Attune to soul's divine ray: Love, Power or Serenity Discover and pursue soul's task. Work with ritual and ceremony. Seek and heed spirit guides; Surrender to spiritual masters. Commit life and will to God.	Discover and work with negative intentions. Feel and release pain behind revenge, bitterness, withholding. Uncover and discharge karmic imprints from past lives. Take full responsibility for creation of own life. Work with archetypes, dreams, inner journeys, creative visualizations. Work with Breath and Rhythm.	Notice how deeper soul issues are re-created in helping relationship. Model appropriate relatedness. Thin own boundaries to allow soul level contact. Step out of the way; enter space beyond ego limits; channel higher energies. Allow personal transparency.
PRAYER ...	Worship the Divine in all forms. Practice moment-to-moment awareness.	Allow spontaneous, creative impulses. Relax into Breath, Rhythm, God.	Allow the work to be a constant co-creation between teacher and student, both accessing the Divine, without boundaries or separation.

List of Pathwork Guide Lectures

1. The Sea of Life
2. Decisions and Tests
3. Choosing Your Destiny
4. World Weariness
5. Happiness as a Link in the Chain of Life
6. Man's Place in the Spiritual and Material Universes
7. Asking for Help and Helping Others
8. Contact with God's Spirit World—Mediumship
9. The Lord's Prayer
10. Male and Female Incarnations—Their Rhythm and Causes
11. Know Thyself
12. The Order and Diversity of the Spiritual Worlds—
    The Process of Reincarnation
13. Positive Thinking
14. The Higher Self, the Lower Self, and the Mask
15. Influence between the Spiritual and Material Worlds
16. Spiritual Nourishment
17. The Call
18. Free Will
19. Jesus Christ
20. God—the Creation
21. The Fall
22. Salvation
25. The Path
26. Finding One's Faults
27. Escape Possible Also on the Path
28. Communication with God
29. Activity and Passivity
30. Self-Will, Pride, and Fear
31. Shame
32. Decision-Making
33. Occupation with Self
34. Preparation for Reincarnation
35. Turning to God
36. Prayer
37. Acceptance—Dignity in Humility
38. Images
39. Image-Finding
40. More on Images
41. Images – the Damage They Do
42. Objectivity and Subjectivity
43. Three Basic Personality Types: Reason, Will, Emotion
44. The Forces of Love, Eros, and Sex
45. Conscious and Unconscious Desires
46. Authority
47. The Wall Within
48. The Life Force
49. Guilt: Justified and Unjustified—Obstacles on the Path

These lectures are available from the centers listed on the following page.

"Be blessed, every one of you.

"Those of you who want to make a commitment to your inner being and avail yourselves of the help this particular path can give are blessed and guided in all your efforts. And those who do not wish to take this step yet, or are drawn elsewhere, you too are being blessed.

"Be in peace."
—The Guide

For Further Information About the Pathwork

We welcome the opportunity to support you in connecting with others worldwide who are interested in exploring this material further. To order any Pathwork Guide Lecture or books, or for further information, please contact the following regional centers:

California & Southwest:
Pathwork of California, Inc.
1355 Stratford Court #16
Del Mar, California 92014
(619) 793-1246 Fax (619) 259-5224

Path to the Real Self/Pathwork
Box 3753
Santa Fe, New Mexico 87501-0753
(505) 455-2533

Central:
Pathwork of Iowa
24 Highland Drive
Iowa City, Iowa 52246
(319) 338-9878

Great Lakes Region:
Great Lakes Pathwork
1117 Fernwood
Royal Oak, Michigan 48067
(810) 585-3984

Mid-Atlantic:
Sevenoaks Pathwork Center
Route 1, Box 86
Madison, Virginia 22727
(703) 948-6544 Fax (703) 948-5508

New York, New Jersey, New England:
Phoenicia Pathwork Center
Box 66
Phoenicia, New York 12464
(914) 688-2211 Fax (914) 688-2007

Northwest:
Northwest Pathwork/Core Energetics
811 NW 20th, Suite 103C
Portland, Oregon 97209
(503) 223-0018

Philadelphia:
Philadelphia Pathwork
910 S. Bellevue Avenue
Hulmeville, Pennsylvania 19407
(215) 752-9894

Southeast:
Pathwork of Georgia
1765 Blue Pond Drive
Canton, Georgia 30115
(404) 889-8790

Brazil:
Aidda Pustilnik
Rua da Graviola #264, Apt. 1003
41810-420 Itaigara, Salvador, Brasil
Ph. 71-2470068 Fax 71-245-3089

Canada:
Ottawa/Montreal Pathwork
Roddy Duchesne
604-222 Guigues Ave.
Ottawa, Ontario K1N 5J2 Canada
Ph. (613) 241-4982

Germany:
Pfadgruppe Kiel
Rendsburger Landstrasse 395
24111 Kiel, Germany
Alf Girtler   Ph. 0431-69-74-73
Paul Czempin   Ph. 0431-66-58-07

Italy:
Il Sentiero
Raffaele Iandolo
Campodivivo, 43. 04020 Spigno
Saturnia (LT) Italy
Ph. (39) 771-64463 Fax 39-771-64693

Luxembourg:
Pathwork Luxembourg
Maria van Eyken
21 rue de Capellen
L-8279 Holzem, Luxembourg
Ph. 0/352-38515

Mexico:
Andres Leites
Pino 1, Col Rancho Cortes
Cuernavaca, Mor 62130 Mexico
Ph. 73-131395 Fax 73-113592

The Netherlands:
Padwerk
Johan Kos
Boerhaavelaan 9
1401 VR Bussum, Holland
Ph/Fax 02159-35222